Keys to Success

IN COLLEGE, CAREER, AND LIFE

How to Achieve Your Goals

BRIEF THIRD EDITION

Carol Carter

Joyce Bishop

Sarah Lyman Kravits

Editorial Consultant

Richard D. Bucher

*Professor of Sociology,
Baltimore City Community College*

Prentice
Hall

*Upper Saddle River, New Jersey
Columbus, Ohio*

Library of Congress Cataloging-in-Publication Data

Carter, Carol.
    Keys to success in college, career, and life : how to achieve your goals / Carol Carter,
Joyce Bishop, Sarah Lyman Kravits : editorial consultant, Richard D. Bucher.—Brief 3rd ed.
      p. cm.
    Includes bibliographical references and index.
    ISBN 0-13-098634-8
    1. College student orientation—United States—Handbooks, manuals, etc. 2. Study
skills—Handbooks, manuals, etc. 3. College students—Unted States—Life skills guides.
4. Career development—United States—Handbooks, manuals, etc. I. Title: Keys to
success. II. Bishop, Joyce (Joyce L.). III. Kravits, Sarah Lyman. IV. Bucher,
Richard D. V. Carter, Carol. Keys to success. VI. Title.

LB2343.32 .C37 2003
379.1'98—dc21

2002072294

Vice President and Publisher: Jeffery W. Johnston
Senior Acquisitions Editor: Sande Johnson
Assistant Editor: Cecilia Johnson
Production Editor: Holcomb Hathaway
Design Coordinator: Diane C. Lorenzo
Cover Designer: Thomas Borah
Cover Photos: Corbis Stock Market
Production Manager: Pamela D. Bennett
Director of Marketing: Ann Castel Davis
Director of Advertising: Kevin Flanagan
Marketing Manager: Christina Quadhamer

This book was set in Sabon by Aerocraft Charter Art Service. It was printed and
bound by Banta Book Group. The cover was printed by The Lehigh Press, Inc.

Pearson Education Ltd.
Pearson Education Australia Pty. Limited
Pearson Education Singapore Pte. Ltd.
Pearson Education North Asia Ltd.
Pearson Education Canada, Ltd.
Pearson Educación de Mexico, S.A. de C.V.
Pearson Education–Japan
Pearson Education Malaysia Pte. Ltd.
Pearson Education, *Upper Saddle River, New Jersey*

Reprinted with corrections January, 2003.

Photo Credits, by page
p. 2, Dynamic Graphics; p. 15,
Breton Littlehales; p. 24 Dyna-
mic Graphics; p. 44, Tomi/
Getty Images, Inc./PhotoDisc,
Inc.; p. 46, D. Berry/Getty
Images, Inc./PhotoDisc, Inc.;
p. 56, Dynamic Graphics; p. 62,
Mary Kate Denny/PhotoEdit;
p. 77, Gabe Palmer/Corbis/
Stock Market; p. 88, Dynamic
Graphics; p. 99, Robert Harbi-
son; p. 109, Jeff Greenberg/
PhotoEdit; p. 124, Dynamic
Graphics; p. 129, Dynamic
Graphics; p. 152, Mark
Richards/PhotoEdit; p. 162,
Copyright Images 100 LTD;
p. 170, Doug Menuez/Getty
Images, Inc./PhotoDisc, Inc.;
p. 184, Gary Conner/PhotoEdit;
p. 196, Corbis Images; p. 200,
Kevin Horan/Getty Images,
Inc.; p. 213, Ulrike Welsch/
PhotoEdit; p. 217, Jared Leeds,
2001; p. 228, Dynamic Graph-
ics; p. 234, Gallaudet Univer-
sity; p. 247, Tony Freeman/
PhotoEdit; p. 264, Dynamic
Graphics; p. 271, Stewart
Cohen/Getty Images, Inc.;
p. 281, Jack Star/Getty Images,
Inc./PhotoDisc, Inc. All other
photographic images ©Hemera
Technologies, Inc.

Prentice Hall

10 9 8 7 6 5 4 3 2
ISBN 0-13-098634-8

Dedication

HEALING OUR HEARTS

We dedicate this edition to the lives and the loved ones of those lost in the terrorist attacks on America on September 11, 2001. We ask that all of us remember that day by taking more time to be with those we care about, by living our lives to the fullest, and by replacing hatred with kindness in our neighborhoods, our country, and the world. We ask that you keep your spirit strong in times of adversity and be true to the resources, talents, and greatness within you.

Mission Statement

Our mission is to help students know and believe in themselves, take advantage of resources and opportunities, set and achieve their goals, learn throughout their lives, discover careers that fulfill and support them, build fruitful and satisfying relationships with others from all backgrounds and walks of life, and experience the challenges and rewards that make life meaningful.

Contents

Part I
Defining Yourself and Your Goals   1

Chapter 1

Welcome to College: *Opening Doors*   2

Chapter 2

Self-Awareness: *Knowing How You Learn and How to Choose a Major*   24

Chapter 3

Goal Setting and Time Management: *Using Values to Map Your Course*   56

Part II
Developing Your Learning Skills   87

Chapter 4

Critical and Creative Thinking:
Becoming an Active Learner   88

Chapter 5

Reading and Studying:
Focusing on Content   124

Chapter 9

Wellness, Career, and Money:
Building Skills for Life Success   264

NOTE: Every effort has been made to provide accurate and current Internet information in this book. However, the Internet and information posted on it are constantly changing, so it is inevitable that some of the Internet addresses listed in this textbook will change.

Foreword

BY THE STUDENT EDITORS

Certainly college is a wonderful key to opportunities never imagined! I had great expectations before my entrance into the "Inferno." The most important aspect of attending college seemed to be the Spirit of Success. Yet, I could not feel this spirit without the costs of failure. My first days as a college student were extremely difficult to cope with academically and socially. The Herculean workload weighed me down. Getting help seemed like the best answer, but talking did not bring solutions. I had to get involved.

The contents of *Keys to Success* made learning personal, providing insight into the obstacles that confronted me. The "learn-by-doing" emphasis took me from the trenches of failure and turned me into a student who could set priorities and manage time. Writing definitely brought abundance to my table in note taking and studying. Curriculum planning, cultural issues, and wellness are topics I found useful due to personal struggles in these areas.

Self-awareness, confidence, and responsibility are three pillars that support a life I can call my own. I have been provided "keys" to set goals in areas I never imagined embarking upon, such as research in gender studies, taking courses in multiple intelligences, and continuing Model United Nations. Once I had organized my academic life, my social life returned again, and the task of lifelong learning evolved into a goal I seek today.

As you embark on your journey to success, know that the tools in *Keys to Success* can assist you not only in college, but for a lifetime. Pay attention to the information on technology because it connects you with peers, instructors, and the resources of the world. Check out issues on sexual decisions and substance abuse, diversity, and managing finances; these will be helpful long after graduation. Information on goal setting and critical thinking will inspire you to grow into a responsible and well-organized individual. *Keys to Success* reveals the extraordinary through the practical. It is certainly a book that I will refer to often for the rest of my life.

My goal as student editor is to inspire you to aim for goals compassionately and extraordinarily. You, too, can be successful with this book! All that you need to succeed in college is available within it. Opportunities are all around you, and *Keys to Success* will help you unlock the benefits of these opportunities. So have a look for yourself. A warm thank you goes out to the authors and editors; and to the reader, my best to you in all your endeavors.

Jason Kim

**Undergraduate student,
The Johns Hopkins University**

No matter how well you perform in school, there is always something more that can be done to improve the way you learn. *Keys to Success* will equip you with learning strategies designed to produce success not only in school but also in life. Time management, for example, is a skill that nourishes and sustains our accomplishments; it is the gateway to personal satisfaction and workplace innovation.

As a senior majoring in English at Northwestern University, I've found that applying the strategies found in *Keys to Success* promotes facility in learning and even improves the general quality of my life. The learning skills described in this book have helped me to study more efficiently, and thereby create time for my passions in life—literature, music, and writing. I'm confident they will do the same for you.

Alexander Stacey

Undergraduate student,
Northwestern University

My decision to go back to school after 18 years has been a hard one and I have had to overcome a lot of inner obstacles. I was worried about having enough time to study as well as taking care of my three children. After finishing *Keys to Success,* I have come to realize that once you set a goal for yourself there is nothing you can't achieve.

The confidence and knowledge I have gained after reading *Keys to Success* have been immeasurable and have seeped into every aspect of my life. I have learned that I'm a visual learner, which has helped me with the way I take my class notes as well as the way I study for my tests. The straightforward format made it easy to read and understand. At my community college, I'm enrolled in a 2 + 2 program that will let me get my AA degree here and then transfer to Florida Atlantic University to finish my bachelor's degree in Elementary Education.

Coming back to school has been a positive and enriching life experience and has shown my children how important it is to have an education. I am very proud to have been a part of the revision process for *Keys to Success.*

Patricia Wright

Undergraduate student,
Indian River Community College

Preface

Owner's Manual

PLEASE READ THIS FIRST

You are living in a world of enormous change, a world where technology turns dreams into reality, where people from every land and culture communicate and interrelate—often for the first time—and where new opportunities are created as quickly as old ones fade away. The world may seem bright with promise, even as the choices you face feel overwhelming—what to study, what career to pursue, what lifestyle to adopt, what to believe.

Two keys will help you get where you want to go. The first is *an open mind*—being a receptive learner. Only when you are open to information, choices, and situations can you hope to see the possibilities that are often right in front of you. The second is *motivation*. Throughout life, you will need the determination and drive to take advantage of those possibilities and achieve your goals.

Open Your Mind to *Keys to Success*

Start by opening your mind to the many features in this text and to the resources available in your course. *Keys to Success,* Brief Third Edition, is filled with tools that will help you to develop the attitudes, ideas, and skills that are the building blocks of future success. Among the tools you will encounter are:

Skills that prepare you for college, career, and life. The ideas and strategies that help you succeed in college also take you where you want to go in your career and personal life. The three parts of this text help you develop a firm foundation for lifelong learning.

- *Part I: Defining Yourself and Your Goals.* **Chapter 1** provides an **overview** of today's college experience and an opportunity to evaluate your personal starting point. **Chapter 2** helps you identify complementary aspects of your **learning style**—your Multiple Intelligences and your Personality Spectrum profile—and choose strategies that make them work for you. **Chapter 3** helps you master valuable **goal-setting and time-management** skills that keep you moving forward.

- *Part II: Developing Your Learning Skills.* **Chapter 4** puts your learning into action, introducing you to an array of **critical-thinking skills**—how to take in, question, and use information so that you can solve problems, make decisions, and plan strategically. The remaining chapters in Part II build crucial skills for the classroom and beyond—**Reading and Studying (Chapter 5), Listening, Note Taking, and Memory (Chapter 6),** and **Test Taking (Chapter 7).**

- *Part III: Creating Success.* Recognizing that success includes more than academic achievement, **Chapter 8** focuses on developing the **interpersonal and communication skills** you need in a diverse society. **Chapter 9** helps you to manage **stress and wellness** issues, develop the **money-management and career-planning** skills that you need in college and beyond, and **think expansively:** What path have you traveled during the semester? What plans do you have for your future?

Skill-building exercises. Today's graduates need to be effective thinkers, team players, writers, and strategic planners. The set of exercises at the end of each chapter—"Building Skills for College, Career, and Life Success"—encourages you to develop these valuable skills and to apply thinking processes to any topic or situation:

- *The Big Picture: Combining Thinking, Strategy, and Teamwork.* This exercise encourages you to apply critical thinking and strategy to chapter topics in ways that take your personal goals into account. It also gives you a chance to interact and learn in a group setting, building your teamwork and leadership skills in the process.

- *Writing: Discovery Through Journaling.* This journal exercise provides an opportunity to express your thoughts and develop your writing skills.

- *Career Portfolio: Charting Your Course.* This exercise helps you gather evidence of your talents, skills, interests, qualifications, and experience. At the end of the semester, you will have created a portfolio of information and insights that will help you find the right career and job.

- *Assess Yourself: Student Success Strategies.* If you have access to the CD-ROM *Strategies for Success,* this exercise provides more ways to broaden your understanding of the chapter material.

Diversity of voice. The world is becoming increasingly diverse in ethnicity, perspective, culture, lifestyle, race, choices, abilities, needs, and more. In recognition of this fact, many voices speak to you from these pages, through the following features:

- *Personal Triumph* presents a real-life story of a person who has overcome difficult circumstances in the pursuit of education and fulfillment. You may relate personally to the people profiled, but even if you don't, you will be inspired by their stories. What you read of their courage and perseverance will motivate you to step up your personal efforts to succeed. You will find a Personal Triumph story in each chapter.

- *Chapter opening Q & As* highlight questions posed by actual students as they begin college. Each question is answered by another person who has had similar experiences.

- *Text examples* deal with the realities that students face—balancing school with work; returning to school as an older student; dealing with financial needs, parenting, supporting various lifestyles and schedules; and so on.

- *Chapter summaries* introduce a word or phrase from a language other than English and suggest how you might apply the concept to your own life.

What's new in this edition. As we revise, we are in constant touch with students and instructors who tell us how we can improve. For this edition we worked with student editors and contributors gathered from all over the country. Some provided the real-life stories for Personal Triumph and chapter opening Q & As; others read our manuscript in detail and gave us honest and valuable feedback. More than ever before, this edition contains what students taking this course have told us that they want and need—and it reflects their hard work and dedication.

In addition to the personal stories found throughout the text, other new elements include:

- Multiple Intelligence charts throughout the text that demonstrate, in specific, concrete ways, how to apply MI strategies to chapter topics.

- Expanded discussion of academic integrity (Chapter 1).

- Expanded discussion of choosing a major (Chapter 2).

- Strategies for finding the main idea in reading (Chapter 5).

- A look at the unique choices faced by minority students (Chapter 8).

- Increased focus on stress management (Chapter 9).

- Expanded coverage of the pitfalls of credit card debt (Chapter 9).

Be Motivated to Achieve Your Goals

Now that you are open to what is available to you within these pages, the next step depends on your motivation—your ability to get yourself moving toward your goal. In this case, being motivated means studying *Keys to Success* and taking specific actions to use what you learn to create options and opportunities.

You are responsible for your education and your future. We can offer helpful suggestions, strategies, and ideas, but ultimately it's up to you to use them. We challenge you to start now to make the most of the opportunities before you. If you know yourself, choose the best paths available to you, and follow them with determination, you will earn the success that you deserve. You've made a terrific start by choosing to pursue an education—now you can build the future of your dreams.

Students and instructors: Send your questions, comments, and ideas about *Keys to Success* to us at www.caroljcarter.com. We look forward to hearing from you.

Acknowledgments

This book has come about through a heroic group effort. We would like to take this opportunity to acknowledge the people who have made it happen. Many thanks to:

• Our savvy student editors, for their wisdom and guidance. They read manuscript in detail, gave us the benefit of their best instincts, and even got advice from friends. Their high level of constructive criticism has made this edition stronger than ever. Student editors are: Jason Kim, The Johns Hopkins University; Alexander Stacey, Northwestern University; Patricia Wright, Indian River Community College

• Other helpful student contributors include: Jemma Erikson, Pepperdine University; Jeremy Hawn, University of Denver; Elena Rodriguez, University of Colorado at Boulder; Sandi Armitage; Marisa Connell; Jennifer Moe; Alex Toth

• Our esteemed reviewers, whose input has made an incalculable difference.

Third edition reviewers: Fred Amador, Phoenix College; Leslie Chilton, Arizona State University; Jim Coleman, Baltimore City Community College; Sara Connolly, Florida State University; Skye Gentile, California State University, Hayward; Karen Hardin, Mesa Community College; Patricia Hart, California State University, Fresno; Laura Kauffman, Indian River Community College; Kathy Masters, Arkansas State University; Sue Palmer, Brevard Community College; Marsha Walden, Valdosta State University; Angela Williams, The Citadel

Reviewers from previous editions: Manual Aroz, Arizona State University; Glenda Belote, Florida International University; Todd Benatovich, University of Texas at Arlington; John Bennett, Jr., University of Connecticut; Ann Bingham-Newman, California State University–LA; Mary Bixby, University of Missouri–Columbia; Barbara Blandford, Education Enhancement Center at Lawrenceville, NJ; Jerry Bouchie, St. Cloud State University; Mona Casady, SW Missouri State University; Kara Craig, University of Southern Mississippi; Janet Cutshall, Sussex County Community College; Valerie DeAngelis, Miami-Dade Community College; Rita Delude, NH Community Technical College; Marianne

Edwards, Georgia College and State University; Judy Elsley, Weber State University in Utah; Bob Gibson, University of Nebraska–Omaha; Sue Halter, Delgado Community College; Suzy Hampton, University of Montana; Maureen Hurley, University of Missouri–Kansas City; Karen Iversen, Heald Colleges; Kathryn K. Kelly, St. Cloud State University; Nancy Kosmicke, Mesa State College; Frank T. Lyman, Jr., University of Maryland; Marvin Marshak, University of Minnesota; Barnette Miller Moore, Indian River Community College; Rebecca Munro, Gonzaga University; Bobbie Parker, Alabama State University; Virginia Phares, DeVry of Atlanta; Brenda Prinzavalli, Beloit College; Jacqueline Simon, Education Enhancement Center at Lawrenceville, NJ; Carolyn Smith, University of Southern Indiana; Joan Stottlemyer, Carroll College; Thomas Tyson, SUNY Stony Brook; Eve Walden, Valencia Community College; Rose Wassman, DeAnza College; Don Williams, Grand Valley State University; William Wilson, St. Cloud State University; Michelle G. Wolf, Florida Southern College

• The PRE 100 instructors at Baltimore City Community College, Liberty Campus, for their ideas, especially college President Dr. Jim Tschechtelin, Co-ordinator Jim Coleman, and Sonia Lynch, Jack Taylor, and Peggy Winfield. Thanks also to focus group participants Stan D. Brown, Frederick W. Campbell, Jr., James E. Coleman, Joseph A. Faw, Lyllis M. Green, and Marjorie E. Hunt. Special thanks to the late Rita Lenkin Hawkins for her support.

• Those who generously contributed personal stories, exhibiting courage in being open and honest about their life experiences:

Beverly Andre, Triton College; Edhilvia Campos, Parkland Community College; Chip Case, Piedmont Virginia Community College; Shera Chantel Caviness, University of Memphis; Peter Changsak, Sheldon-Jackson College; Rosalia Chavez, University of Arizona; Carol Comlish, University of Alabama; Brett Cross, University of Washington; Dani E. Day, Community College of Denver; Darrin Estepp, Ohio State University; Katherine Freeman, University of Akron; Chris Wong Sick Hong, Texas A & M; Erin Hughey-Commers, St. John's College;

Susie Ivy, Dominican University; Kevin Leman, Psychologist, Speaker, and Author; Ramona Z. Locke, Vice President Senior Financial Consultant, Merrill Lynch Private Client Group; Joe A. Martin, Jr., Professor of Communications, University of West Florida; Matt Millard, University of Wyoming; Gustavo Minaya, Essex Community College; Todd Montalbo, University of Alaska; Raymond Montolvo, Jr., University of Southern California; Julia Nolan, University of California, Davis; Michael Nolan, Oregon State University; Tim Nordberg, Chicago Youth Project; Morgan Paar, Academy of Art College; Morgan Packard, Tulane University; Richard Pan, Columbia University; Nathalie Piraino, Essex Community College; Gloria Finn Porter, Attorney at the Center for Justice; Jo Anne Roe, Instructor, Oak Park–River Forest High School; Norma Seledon, Director, Las Mujeres en Accion; Carlos Vela Shimano, ITESM Campus, Mexico; Tim Short, Washington State University; Litzka Stark, Sarah Lawrence College; Randy Ust, University of Mary; Tracy Ust, St. Cloud University

• The instructors at DeVry, especially Susan Chin and Carol Ozee, for their suggestions.

• The folks at California State University at Fresno, for their support and ideas: Patricia B. Hart, Phyllis Khuen, Scott Sailor, and Timothy Stearns. Special thanks to Candace Lee Egan for her work on the Keys to Lifelong Learning Telecourse and Marie E. Provencio for her help with the instructor's manual.

• Vikki and Eric Mayberry, Jeff and Margo McIlroy, Kate Lareau, Carol Abolafia, and Sue Bierman for their invaluable assistance.

• Cynthia Nordberg, for her work with contributors and her particular talent in gathering true and important stories.

• Michael Jackson for his writing samples and advice.

• Our editorial consultant Rich Bucher, professor of sociology at Baltimore City Community College, who provided important advice and consultation on diversity.

• Dr. Frank T. Lyman, Jr., educational consultant and innovator, for his invaluable advice on the text and for his generous permission to use and adapt his Thinktrix critical thinking system. Dr. Lyman is nationally recognized for innovations in curriculum and instruction including Think-Pair-Share and the Thinktrix.

• Marjorie Freilich-Den, Sheri Garrou, Ross T. Labaugh of California State University at Fresno, and Bobbie Stevens of University of Texas at Arlington, for their reviews of the revised material on library research.

• Our terrific editor Sande Johnson and assistant editor Cecilia Johnson for their hard work, candid comments on the manuscript, and belief in the cause.

• Those who reviewed and contributed to the instructors' manual, for their insight:

Todd Benatovich, University of Texas at Arlington; Amy Bierman, student, Old Dominion University; Jennifer Cohen; Jodi Levine, Temple University; Geri MacKenzie, Southern Methodist University; Gene Mueller, Henderson State University; Tina Pitt, Heald College; Dan Rice, Iowa State University; Michael and Frances Trevisan, Washington State University; Karen Valencia, South Texas Community College; Eve Walden, Valencia Community College; Don Williams, Grand Valley State University; William Wilson, St. Cloud State University; Nona Wood, North Dakota State University

• Sara Stensgaard of the University of Buffalo, for her work in integrating Web activities.

• Our fabulous production team, especially Gay Pauley.

• Our marketing gurus, especially Christina Quadhamer and Barbara Rosenberg.

• Jeff Johnston, Robin Baliszewski, Gary June, Tim Bozik, Will Ethridge, and Rit Dojny, for their vision and commitment to these books and to the success of all students.

• The Prentice Hall representatives and the management team led by David Gillespie, who, since getting his masters in student affairs, has always had a passion for student success and communicates that passion to those with whom he works.

• Our families and friends, who have encouraged us and put up with our commitments. Special thanks to Josephine and Louis Kravits for accommodating their mother's work schedule.

• We extend a very special thanks to Judy Block, whose research, writing, and editing work was essential and invaluable.

Finally, for their ideas, opinions, and stories, we would like to thank all of the students and professors with whom we work. Joyce in particular would like to thank the thousands of students who have allowed her, as their professor, the privilege of sharing part of their journey through college. We appreciate that, through reading this book, you give us the opportunity to learn and discover with you—in your classroom, in your home, on the bus, and wherever else learning takes place.

About the Authors

Carol Carter is founder and president of LifeBound, which provides seminars, coaching and resources for high school and college students. In addition, as Director of Faculty Development at Prentice Hall, Carol puts together and runs faculty symposia and workshops in student success across the country.

She has written *Majoring in the Rest of Your Life: Career Secrets for College Students* and *Majoring in High School*. She has also co-authored *Keys to Preparing for College, Keys to College Studying, The Career Tool Kit, Keys to Career Success, Keys to Study Skills, Keys to Thinking and Learning,* and *Keys to Success*. She has taught welfare-to-work classes, team taught in the La Familia Scholars Program at Community College of Denver, and has conducted numerous workshops for students and faculty around the country. She is the host of the Keys to Lifelong Learning Telecourse, a 26-episode telecourse to help students at a distance prepare for college, career, and life success. In addition to working with students of all ages, Carol thrives on foreign travel and culture; she has been fortunate enough to have been a guest in more than 40 countries. Please visit her Web site and write her at www.caroljcarter.com.

Joyce Bishop holds a Ph.D. in psychology and has taught for more than 20 years, receiving a number of honors, including Teacher of the Year for 1995 and 2000. For five years she has been voted "favorite teacher" by the student body and Honor Society at Golden West College, Huntington Beach, CA, where she has taught since 1987 and is a tenured professor. She has worked with a federal grant to establish Learning Communities and Workplace Learning in her district, and has developed workshops and trained faculty in cooperative learning, active learning, multiple intelligences, workplace relevancy, learning styles, authentic assessment, team building, and the development of learning communities. She is currently teaching on-line and multimedia classes, and training other faculty to teach on-line in her district and region of 21 colleges. She also co-authored *Keys to College Studying, Keys to Success, Keys to Thinking and Learning,* and *Keys to Study Skills*. Joyce is the lead academic of the Keys to Lifelong Learning Telecourse, distributed by Dallas Telelearning.

Sarah Lyman Kravits comes from a family of educators and has long cultivated an interest in educational development. She co-authored *Keys to College Studying, The Career Tool Kit, Keys to Success, Keys to Thinking and Learning,* and *Keys to Study Skills* and has served as Program Director for LifeSkills, Inc., a non-profit organization that aims to further the career and personal development of high school students. In that capacity she helped to formulate both curricular and organizational elements of the program, working closely with instructors as well as members of the business community. She also gives faculty workshops in student success and in critical thinking. Sarah holds a B.A. in English and drama from the University of Virginia, where she was a Jefferson Scholar, and an M.F.A. from Catholic University.

I

Defining Yourself and Your Goals

CHOOSE

1

IN THIS CHAPTER

In this chapter you explore answers to the following questions: • How will college prepare you for life? • How can you get motivated? • What is the connection between college and lifelong learning?

Welcome to college

WELCOME—or welcome back—to your education.

Like Matt Millard (see next page), you are embarking

on a new phase of life that may bring all kinds of

questions and concerns. This chapter will give you

a preview of how college will prepare you for life.

You will explore specific strategies that will help

motivate you. Finally, you will see how the skills

you build in college can help you become a lifelong

learner—and why that means

greater success for you.

opening doors

Matt Millard, University of
Wyoming, Laramie, Wyoming

Todd Montalbo,
University of Alaska, Anchorage, Alaska

*How can I get the
most out of college?*

*I think it's very important to do what
you love.*

I decided to attend college so I could have a job doing what I really like instead of just doing it for the money. Even though I haven't decided what I want to do when I graduate, I know that I want to continue learning for a long time. I'd even like to continue on to get a Masters and maybe even a Ph.D. someday. So far, I'm mainly interested in the theater and English, but I'm not quite sure where to go with it.

I try to take steps to better myself. Even though I'd like it to be more often, I work out at racquetball a couple of times a week. I also think it's important to help other people, so I make time to help my friends with their homework and stuff like that. My grades are average so I'd like them to get better. I'd also like to get a little more focused on what I want to declare as a major. What steps do you think I need to take in order to get the most out of my learning?

I think it's very important to do what you love. That will really help your goal of lifelong learning. Even though having money is important, it's more important to enjoy what you're doing and feel like you're making a difference. I chose education as my major because I really like being with young people and feel I can influence their lives in a positive way. Plus, my mother is a teacher. After going to her classes and seeing her teach, I decided it was something I'd enjoy. I've changed my major twice, though, since I started school. I tried the business department, but realized after taking an economics class that I just wasn't that interested.

It might be beneficial for you to try different classes in the subjects that really interest you. That way you'll know if you're on the right track. Another suggestion is to join a drama club or try out for a local theater production. You might want to get to know someone who makes a living teaching English. He may be able to help you decide if it's the career for you. I also recommend that you try to have balance in your life. I'm a member of the ski team at my school. Whenever I come back from skiing and sit down to study, I feel like I'm more focused and I feel like my whole life isn't just studying. I'm more motivated that way. I also get a lot more done in a shorter time because I have more energy.

Your first year can be a big adjustment. I can guarantee you, it will get better. You can help make it easier by exploring different professions, changing some of your normal routines, and trying classes that other students say are interesting or exciting.

How will college prepare you for *life?*

I n choosing to pursue an education, you are building your power to create a better world. Whatever your reasons for attending college, what you do today—in a writing classroom, a study session, a conference with an instructor, or other educational setting—will help you navigate what lies ahead.

Education Promotes Success

If you take advantage of all your college has to offer, you will develop the skills and talents you need to succeed in your career and life.

Education prepares you for career success. This happens in two ways. First, education expands your career choices by teaching you, through your courses and the people you meet, more about potential careers and jobs than you ever imagined. Second, your day-to-day course work gives you the hands-on skills you need to achieve the career goals you choose. Education makes you a more *literate* person—able to use written and mathematical skills to learn and to improve your life.

Education improves your employability and earning potential. Although education doesn't automatically guarantee a high-level, well-paying job, it greatly increases the probability you will find one (see Figure 1.1 and Figure 1.2

Figure 1.1	Education and income.

Median annual income of persons with income 25 years old and over, by highest degree attained and gender, 1998.

Source: U.S. Department of Commerce, Bureau of the Census, *Current Population Reports,* Series P-60, Money Income in the United States: 1998.

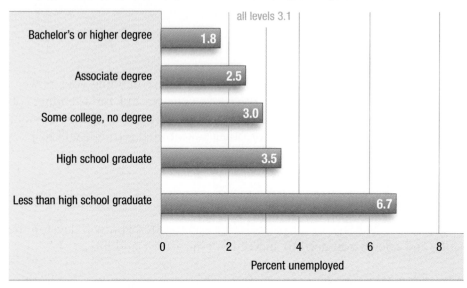

Figure 1.2 **Education and employment.**

Unemployment rates of persons 25 years old and over, by highest degree attained.*

all levels 3.1

- Bachelor's or higher degree — 1.8
- Associate degree — 2.5
- Some college, no degree — 3.0
- High school graduate — 3.5
- Less than high school graduate — 6.7

Percent unemployed
(0, 2, 4, 6, 8)

Source: U.S. Department of Labor, Bureau of Labor Statistics, Office of Employment and Unemployment Statistics, *Current Population Survey,* 1999.

for details). Having a college degree makes an impression on potential employers and makes you eligible for higher-salaried positions. In basic terms, there is a significant wage gap between high school and college graduates, and you want to be on the winning side of it.

Education broadens your worldview. As it introduces you to new ways of learning, doing, being, and thinking, education increases your understanding of diversity and your appreciation of areas that affect and enrich human lives, such as music, art, literature, science, politics, and economics.

Education helps you develop flexibility. Today's world is marked by rapid workplace change, ever-increasing loads of information, and booming technology growth. What you learn in college will help you handle whatever comes your way with flexibility. You will develop the ability to embrace change by taking risks, being self-directed, and keeping an open mind about what lies in store.

Education Helps You Build Teamwork Skills

Think of your accomplishments and you will find that rarely do you achieve anything alone. Your success at school and at work depends on your ability to cooperate in a team setting. Teams gain strength from the diversity of their members, because the greater the diversity of a team, the greater the number of choices or solutions when problem solving.

The needs of an increasingly diverse student body have molded a new educational experience. So-called traditional students—18 years old, just out of high school, and living in on-campus dorms—now often share classrooms with less traditional students. Figures 1.3, 1.4, and 1.5 indicate how the student population has changed since the 1980s.

Figure 1.3   Students are more diverse.

Unemployment rates of persons 25 years old and over, by highest degree attained.*

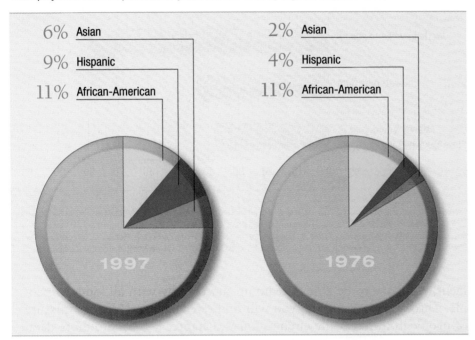

6% Asian

9% Hispanic

11% African-American

2% Asian

4% Hispanic

11% African-American

1997

1976

Source: U.S. Department of Education, National Center for Educational Statistics, Digest of Education Statistics 2000, NCES 2001–034, by Thomas D. Snyder. Washington D.C.: U.S. Government Printing Office, 2001, pp. 194–195

Furthermore, diversity is part of the reality of living in the United States today. The year 2000 census reports that one in four Americans is a member of a minority group as compared to 1980, when only one in five reported minority status. The nation's diversity is expected to grow.

What does this mean for you? In order to succeed postgraduation in a world where you will almost certainly be working in a diverse environ-

Figure 1.4   Students are older and have varied responsibilities.

Percentage of undergraduate student body, academic year 1995–1996

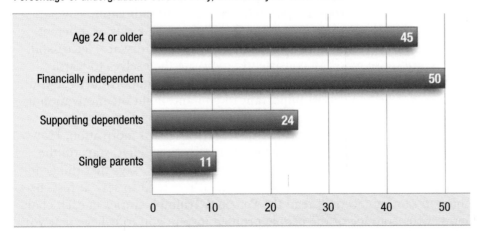

Category	Percentage
Age 24 or older	45
Financially independent	50
Supporting dependents	24
Single parents	11

Source: U.S. Department of Education, National Center for Educational Statistics, Digest of Education Statistics 2000, NCES 2001–034, by Thomas D. Snyder. Washington D.C.: U.S. Government Printing Office, 2001, pp. 274, 374; and U.S. Department of Education, National Center for Education Statistics, Profile of Undergraduates in U.S. Postsecondary Education Institutions: 1995–96, NCES 98-084, by Laura J. Horn, Jennifer Berktold, and MPR Associates, Inc. Washington D.C.: U.S. Government Printing Office, 1998, p. 77.

Figure 1.5 Students are following less traditional educational paths.

Percentage of undergraduate student body, academic year 1995–1996

Working while in school	full time 37 80
Enrolled part-time	43
Attending two-year or less-than-two-year schools	38

Source: U.S. Department of Education, National Center for Educational Statistics, *Digest of Education Statistics 2000,* NCES 2001–034, by Thomas D. Snyder. Washington D.C.: U.S. Government Printing Office, 2001, pp. 234–235; and U.S. Department of Education, National Center for Education Statistics, *Profile of Undergraduates in U.S. Postsecondary Education Institutions: 1995–96,* NCES 98-084, by Laura J. Horn, Jennifer Berktold, and MPR Associates, Inc. Washington D.C.: U.S. Government Printing Office, 1998, p. 5.

ment, you have to be able to team up successfully with all kinds of people. Throughout this book, you will find references to a diverse mixture of people in different life circumstances. Chapter 8 goes into more detail about communicating across lines of difference.

You are responsible for examining your unique challenges and seeking out the educational opportunities that help you meet them. Particular strategies help you build and maintain your motivation to learn and succeed.

How can you get *motivated?*

MOTIVATION

A force that moves
a person to action;
often inspired by an
idea a fact, an
event, a goal.

Success is a process, not a fixed mark—and **motivation** is what keeps the process in motion. People have all kinds of different *motivators*—goals or ideas that move them forward. Successful people are those who can consistently motivate themselves to learn, grow, and work toward goals. College provides an opportunity for you to discover the goals most important to you and build the motivation it takes to achieve them.

From time to time, everyone experiences a loss of motivation. How can you build motivation or renew lost motivation? First, start on the path. Newton's first law of motion, a law of physics, says that things in motion tend to stay in motion and things at rest tend to stay at rest. Be a thing in motion. Second, read the Personal Triumph stories in each chapter. Let the courage of the people profiled inspire you to believe that you can leap your own hurdles successfully. Finally, explore the following motivation-boosting strategies.

Make a Commitment

How do you focus the energy of motivation? Make a commitment. Commitment means that you do what you say you will do. When you honor a commitment to an academic goal, a career dream, or a self-improvement task, you prove to yourself and others that your intentions can be trusted.

How do you go about making and keeping a commitment?

- *State your commitment concretely.* Set a clear goal and break it into manageable pieces. Emphasize to yourself what you will gain from this commitment.

- *Take the first step.* Decide on the first step of your commitment and take it today. Then continue a day at a time, breaking tasks into small steps.

- *Stay aware of each commitment.* Keep a list of commitments where you can see it. Talk about them with someone you trust to help you stay on track.

- *Reward yourself as you move ahead.* Rewards help you feel good about what you've accomplished so far and can help keep you going. Treat yourself to dinner with a friend, a new CD, a movie night.

Making commitments helps you keep a steady focus on your most important goals. It gives you a sense of accomplishment as you experience gradual growth and progress.

> "A journey of a thousand miles begins with a single step."

LAO TZU

COMMITMENT

1) A pledge or promise to do something, or 2) dedication to a long-term course of action.

Develop Positive Habits

People have all kinds of habits; some you may consider "bad" and others "good." Bad habits stall motivation and prevent you from reaching important goals. Good habits are those that bring the kind of positive effects that keep motivation high.

Look at the positive and negative effects of your habits to decide which you want to keep and which you need to change or improve. Take the following steps to evaluate a habit and, if necessary, make a change (if the habit has more negative effects than positive ones).

HABIT

A preference for a particular action that you do a certain way, and often on a regular basis or at certain times.

1. *Define and evaluate the habit.* Name your habit and look at the negative and positive effects. If there are more negatives than positives, it is most likely a habit worth changing.

2. *Decide to keep or change the habit.* Until you are convinced that you will receive a benefit, efforts to change will not get you far. Commit to a change if you see too many negative effects.

3. *Start today—and keep it up.* Each day is a day you can benefit from a new lifestyle. Be consistent for at least three weeks so that you become accustomed to the new habit.

4. *Reward positive steps.* Choose a reward that encourages you to stay on target. If you earn a good grade, for example, treat yourself to one night out instead of slacking off on studying the following week.

Finally, don't get too discouraged if the process seems difficult. Rarely does someone make the decision to change and do so without a setback or two. Take it one step at a time; when you lose steam, reflect on what you stand to gain. With persistence and positive thinking, you can reach your goal.

Be Responsible

In college, you are responsible for making decisions that keep you in motion and avoiding choices that stall you in your tracks. You are your own manager. Taking responsibility is all about living up to your obligations. Through action, you prove that you are responsible—"response-able"—able to respond.

Taking responsibility is taking action—and doing it reliably. In college, responsible people can be trusted to live up to obligations like these:

- Attending class and participating in activities and discussions
- Completing reading and assignments on time
- Communicating with instructors and fellow students

These actions may sound mundane. However, these building blocks of responsibility will get you where you want to go. Here's why:

- *Everyday responsibilities get you in the action habit.* As with any other habit, the more you do something, the more it becomes second nature. The more often you complete and turn in assignments on time, for example, the more likely you are to stay on top of your job tasks down the road when you are on a tight deadline.

- *The small accomplishments make a big impression.* When you show up to class, pay attention, contribute, and work hard, you send a message. An instructor who observes these behaviors is more likely to trust and respect you. People who trust you may give you increasing power and opportunities for growth.

- *Fulfilling day-to-day responsibilities gives you freedom.* The more responsible you are, the more those around you will give you the freedom to handle situations and problems on your own.

INITIATIVE

The power to begin or to follow through energetically with a plan or task; determination.

Responsibility also means showing initiative. Initiative means that you make a move on your own instead of waiting for people, rules, requirements, or circumstances to push you. You show initiative when you make an appointment with an instructor to discuss a paper, find a better way to do a task at work, vote, or start an exercise program. Once you take that first step, it is often easier to keep your momentum going and continue to act responsibly.

Face Your Fears

Everyone experiences fear. Anything unknown—new people, experiences, challenges, situations—can be frightening. The challenges you face as you work toward your goals demand a willingness to face your fears and push your limits. The following steps will help you work through fear with courage:

1. *Acknowledge fears.* The act of naming your fear begins to lessen its hold on you. Be specific.
2. *Examine fears.* Sometimes one fear hides a larger one. If you fear a test, determine whether you fear the test itself or the fact that if you pass it, you will have to take a tougher class next.

"He has not learned the lesson of life who does not every day surmount a fear."

RALPH WALDO EMERSON

3. *Develop a plan.* Evaluate what will help you overcome your fear. For example, if you are scared of Shakespeare, consider asking your instructor for advice or watching a Shakespeare movie.
4. *Move ahead with your plan.* Courage is the key to moving ahead. Take the steps that help you to confront and move beyond your fears.

As you work through your fears, talk about them with people you trust. Everyone has fears, and when people share strategies, everyone benefits.

Build Self-Esteem

When people believe in their value and capabilities, their self-esteem fuels their motivation to succeed. Belief, though, is only half the game. The other half is the action and effort that help you feel that you have earned your self-esteem. Rick Pitino discusses self-esteem in his book *Success Is a Choice:* "Self-esteem is directly linked to deserving success. If you have established a great work ethic and have begun the discipline that is inherent with that, you will automatically begin to feel better about yourself. It's all interrelated. You must deserve victory to feel good about yourself."[1]

Building self-esteem, therefore, involves both *thinking positively* and *taking action.* Together, they help you generate the belief in yourself that keeps you motivated.

SELF-ESTEEM

A strong and deeply felt belief that you as a person have value in the world.

Think Positively

Attitudes influence your choices and affect how you perceive and relate to others. A positive attitude can open your mind to learning experiences and inspire you to action. One way to create a positive attitude is through positive self-talk. These hints will help:

+ + +
POSITIVE SELF-TALK

Supportive and positive thoughts and ideas that a person communicates to himself or herself.

- *Stop negative talk in its tracks.* If you catch yourself thinking, "I can never write a decent paper," stop and say to yourself, "I can write better than that and next time I will." Then think about some specific steps you can take to improve.
- *Pay yourself a compliment.* Note your successes. Be specific: "I have really improved my spelling and proofreading."
- *Replace words of obligation with words of personal intent.*

| I should | *becomes* | I choose to |
| I'll try | *becomes* | I will |

Words of intent give you power and control because they imply a personal decision to act.

Take Action

Although thinking positively sets the tone for success, it cannot get you there by itself. You have to take action. Without action, positive thoughts become empty statements or even lies.

Consider, for example, a student in a freshman composition class. This student thinks every possible positive thought: "I know how to write well. I can get a B in this class. I will succeed in school." And so on. Then, during the semester, she misses about one-third of the class meetings, turns in some of her papers late, and completely forgets a couple of assignments. At the end of the course, when she barely passes the class, she wonders how things went so wrong when she had such a positive attitude.

This student did not succeed because she did not earn her belief in herself through action and effort. By the end of a semester like this, positive thoughts look like lies. "If I can get a B, why did I get a D? If I am such a great student, why did I barely make it through this course?" Eventually, with no action to support them, the positive thoughts disappear.

Following are some ways to get moving in a positive direction:

- *Build your own code of discipline.* Develop general guidelines to follow, based on your top priorities. Construct each day's goals and actions so that they help you achieve your larger objectives.
- *Make action plans and follow through.* Figure out how you plan to take action for any situation, so that, for example, "I am a great student" is backed up by specific actions to ensure success.
- *Acknowledge every step.* Even the smallest action is worth your attention because every action reinforces a positive thought and builds self-esteem.

Believing in yourself helps you make good choices. When your self-esteem is strong, you are more likely to choose actions that you can be proud of.

What is the connection between college and *lifelong learning?*

I n his book *TechnoTrends—24 Technologies That Will Revolutionize Our Lives,* futurist Daniel Burns describes a tomorrow that is linked to continuing education: "The future belongs to those who are capable of being retrained again and again," he says. "Think of it as periodically upgrading your human assets throughout your career. . . . Humans are infinitely upgradeable, but it does require an investment" in lifelong learning.[2] College is the ideal training ground for learning skills that will serve you throughout your life.

College Prepares You to Learn from Failure and Celebrate Success

College brings new challenges and with them come situations in which you may fail. Failure is an opportunity to realize what you didn't know so that you can learn and improve; in fact, what you learn from a failure will most likely guide you more effectively than many other things you learn. If you can accept failure as part of life, forgive yourself, and learn from it, you will be able to pick yourself up and keep improving.

Learning from Failure

Learning from your failures and mistakes involves careful thinking. One useful course of action is to first look at what happened, then make any improvements that you can, and finally decide how to change your action or approach in the future. For example, imagine that after a long night of studying for a test, you forgot that you had a deadline for a five-page paper the next day.

Look at what happened. Your exhaustion and concern about the test caused you to forget to check your planner to see what else was on your plate. Now you may face a lower grade on your paper if you turn it in late, plus you may be inclined to rush it and quickly turn in a paper that isn't as good as it could be.

Make any possible improvements on the situation. You could visit your instructor during office hours, or send an e-mail, explain the situation and ask if you can have a brief extension on the paper.

Make changes for the future. You can set a goal to note deadlines in a bright color and to check your planner more often. You can also try arranging your study schedule so that you will be less exhausted.

Keep in mind that your value as a human being does not diminish when you make a mistake. Expect that you always will do the best that you can, knowing that just getting through another day as a student, employee, or parent is a success.

Celebrating Success

Success is being who you want to be and doing what you want to do. In addition, although you may not feel successful until you reach an important goal, success is a process. Each step along the way to improvement and growth, no matter how small, is a success worth acknowledging.

Here are some ways to celebrate successes big and small:

- *Appreciate yourself.* Take time to congratulate yourself for a job well done—whether it is a good grade, a job offer, or a personal victory over substance abuse.

- *Build your confidence for future challenges.* Let this experience help you to solidify your confidence. Show yourself and others that you are capable of building on and continuing your success.

- *Stay sensitive to others.* Some people around you may not have been as successful. Remember that you have been in their place and they in yours. Enjoy what you have and support others as they need it.

Both failure and success will be a bottomless source of learning as you move through college and beyond. The better coping skills you build now, the more you benefit in the future.

College Helps You Become a Person of Integrity

Integrity is at the heart of your actions as a member of your academic community. Having integrity implies that you adhere to a code of moral values, prizing honesty and fairness in all aspects of life. Academic integrity, specifically, refers to integrity in academic situations: classes, assignments, tests, papers, projects, and relationships with students and faculty.

When you register for college, you agree, either implicitly or explicitly, to a code of academic conduct consisting of positive actions as well as actions to avoid. Your school's code of honor, or academic integrity policy, should be printed in your student handbook. Following this code—doing what is asked of you honestly and in a manner that promotes learning—ensures a quality education based on ethics and hard work. Furthermore, it helps you develop a habit of integrity that will make you a desirable and trustworthy employee, friend, and family member.

The Center for Academic Integrity, part of the Kenan Institute for Ethics at Duke University, defines academic integrity as a commitment to five fundamental values: honesty, trust, fairness, respect, and responsibility.[3] These values form the basis of acceptable behaviors for students and instructors.

- *Honesty.* The most fundamental value in college is honesty. Honesty defines the pursuit of knowledge and implies a search for truth in your class work, papers and lab reports, and teamwork with others.

INTEGRITY

Adherence to a code of moral values; incorruptibility, honesty.

PERSONAL TRIUMPH

You have begun a journey of self-discovery that will help you define who you are and what you want out of life. What Bryan M. Johnson has learned about himself and the world from his own journey has led him to goals that have great meaning for him.

I still remember a good friend's concern when I joined the Navy a year out of high school. I understood his sentiments. I thought of military enlistment as custom-made for boneheads not bright enough to further their education or talented enough to do anything else.

If that was the case, then I fit the mold at 19. I barely graduated from high school with an abysmal 1.8 GPA; my most formidable accomplishment was holding the senior-year record for skipping classes. After high school, I drove a patio furniture delivery van. I had "quit" my other job as a cashier after being accused of fingering money from the register (truthfully, I just couldn't add or subtract). Faced with a life of delivering windproof side tables, I decided to give the military a shot. When I bid farewell at the patio store, the manager laughed. "You'll be back," he said. I walked out thinking he was probably right.

After naval boot camp, I was assigned on a destroyer, my days filled with backbreaking hours of sanding and painting in a never-ending battle to preserve the ship's exterior. I learned the value of an honest day's work, but soon began looking for a way out of a dull, weary routine. I found it that first Christmas home, when I spent my stocking money on remedial math and reading texts. I returned to the ship with a backpack full of scholarly spoils, and the tiny bulb over my rack burned every night for almost a year. My hard work paid off when I landed a position standing navigation watch.

As he showed me how to plot our destroyer's course, my new supervisor said something that made a lasting impression. "If you don't do your job right, don't pay attention, people could die." Lives were at stake and someone was trusting me to make good decisions. I was honored.

Bryan M. Johnson, medical student,
Uniformed Services University, Bethesda, Maryland

What an odd yet wonderful feeling that was. More important, a fire had ignited inside me. I now rose to challenges instead of avoiding them, and loved the sense of self-worth I felt at a job well done.

To fill in dozens of empty hours at sea, crew members talked with one another. I learned that a person's skin color, or where he came from, wasn't a very good indicator of his character. I also realized that my preconceived notion of a military consisting of losers was completely unfounded. I knew one sailor, for instance, who joined the Navy because he cherished his country's freedom and wanted to give his time and energy in return.

Despite a worthwhile four years, I decided not to re-enlist and to give college a try. I diligently pursued a B.S. degree, and graduated with honors and hopes of attending medical school. Yet something was missing. I recalled the pride I had felt in my uniform, a symbol of something greater than myself. I applied to the United States' only military school of medicine and started classes.

Going home these days is a bit like winding back the clock 10 years—old friends look bewildered when I mention that I've rejoined the service. Don't think I'm offended: I belong to an organization that defends the rights of Americans to have their own opinions.

Although I've put the past behind me, I often wonder what the manager would say if I dropped by the patio store. But then he'd be right: I would be back—but only to buy a ceramic yard frog.

Take a moment to consider . . .

- *What you feel has been the most significant learning experience in your life so far.*
- *What you would like to be most proud of when you graduate from college.*

- *Trust.* Mutual trust—between instructor and student, as well as among students—forms the basis for the free exchange of ideas that is fundamental to learning. Trust means that you are true to your word.

- *Fairness.* Instructors must create a fair academic environment in which students are judged against clear standards and in which procedures are well defined.

- *Respect.* In a respectful academic environment, both students and instructors accept and honor a wide range of opinions, even if the opinions are contrary to core beliefs.

- *Responsibility.* You are responsible for your own choices in school and in striving for the best education. Personal responsibility implies a commitment to choices that reflect fairness and honesty.

Having academic integrity has important positive effects on the following:

Your behavior patterns. When you condition yourself to play fair now, you set a pattern that follows you on the job and in your personal relationships.

Your knowledge level. If you cheat on a test you might pass the test—and the course—but what do you remember after you receive your grade? The point of college is to acquire knowledge and skills that you will use long after you graduate. Retaining knowledge leads to obtaining—and retaining—jobs.

Your interaction with others. When you act with academic integrity, you show respect for the work of others. In turn, you earn trust and respect from them, which may lead to friendships and opportunities.

Your self-esteem. Remember that self-esteem is tied to action. The more you act in respectful and honorable ways, the better you feel about yourself, and the more you are able to succeed.

Above all, you are responsible for your own integrity. You can choose actions that build your confidence, ability, knowledge, and reputation. Make choices that serve you well. With a strong sense of integrity, you are able to learn throughout your life.

College Provides an Opportunity to Examine Your Life

Making the commitment to work toward a college education means putting energy into thinking about yourself on a big-picture level. What do you do well? What do you want out of life? What can you improve? College gives you the chance to evaluate where you are and to make some concrete decisions about how to get to where you want to be.

This course is an ideal opportunity to kick off this exploration, and one place to begin is with The Wheel of Life, an assessment that helps you get an idea of your starting point. The image of the wheel has been used for centuries as a way to help people understand themselves and

"If you don't risk anything, you risk even more."

ERICA JONG

their world. Some Native American cultures, for example, use the "medicine wheel" to reflect the life cycle. In different regions (North, South, East, and West), qualities represented by colors and animals, seasons, and stages of life are honored on the wheel, providing a way to understand each experience as one progresses through life.

Think of the wheel in Figure 1.6 as a circle of your lessons and growth areas at this time in your life. Look at each area on the wheel and ask yourself where you feel accomplished and where you would like to improve. At the end of this course, you will do this exercise again. This wheel is based on one used by an organization that trains personal coaches.

As you move through this course and through your educational experience, seek continual change and improvement. Take to heart this quotation from a student in Mississippi: "Without an education in the [new millennium], we the people will be in serious trouble. Because now everything is moving forward fast and without an education you will be moving nowhere."[4] Let your ability to make change happen keep you on the move.

In Chinese writing, this character has two meanings: One is "chaos"; the other, "opportunity." The character communicates the belief that every chaotic, challenging situation in life also presents an opportunity. By responding to challenges actively, you can discover the opportunity within the chaos.

Let this concept reassure you as you begin college. You may feel that you are going through a time of chaos and change. Remember that no matter how difficult the obstacles, you have the ability to persevere. You can create opportunities for yourself to learn, grow, and improve.

Figure 1.6 The wheel of life.

Rate yourself in each area of the wheel on a scale of 1 to 10, 1 being least developed (near the center of the wheel) and 10 being most developed (the outer edge of the wheel). In each area, at the level of the number you choose, draw a curved line to create a new outer edge for that segment of the chart. Remember, this is for your benefit only, so be honest. Finally, look at your wheel as a whole. What does it say about the balance in your life? If this were a real wheel, how well would it roll?

Sample Wheel

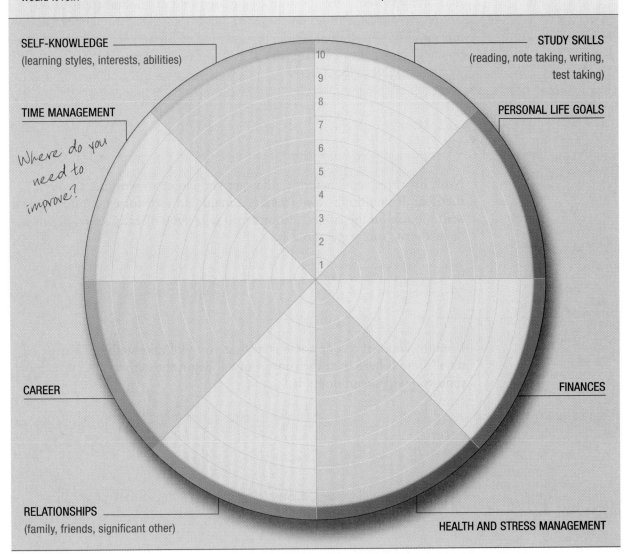

SELF-KNOWLEDGE
(learning styles, interests, abilities)

STUDY SKILLS
(reading, note taking, writing, test taking)

TIME MANAGEMENT

PERSONAL LIFE GOALS

CAREER

FINANCES

RELATIONSHIPS
(family, friends, significant other)

HEALTH AND STRESS MANAGEMENT

Source: Based on "The Wheel of Life" model developed by the Coaches Training Institute, © Co-Active Space 2000.

Building Skills

FOR COLLEGE, CAREER, AND LIFE SUCCESS

The Big Picture *Combining Thinking, Strategy, and Teamwork*

Get Motivated[5]

One strategy for boosting motivation is to let go of the need to be perfect that often prevents people from doing anything at all, and to *do something*. The easiest way to do this is to break the task into manageable units and do one step at a time. First, think of an activity you have been postponing because of fear (fear of success, of failure, of the task, of perfectionism). Describe it here.

_____

_____

_____

Now, list three small activities that get you closer to working through that fear. If you don't want to start a major project, for example, you can read a book on the subject, brainstorm what you already know about it, or just write one page about it.

1. _____

2. _____

3. _____

Commit yourself to one small step that you will take within the next two days. State it here. List the time you will begin the activity and how much time you will spend doing it.

_____

_____

_____

What reward will you give yourself for having taken that step?

_____

_____

After taking the step, describe how it felt.

_____

_____

Affirm that you have taken that first step and are on the way to success by signing your name here and writing the date. Use motivation strategies to continue on the road toward conquering your fear.

Signature _____ *Date* _____

Exchanging ideas with others can also boost motivation. Gather in a group of three to five students. Each person should take out a blank sheet of paper and write at the top what he or she thinks is his or her biggest motivation problem; that is, the situation or thing that most often kills that person's motivation. Don't include names on the pages. When everyone is finished, each person should pass his or her page to the person to the left. On the page you receive, you should list one idea you have about fighting the particular motivation problem that is at the top of the page. Again, when everyone is finished, pass the pages to the left. Continue until your page comes back to you.

Then, discuss the ideas together. Offer thoughts about which ideas might work better than others. Add other ideas to the list if you think of them. You may want to combine everyone's lists together so that each group member has a copy. You may also want to share your ideas with the class if you have time.

Writing *Discovery Through Journaling*

To record your thoughts, use a separate journal or the lined pages at the end of the chapter.

REASONS FOR COLLEGE. Think back to the section describing various reasons that people decide to go to college. Now describe your own: Why are you here? How do you feel about your reasons for being here? Next, describe your educational goals: What do you want out of college?

Career Portfolio *Charting Your Course*

SETTING CAREER GOALS. Whether you have a current career, have held a few different jobs, or have not yet entered the workplace, college is an ideal time to take stock of your career goals. Even if you won't enter the workplace for a few years, now is not too early to consider what you might like to do after you have finished school. The earlier in your college education that you consider your career goals, the more you can take advantage of how college can help prepare you for work, in both job-specific and general ways.

Take some time to think about your working life. Spend 15 minutes brainstorming everything that you wish you could be, do, have, or experience in your career—the career area, finances, benefits, experiences, travel, anything you can think of. List your wishes on a blank piece of paper, draw them, depict them using cutouts from magazines, or combine these ideas—whatever you like best.

Now, look at your list. To discover how your wishes relate to one another, group them in order of priority. Take three pieces of paper and label them Priority 1, Priority 2, and Priority 3. Write each wish on the piece of paper where it fits, with Priority 1 being the most important, Priority 2 the second most important, and Priority 3 the third.

Look at your priority lists. What do they tell you about what is most important to you? What wishes are you ready to work toward right now? Circle the three highest-priority wishes that you want to achieve with your entry into a new career.

Assess Yourself *Student Success Strategies*

If you have access to the CD-ROM Strategies for Success, use the following questions to assess your thoughts and enhance your understanding of the chapter. The questions below represent only some of the activities provided on the CD for the chapter topics—try others if you have time.

Click on the **Where Are You Now?** bookmark. Use the following activities to prime your mind for making the most of your education:

1. Take the pre-assessment to consider how you believe education is involved in your drive toward success.

2. Watch the video and think about education's six areas of influence: lifelong learning, self-concept, extended possibilities, community service, personal health and well-being, and quality of life. In the field provided, type these in priority order from most important to least important.

3. Click on **Activity One: Educational Contract.** Fill in the Educational Contract and experience the clarity and motivation that often come from putting your thoughts down on paper. Print it out to keep in your portfolio.

4. Take the post-assessment to clarify what you know about how education can help you achieve your goals.

SUGGESTED READINGS

Baker, Sunny and Kim Baker. *College After 30: It's Never Too Late to Get the Degree You Need!* Holbrook, MA: Bob Adams, 1992.

Cobb, Joyanne. *Learning How to Learn: A Guide for Getting Into College with a Learning Disability, Staying In, and Staying Sane.* Washington, DC: Child Welfare League of America, 2001.

Evers, Frederick T., James Cameron Rush, and Iris Berdow. *The Bases of Competence: Skills for Lifelong Learning and Employability.* San Francisco, CA: Jossey-Bass, 1998.

Jeffers, Susan. *Feel the Fear and Do It Anyway.* New York: Fawcett Columbine, 1992.

Lewis, Erica-Lee and Eric L. Lewis. *Help Yourself: Handbook for College-Bound Students with Learning Disabilities.* New York: Princeton Review, 1996.

Shields, Charles J. *Back in School: A Guide for Adult Learners.* Hawthorne, NJ: Career Press, 1994.

Weinberg, Carol. *The Complete Handbook for College Women: Making the Most of Your College Experience.* New York: New York University Press, 1994.

INTERNET RESOURCES

Student Center: www.studentcenter.org

Student.Com: College Life Online: www.student.com

Attention Deficit Disorder Association: www.add.org

National Center for Learning Disabilities: www.ncld.org

Prentice Hall Student Success Supersite: Student Union: www.prenhall.com/success/StudentUn/index.html

Success Stories: www.prenhall.com/success/Stories/index.html

ENDNOTES

1. Rick Pitino, *Success Is a Choice.* New York: Broadway Books, 1997, p. 40.

2. Cited in Colin Rise and Malcolm J. Nicholl, *Accelerated Learning for the 21st Century.* New York: Dell, 1997, pp. 5–6.

3. Center for Academic Integrity, Kenan Institute for Ethics, Duke University. A Report from the Center for Academic Integrity, October 1999. Downloaded March 19, 2001 from www.academicintegrity.org.

4. National Institute for Literacy Web site: www.nifl.gov/reders/!intro.htm#C

5. Rita Lenken Hawkins, Baltimore City Community College, 1997.

JOURNAL

name   date

visit: www.prenhall.com/carter NY Times link for this chapter

In this chapter you explore answers to the following questions: • **What is a learning style?** • **How can you discover how you learn?** • **Why is it important to know how you learn?** • **How can you start thinking about choosing a major?**

IN THIS CHAPTER

24

Self-awareness

EXPLORE

MANY STUDENTS do what they have to do in school without any idea of how they learn best. What Michael Nolan (see next page) already knows about himself serves as an excellent jumping-off point for his exploration of the college courses and the major that will make sense for him. Combining what you already know about yourself with the two different learning-style assessments in this chapter will help you further clarify your personal path. You can then apply what you have dis-covered as you consider your major and what it means for your life.

knowing how you learn and how to choose a major

Michael Nolan, Oregon State University, Corvallis, Oregon

Julia Nolan, University of California, Davis, California

How can I find the right major for me?

I encourage you to take internships in your field . . .

I have loved sports as long as I can remember. I love the strategy, the thought, and the decisions involved as much as I do the athletics. In fact, to me, the creation of a winning team from a jumble of talented players is often more interesting than the game itself.

Because of this, the business of sports is fascinating to me. One problem is that it's hard to get experience in as competitive a field as sports business. Also, there aren't a lot of sports business programs in the country, particularly at schools that interest me and have strong sports programs. Ideally, I'd also like to have a major that could be used somewhere else, in case I can't find a job in sports.

How can I find a major that appeals to my interests and that leads to a good career? How can I make sure that I like my chosen occupation and test its compatibility with me at school? And how can I learn what classes I should take to learn the most about sports business and excel in my field?

From early childhood, I wanted to be a scientist. I lived for the day when I'd be able to go to a *real* university and do *real* research in a *real* lab and contribute to the growing body of scientific knowledge. So, when one of my professors asked me to work for him on some antibiotics research at the end of my freshman year, I was ecstatic. After years of anticipation, I'd finally get to do what I'd dreamed of.

And I found that I hated it. Most of what I did was repetitive, such as reacting the product, identifying the product, purifying the product; all in long, laborious tasks for which I couldn't see the end result. Even worse, even if what I was working on did turn into a lifesaving antibiotic, it would likely take decades before anyone could use it. I found I just didn't have the patience for research. I don't like long hours of repetitive lab work and I don't want to wait for decades for a theory to become useful.

So, I discovered engineering. And I found a career that seems perfect for me, even though I couldn't have imagined myself as an engineer when I started college. Yet, the irony is that I only discovered that I love engineering and don't adore scientific research because I did an internship.

Had I not decided to do research in college, I'd probably be looking for a good Ph.D. program now, rather than doing something I love. I still like research and I still love reading about what's on the cutting edge of technology, but I also realize that a life of pure research isn't for me. That's probably the most important thing that I learned from my internship. I encourage you to take internships in your field because it was a lot better for me to learn that I didn't like lab work in college than it would have been several years into my first job.

What is a *learning style?*

t happens in nearly every college course: Students listen to lectures throughout the semester. Each student hears the same words at exactly the same time and completes the same assignments. However, after finals, student experiences with the course range from fulfillment and high grades to complete disconnection and low grades or withdrawals. Many causes may be involved—different levels of interest and effort, different levels of ability, outside stresses. Another major factor that often is not considered is **learning style.**

Although presentation styles vary, the standard lecture is still the norm in the majority of classrooms. This might lead you to assume that most students learn best in a lecture setting. Unfortunately, this is not the case, and students who don't learn as well from a lecture course may develop doubts about their competence. However, there are many different and equally valuable ways to learn. To succeed in any kind of course—and in life—you have to know how you learn, understand the strategies that heighten your strengths and boost your weaknesses, and know when to use them.

LEARNING STYLE

A particular way in which the mind receives and processes information.

The Two Parts of Learning Style

Students process information in different ways and have varied styles of interaction with others. Say, for example, that a group of students is taking a freshman composition class that is broken up into study groups during two out of three class meetings. Students who are comfortable working with words or happy when engaged in discussion with a study group may do well in the course. Students who are more mathematical than verbal, or who prefer to work alone, might not do as well. The learning-style factor results in different levels of success with the course.

This example shows that learning style is about more than just what kinds of courses or topics you prefer. Learning style can be seen as having two equally important aspects:

- Learning preferences—what abilities and areas of learning interest you and come most easily to you
- Personality traits—how you interact with information and with others

These two aspects are important partners in defining how you learn—and how you succeed in college and beyond. Neither one gives you a complete picture without the other. Imagine that a freshman composition instructor discovers that her entire class has strong verbal learning preferences. Thrilled, she proceeds with her group discussion-based course, figuring that the students will continue to do well. After finals, she is surprised to find a wide array of grades. A possible reason: Not everyone functions well in small group discussions.

Likewise, suppose another instructor chances on a course section composed entirely of students who love the experience-based, hands-on style of his biology course. He assumes that everyone will pass with flying colors. They don't, however—because, of course, not everyone has a natural learning preference in the sciences, no matter how much they like the style of interacting with the course material.

Getting Perspective on Learning Style

What you find out about your learning style through the assessments in this chapter can help you manage yourself effectively at school, work, and home. However, no assessment has the final word on who you are and what you can and cannot do. It's human to want an easy answer—a one-page printout revealing the secrets of your identity—but this kind of quick fix does not exist.

Your thinking skills—your ability to evaluate information—enable you to see yourself as a whole, including your strengths and weaknesses. Your job is to analyze the information you gain from the assessments in this chapter to arrive at an accurate self-portrait. Before you get into the heart of the assessments and what they mean, consider how to best use what you learn from them.

Using Assessments for Reference

Approach any assessment as a tool with which you can expand your idea of yourself. There are no "right" answers, no "best" set of scores. Think of it in the same way you would a new set of eyeglasses for a person with somewhat blurred vision. The glasses will not create new paths and possibilities, but will help you see more clearly the ones that already exist.

You continually learn, change, and grow throughout your life. Any evaluation is simply a snapshot, a look at who you are in a given moment. Your answers can, and will, change as you change and as circumstances change. They provide an opportunity for you to look at the present moment by asking questions: Who am I right now? How does this compare to who I want to be?

Using Assessments for Understanding

Understanding your preferred learning styles helps to prevent you from boxing yourself into categories that limit your life. Instead of saying, "I'm no good in math," someone who is not a natural in math can make the subject easier by tapping into learning style-related strategies. For example, a learner who responds to visuals can learn better by drawing diagrams of math problems; a learner who benefits from discussing material with others can improve comprehension by talking out problems with a study partner.

Most people have one or two dominant learning styles. In addition, you may change which abilities you emphasize, depending on the situation. For example, a student with a highly developed visual sense might find it easy to take notes in think link style (see Chapter 6 for an explanation of different note-taking styles). However, if an instructor writes an outline on the board as a guide to a detailed topic, the same student might work with the outline. The more you know yourself, the more you are able to assess and adapt to any situation.

Facing Challenges Realistically

Any assessment reveals areas of challenge as well as ability. Rather than dwelling on limitations (which often results in a negative self-image) or ignoring them (which often leads to unproductive choices), use what you know from the assessment to face your limitations and work to improve them.

> "To be what we are, and to become what we are capable of becoming, is the only end of life."

ROBERT LOUIS STEVENSON

In any area of challenge, look at where you are and set goals that help you reach where you want to be. If a class is difficult, examine what improvements to make in order to succeed. If a work project involves tasks that give you trouble, face your limitations head-on and ask for help. Exploring what you gain from working on a limitation helps you build the motivation you need to move ahead.

How can you *discover* how you learn?

This chapter presents two assessments that help you discover your style of learning and personality traits. View these as two equally important halves that help you form a whole picture of who you are as a learner.

The first assessment focuses on learning preferences and is called *Multiple Pathways to Learning*. It is based on the Multiple Intelligences Theory developed by Howard Gardner.

The second assessment is geared toward personality analysis and is based on the Myers-Briggs Type Inventory® (MBTI). The assessment is called *Personality Spectrum* and helps you evaluate how you react to people and situations.

Multiple Intelligences

There is a saying, "It is not how smart you are, but how you are smart." In 1983, Howard Gardner, a Harvard University professor, changed the way people perceive intelligence and learning with his theory of Multiple Intelligences. This theory holds that there are at least eight distinct intelligences possessed by all people, and that every person has developed some intelligences more fully than others. According to the Multiple Intelligences Theory, when you find a task or subject easy, you are probably using a more fully developed intelligence; when you have more trouble, you may be using a less developed intelligence.[1]

Gardner believes that the way you learn is a unique blend of intelligences, resulting from your distinctive abilities, challenges, experiences, and training. In addition, how you learn isn't necessarily set in stone—particular levels of ability in the intelligences may develop or recede based on changes in your life. Traditionally, the notion of intelligence has been linked to tests such as the Stanford-Binet IQ test and others like it that rely on mathematical, logical, and verbal measurements. Gardner, however, thinks that this doesn't accurately reflect the entire spectrum of human ability:

> I believe that we should . . . look . . . at more naturalistic sources of information about how peoples around the world develop skills important to their way of life. Think, for example, of sailors in the South Seas, who find their way around hundreds, or even thousands, of islands by looking at the constellations of stars in the sky, feeling the way a boat passes over the water, and noticing a few scattered landmarks. A word for intelligence in a society of these sailors would probably refer to that kind of navigational ability.[2]

Table 2.1 offers brief descriptions of the focus of each of the intelligences. You can find information on related skills and study techniques on page 34. The Multiple Pathways to Learning assessment helps you determine the levels to which your intelligences are developed.

Personality Spectrum

Personality assessments indicate how you respond to both internal and external situations—in other words, how you react to information, thoughts, and feelings, as well as to people and events. Employers may give such assessments to employees and use the results to set up and evaluate teams.

The Myers-Briggs Type Inventory is one of the most widely used personality inventories in both psychology and business, and was one of the first instruments to measure psychological types. Katharine Briggs and her daughter, Isabel Briggs Myers, together designed the MBTI. Later, David Keirsey and Marilyn Bates combined the 16 Myers-Briggs types into four temperaments and developed an assessment called the Keirsey Sorter based on those temperaments.

INTELLIGENCE

As defined by H. Gardner, an ability to solve problems or fashion products that are useful in a particular cultural setting or community.

Table 2.1	Multiple intelligences.
INTELLIGENCE	**DESCRIPTION**
Verbal–Linguistic	Ability to communicate through language (listening, reading, writing, speaking)
Logical–Mathematical	Ability to understand logical reasoning and problem solving (math, science, patterns, sequences)
Bodily–Kinesthetic	Ability to use the physical body skillfully and to take in knowledge through bodily sensation (coordination, working with hands)
Visual–Spatial	Ability to understand spatial relationships and to perceive and create images (visual art, graphic design, charts and maps)
Interpersonal	Ability to relate to others, noticing their moods, motivations, and feelings (social activity, cooperative learning, teamwork)
Intrapersonal	Ability to understand one's own behavior and feelings (self-awareness, independence, time spent alone)
Musical	Ability to comprehend and create meaningful sound and recognize patterns (music, sensitivity to sound and patterns)
Naturalistic	Ability to understand features of the environment (interest in nature, environmental balance, ecosystem, stress relief brought by natural environments)

Derived in part from the Myers-Briggs and Keirsey theories, the Personality Spectrum assessment adapts and simplifies their material into four personality types—Thinker, Organizer, Giver, and Adventurer—and was developed by Dr. Joyce Bishop in 1997. The Personality Spectrum gives you a personality perspective on how you can maximize your functioning at school and work. For each personality type, you'll see techniques that improve work and school performance, learning strategies, and ways of relating to others. Page 36 gives you more details about each type.

Scoring the Assessments

The assessments follow this section of text. As you complete them, try to answer the questions objectively—in other words, answer the questions to best indicate who you are, not who you want to be (or who your parents or instructors want you to be). Then, enter your scores on page 37. Don't be concerned if some of your scores are low—that is true for almost everyone.

Following each assessment is information about the typical traits of, and appropriate study strategies for, each intelligence or spectrum dimension. You have abilities in all areas, though some are more developed than others. Therefore, you may encounter useful suggestions under any of the headings. During this course, try a large number of new study techniques and keep what works for you.

Remember, also, that knowing your learning style is not only about guiding your life toward your strongest abilities; it is also about using other strategies when you face challenges. No one goes through life always able to find situations where strengths are in demand and weaknesses are uninvolved. Use the strategies for your weaker areas when what is required of you involves tasks and academic areas that you find difficult. For example, if you are not characteristically strong in logical–mathematical intelligence and have to take a required math or science course, the suggestions geared toward logical–mathematical learners may help you build what skill you have.

IMPORTANT NOTE   *about scoring . . .*

The two assessments are scored *differently.* For *Multiple Pathways to Learning,* each intelligence has a set of numbered statements, and you consider each numbered statement on its own, giving it the number you feel best suits your response to it. You will, therefore, have any combination of numbers for each intelligence, from all 4s to all 1s or anywhere in between.

For *Personality Spectrum,* you rank order the four statements that complete each statement, giving a 4 to the one most like you, a 3 to the next most, a 2 to the next, and a 1 to the one least like you. You will, therefore, have a 4, 3, 2, and 1 for each of the eight numbered questions.

MULTIPLE PATHWAYS TO LEARNING

① ② ③ ④

Directions: Rate each statement as follows. Write the number of your response (1–4) on the line next to the statement and total each set of six questions.

rarely   sometimes   usually   always

1. _____ I enjoy physical activities.
2. _____ I am uncomfortable sitting still.
3. _____ I prefer to learn through doing.
4. _____ When sitting I move my legs or hands.
5. _____ I enjoy working with my hands.
6. _____ I like to pace when I'm thinking or studying.

_____ **TOTAL for Bodily–Kinesthetic**

7. _____ I enjoy telling stories.
8. _____ I like to write.
9. _____ I like to read.
10. _____ I express myself clearly.
11. _____ I am good at negotiating.
12. _____ I like to discuss topics that interest me.

_____ **TOTAL for Verbal–Linguistic**

13. _____ I use maps easily.
14. _____ I draw pictures/diagrams when explaining ideas.
15. _____ I can assemble items easily from diagrams.
16. _____ I enjoy drawing or photography.
17. _____ I do not like to read long paragraphs.
18. _____ I prefer a drawn map over written directions.

_____ **TOTAL for Visual–Spatial**

19. _____ I like math in school.
20. _____ I like science.
21. _____ I problem solve well.
22. _____ I question how things work.
23. _____ I enjoy planning or designing something new.
24. _____ I am able to fix things.

_____ **TOTAL for Logical–Mathematical**

25. _____ I listen to music.
26. _____ I move my fingers or feet when I hear music.
27. _____ I have good rhythm.
28. _____ I like to sing along with music.
29. _____ People have said I have musical talent.
30. _____ I like to express my ideas through music.

_____ **TOTAL for Musical**

31. _____ I need quiet time to think.
32. _____ I think about issues before I want to talk.
33. _____ I am interested in self-improvement.
34. _____ I understand my thoughts and feelings.
35. _____ I know what I want out of life.
36. _____ I prefer to work on projects alone.

_____ **TOTAL for Intrapersonal**

37. _____ I like doing a project with other people.
38. _____ People come to me to help settle conflicts.
39. _____ I like to spend time with friends.
40. _____ I am good at understanding people.
41. _____ I am good at making people feel comfortable.
42. _____ I enjoy helping others.

_____ **TOTAL for Interpersonal**

43. _____ I enjoy nature whenever possible.
44. _____ I think about having a career involving nature.
45. _____ I enjoy studying plants, animals, or oceans.
46. _____ I avoid being indoors except when I sleep.
47. _____ As a child I played with bugs and leaves.
48. _____ When I feel stressed I want to be out in nature.

_____ **TOTAL for Naturalistic**

MULTIPLE INTELLIGENCES

Skills

VERBAL–LINGUISTIC

- Analyzing own use of language
- Remembering terms easily
- Explaining, teaching, learning, using humor
- Understanding syntax and meaning of words
- Convincing someone to do something

MUSICAL–RHYTHMIC

- Sensing tonal qualities
- Creating or enjoying melodies and rhythms
- Being sensitive to sounds and rhythms
- Using "schemas" to hear music
- Understanding the structure of music

LOGICAL–MATHEMATICAL

- Recognizing abstract patterns
- Reasoning inductively and deductively
- Discerning relationships and connections
- Performing complex calculations
- Reasoning scientifically

VISUAL–SPATIAL

- Perceiving and forming objects accurately
- Recognizing relationships between objects
- Representing something graphically
- Manipulating images
- Finding one's way in space

BODILY–KINESTHETIC

- Connecting mind and body
- Controlling movement
- Improving body functions
- Expanding body awareness to all senses
- Coordinating body movement

INTRAPERSONAL

- Evaluating own thinking
- Being aware of and expressing feelings
- Understanding self in relationship to others
- Thinking and reasoning on higher levels

INTERPERSONAL

- Seeing things from others' perspectives
- Cooperating within a group
- Communicating verbally and nonverbally
- Creating and maintaining relationships

NATURALIST

- Deep understanding of nature
- Appreciation of the delicate balance in nature

Study Techniques

VERBAL–LINGUISTIC

- Read text and highlight no more than 10%
- Rewrite notes
- Outline chapters
- Teach someone else
- Recite information or write scripts/debates

MUSICAL–RHYTHMIC

- Create rhythms out of words
- Beat out rhythms with hand or stick
- Play instrumental music/write raps
- Put new material to songs you already know
- Take music breaks

LOGICAL–MATHEMATICAL

- Organize material logically
- Explain material sequentially to someone
- Develop systems and find patterns
- Write outlines and develop charts and graphs
- Analyze information

VISUAL–SPATIAL

- Develop graphic organizers for new material
- Draw mind maps
- Develop charts and graphs
- Use color in notes to organize
- Visualize material

BODILY–KINESTHETIC

- Move or rap while you learn
- Pace and recite
- Move fingers under words while reading
- Create "living sculptures"
- Act out scripts of material, design games

INTRAPERSONAL

- Reflect on personal meaning of information
- Visualize information/keep a journal
- Study in quiet settings
- Imagine experiments

INTERPERSONAL

- Study in a group
- Discuss information
- Use flash cards with others
- Teach someone else

NATURALIST

- Connect with nature whenever possible
- Form study groups of people with like interests

Adapted by Dr. Joyce Bishop from David Lazear, *Seven Pathways of Learning*, 1994.

PERSONALITY SPECTRUM

STEP 1. Rank order all four responses to each question from most like you (4) to least like you (1). Use the circles next to the responses to indicate your rankings.

most like me   more like me   less like me   least like me

1. I like instructors who
   a. ◯ tell me exactly what is expected of me.
   b. ◯ make learning active and exciting.
   c. ◯ maintain a safe and supportive classroom.
   d. ◯ challenge me to think at higher levels.

2. I learn best when the material is
   a. ◯ well organized.
   b. ◯ something I can do hands-on.
   c. ◯ about understanding and improving the human condition.
   d. ◯ intellectually challenging.

3. A high priority in my life is to
   a. ◯ keep my commitments.
   b. ◯ experience as much of life as possible.
   c. ◯ make a difference in the lives of others.
   d. ◯ understand how things work.

4. Other people think of me as
   a. ◯ dependable and loyal.
   b. ◯ dynamic and creative.
   c. ◯ caring and honest.
   d. ◯ intelligent and inventive.

5. When I experience stress I would most likely
   a. ◯ do something to help me feel more in control of my life.
   b. ◯ do something physical and daring.
   c. ◯ talk with a friend.
   d. ◯ go off by myself and think about my situation.

6. I would probably not be close friends with someone who is
   a. ◯ irresponsible.
   b. ◯ unwilling to try new things.
   c. ◯ selfish and unkind to others.
   d. ◯ an illogical thinker.

7. My vacations could be described as
   a. ◯ traditional.
   b. ◯ adventuresome.
   c. ◯ pleasing to others.
   d. ◯ a new learning experience.

8. One word that best describes me is
   a. ◯ sensible.
   b. ◯ spontaneous.
   c. ◯ giving.
   d. ◯ analytical.

STEP 2. Add up the total points for each letter.

TOTAL for a. ◯ Organizer   TOTAL for c. ◯ Giver

TOTAL for b. ◯ Adventurer   TOTAL for d. ◯ Thinker

STEP 3. Plot these numbers on the brain diagram on page 37.

PERSONALITY SPECTRUM

Skills   ## Study Techniques

THINKER

- Solving problems
- Developing models and systems
- Analytical and abstract thinking
- Exploring ideas and potentials
- Ingenuity
- Going beyond established boundaries
- Global thinking—seeking universal truth

THINKER

- Find time to reflect independently on new information
- Learn through problem solving
- Design new ways of approaching issues
- Convert material into logical charts and graphs
- Try to minimize repetitive tasks
- Look for opportunities where you have the freedom to work independently

ORGANIZER

- Responsibility, reliability
- Operating successfully within social structures
- Sense of history, culture, and dignity
- Neatness and organization
- Loyalty
- Orientation to detail
- Comprehensive follow-through on tasks
- Efficiency

ORGANIZER

- Try to have tasks defined in clear, concrete terms so that you know what is required
- Look for a well-structured, stable environment
- Request feedback
- Use a planner to schedule tasks and dates
- Organize material by rewriting and organizing class or text notes, making flash cards, or carefully highlighting

GIVER

- Honesty, authenticity
- Successful, close relationships
- Making a difference in the world
- Cultivating your own potential and that of others
- Negotiation; promoting peace
- Communicating with others
- Openness
- Helping others

GIVER

- Study with others
- Teach material to others
- Seek out tasks, groups, and subjects that involve helping people
- Find ways to express thoughts and feelings clearly and honestly
- Put energy into your most important relationships

ADVENTURER

- High ability in a variety of fields
- Courage and daring
- Approaching problem solving in a hands-on fashion
- Living in the present
- Spontaneity and action
- Ability to negotiate
- Nontraditional style
- Flexibility
- Zest for life

ADVENTURER

- Look for environments that encourage nontraditional approaches
- Find hands-on ways to learn
- Seek people whom you find stimulating
- Use or develop games and puzzles to help memorize terms
- Fight boredom by asking if you can do something extra or perform a task in a more active way

Name: _____   Date: _____

Personality Spectrum: Place a dot on the appropriate number line in the brain diagram for each of your four scores from p. 35; connect the dots; then shade each section using a different color. Write your scores in the four circles just outside the diagram. See information regarding scores below.

Multiple Pathways to Learning: In the vertical bars below the brain diagram, indicate your scores from p. 33 by shading from the bottom going up until you reach the number corresponding to your score for that intelligence. See information regarding scores below.

THINKER
Technical
Scientific
Mathematical
Dispassionate
Rational
Analytical
Logical
Problem Solving
Theoretical
Intellectual
Objective
Quantitative
Explicit
Realistic
Literal
Precise
Formal

GIVER
Interpersonal
Emotional
Caring
Sociable
Giving
Spiritual
Musical
Romantic
Feeling
Peacemaker
Trusting
Adaptable
Passionate
Harmonious
Idealistic
Talkative
Honest

Left Brain   Right Brain

ORGANIZER
Tactical
Planning
Detailed
Practical
Confident
Predictable
Controlled
Dependable
Systematic
Sequential
Structured
Administrative
Procedural
Organized
Conservative
Safekeeping
Disciplined

ADVENTURER
Active
Visual
Risking
Original
Artistic
Spatial
Skillful
Impulsive
Metaphoric
Experimental
Divergent
Fast-paced
Simultaneous
Competitive
Imaginative
Open-minded
Adventuresome

24
20
15

B–K   V–L   V–S   L–M   M   Intra   Inter   N

For the Personality Spectrum, 26–36 indicates a strong tendency in that dimension, 14–25 a moderate tendency, and below 14 a minimal tendency.

For Multiple Pathways to Learning, 21–24 indicates a high level of development in that particular type of intelligence, 15–20 a moderate level, and below 15 an underdeveloped intelligence.

Source for brain diagram: Understanding Psychology, 3/e, by Morris, © 1996. Adapted by permission of Prentice-Hall, Inc., Upper Saddle River, NJ.

Why is it *important* to know *how* you learn?

he knowledge you have gained by taking the assessments in this chapter can guide you to smart choices that will bring success in your studies, the classroom, and the workplace.

Study Benefits

Knowing how you learn helps you choose techniques that maximize what you do best *and* find strategies that help you improve when you have trouble. Say you have discovered that you respond best to information presented in a linear, logical way. You can use that knowledge to select areas of study or courses that have the presentation you like. When you must take a course that doesn't suit you as well, you can find ways to convert the material so that it better matches your learning style.

This text helps you apply what you learn about your learning style to other important topics, in two different ways. First, each of the following chapters has a feature, Multiple Intelligence Strategies, that shows how to improve your mastery of different skill areas through strategies specific to each of the Multiple Intelligences. Second, in the discussion of careers in Chapter 9, a special segment applies the Personality Spectrum to both career choice and work success strategies.

Classroom Benefits

Knowing your learning style can help you make the most of the teaching styles of your instructors (an instructor's teaching style often reflects his or her learning style). Your particular learning style may work well with the way some instructors teach and be a mismatch with other instructors. Occasionally, you may be able to choose an instructor who teaches in a way that maximizes how you learn. Class schedules, however, usually don't make such choices possible.

After several class meetings, you should be able to assess the instructor's teaching styles (it's common for instructors to have more than one). Figure 2.1 sets forth some common styles. If your style doesn't match up well with that of your instructor, you have a number of options.

Bring extra focus to your weaker areas. Working on your weaker points helps you break new ground in your learning. For example, if you're a verbal person in a math- and logic-oriented class, increase your focus and concentration during class so that you get as much as you can from the presentation. Then spend extra study time on the material, ask others

Figure 2.1	Teaching styles reflect instructor learning styles.
LECTURE	Instructor speaks to the class for the entire period, little to no class interaction.
GROUP DISCUSSION	Instructor presents material but encourages class discussion throughout.
SMALL GROUPS	Instructor presents material and then breaks class into small groups for discussion or project work.
VISUAL FOCUS	Instructor uses visual elements such as diagrams, photographs, drawings, transparencies.
VERBAL FOCUS	Instructor relies primarily on words, either spoken or written on the board or overhead projector.
LOGICAL PRESENTATION	Instructor organizes material in a logical sequence, such as by time or importance.
RANDOM PRESENTATION	Instructor tackles topics in no particular order, jumps around a lot, or digresses.

from your class to help you, and search for additional supplemental materials and exercises to reinforce your knowledge.

Ask your instructor for additional help. For example, a visual person might ask an instructor to recommend visuals that help to illustrate the points made in class. Take advantage of your instructor's office hours to talk one-on-one about what's giving you trouble—especially in a large lecture, your instructor won't know what's going on with you unless you speak up.

"Convert" class material during study time. For example, an interpersonal learner takes a class with an instructor who presents big-picture information in lecture format. This student might organize study groups and talk through concepts with other group members while filling in the factual gaps. Likewise, a visual student might rewrite notes in different colors to add a visual element—for example, using one color for central ideas, another for supporting examples.

Instructors are as unique as students, and no instructor can fulfill the particular needs of a whole classroom of individuals. You often have to shift elements of your habitual learning approach to better mesh with how your instructor presents material. Being flexible in this way benefits you throughout life. Just as you can't hand-pick your instructors, in the workplace you are rarely, if ever, able to choose your boss or change his or her style.

Career Benefits

Because different careers require different abilities, there is no one "best" learning style for the workplace. Knowing how you learn brings you the following key benefits on the job:

- *Better performance.* Because so much of what you do at school (e.g., interacting with others, reading, taking notes) is what you do on the job, it follows that your learning style is essentially the same as your working style. If you know how you learn, you can look for a career, position, and environment that suits you best. You can perform at the top of your ability if you work at a job in which you feel competent and happy.

"They are able because they think they are able."

VIRGIL

- *Better teamwork.* Teamwork is a primary feature of the modern workplace. The better your awareness of your abilities and personality traits, the better you are able to communicate with others and identify what tasks you can best perform in a team situation.

- *Better self-awareness.* Knowing how you learn helps you pinpoint roadblocks. This helps you to work on difficult areas; plus, when a task requires a skill that is tough for you, you can either take special care with it or suggest someone else whose style may be better suited to it.

All three of these areas of benefit—study, classroom, and career—come into play as you begin to consider how to focus your studies in college. Take what you have learned about yourself into account when thinking about your choice of a major.

How can you start thinking about
choosing a major?

Sometime during the first half of your time in college, after you complete your general education courses, you will be asked to declare an academic major. Choosing a major is one of the biggest decisions you make in college. It determines many of the courses you take, much of what you learn, many of the people with whom you interact, and often your future career.

First, though, remember that you don't have to decide your future in the next five minutes. Most students come to college with little idea of what they want to study or do for a living. Furthermore, you learn about yourself and make changes as you explore. Many students change their majors one or more times during their college career. And, as career expert and professor Dr. Randall Hansen notes, "Your major in college is important for your first job after graduation, but studies show that most people will change careers about four or five times over the course of their lives."[4]

The key is to *start* now, even though you probably don't have to make a decision right away. It takes time to think through options and get an idea of what is required for different majors and careers. Think of choosing a major as a multistep process that starts with knowing your interests and abilities, continues with looking into career areas, moves to exploring academic options, and concludes with making the choice that is right for you.

MAJOR

An academic subject area chosen as a field of specialization, requiring a specific course of study.

Identify Interests and Abilities

The best majors and careers for you are ones that involve your interests and abilities. You already have some strong clues from the work you have done in exploring how you learn. Take those into consideration and continue the process of learning about yourself by concentrating on your academic interests, abilities, and skills. Asking questions like the following helps to pinpoint your areas of interest and—just as importantly—areas to avoid:

- What courses have I enjoyed the most? What might these courses have in common?

- What subjects are interesting to me when I read and study?

- What school- or career-related activities do I look forward to most?

- In what skills or academic areas do I perform best?

- What areas are most difficult for me? What do I struggle with?

- When I open the college catalog, what areas of study or courses am I drawn to?

- Do I consider myself to be a "natural" in any particular area?

- Am I focused on taking courses that will prepare me for a particular career or is my goal to become well rounded through a broad education?
- Am I willing to go to graduate or professional school to become qualified in a particular field?

In today's flighty economy, it can be hard to take your interests into account if they don't seem to lead you to a well-paying, stable career. Considering your interests, however, can lead you to an area of study or a job that you love—and that won't leave you bored or unfulfilled. Here are three positive effects of focusing on what interests you:

- *You have more energy.* When you're doing something you like, time seems to pass quickly. Contrast this with how you feel about disagreeable activities. You accomplish much more in a subject or career area that you enjoy.
- *You perform better.* When you were in high school, you probably got your best grades in your favorite classes. That doesn't change as you get older. The more you like something, the harder you work at it—and the harder you work, the more you improve and the more job and financial success you have. Do something you love, say career experts, and the money will follow.
- *You have a more positive attitude.* A positive attitude contributes to your success in areas in which you lack natural ability or experience.

Link Interests and Abilities to Careers

The point of declaring and pursuing a major is to help you reach a significant level of knowledge in one subject, often in preparation for a particular career area. So, before you focus on majors, think broadly about the career areas that interest you. Having some idea of career interests helps you narrow the field when looking more carefully at potential majors.

Many students select a major because it prepares them to find work in a particular field after they graduate. An education major, for example, is able to teach in elementary school after fulfilling the departmental requirements

PERSONAL TRIUMPH

Some of the most significant lessons you learn about yourself come from getting through difficult times. Gloria Finn Porter had the drive to succeed, and inspiring mentors helped her find a path that felt right for her.

At an early age, I learned that life can appear unfair. My mother was married seven times, and my father was her third husband. When my mother was 35, she started drinking and was an alcoholic almost immediately. When I was 14, I quit school, left home, and got a job at a fast-food restaurant. My girlfriend had been kicked out of her house, so we rented an apartment together. We drank alcohol and did drugs. I attempted suicide several times.

When I hit my 20s, I picked up a DUI. Getting arrested, however, was the catalyst for change in my life. To expunge the DUI from my record, I went into six months of treatment for alcohol abuse at a halfway house in Wisconsin and earned my G.E.D. When I completed the program, I was sober, but I had no money and no clear idea of what I wanted to do.

On a whim, I decided to move to my grandmother's home in Tennessee and try to start school. I walked into Cumberland University in Lebanon and told them that I wanted to go to school, but couldn't pay for it. Between student loans, grants, and scholarships, it all worked out. I also worked at an all-night truck stop, which was a lot of fun.

Before graduating, I started applying to law schools. I believe that if you keep putting one foot in front of the other, and if you have good motives, you will run into your future. During law school, I volunteered with the Public Defender's office. It was there that I met Jim Sheehan, a veteran public defender, who would teach me not only about the law, but about compassion for others, including those with whom I do not agree.

In 1999, Jim Sheehan founded the Center for Justice. I feel privileged to have been a part of that start-up process. We manage a wide range

Gloria Finn Porter, Cofounder and Attorney at the Center for Justice, Spokane, Washington

of cases including family law, civil rights, environmental, and landlord–tenant issues. Our passion is helping people with modest incomes who are caught in unfair legal situations.

I have learned that to achieve anything, I must ignore the negative voices. When someone says that I can't do something, I see myself achieving that goal. I actually see it; I hold that vision and revisit it each and every day. When someone told me that I would be 35 when I graduated law school, I thought, "Well, I am going to be 35 regardless of what I do—I might as well be a lawyer." I just kept thinking of the little engine that could.

I have also learned to ask for help. No one does it alone. I received so much help from family, friends, counselors, professors, fellow attorneys, my therapist, and mentors and supervisors at the Public Defender's office. People want to help those who want to help themselves.

Last, I have learned to have compassion for those who have harmed me and others. While my mother and father caused us pain, they also loved us very much. They simply did not have the ability to be stable and healthy. It is true that I still see unfairness, but I understand the bigger picture now. It is not about my childhood anymore; it is about me making positive choices and being grateful for my life.

My story was written for those of you who have struggled. You can do anything you want to do—just have faith, get in your little train, and go.

Take a moment to consider . . .

- *How getting through something difficult has fueled your drive to succeed.*

- *A person whose help and attention have helped you learn about yourself and discover goals that feel right to you.*

for undergraduate study. Similarly, an accounting major is prepared for an entry-level job in the accounts payable department of a major corporation.

For many career-oriented majors, students need graduate or professional school to achieve their career goal. For example, in the health sciences field, students who hope to become physicians, physicians' assistants, or dentists have to attend a professional school and be licensed by the state in which they practice. Their undergraduate major is just the beginning of a long journey of learning.

Other undergraduates are looking for intellectual growth and a field that interests them, and they don't focus specifically on a direct career link. These students often gravitate to the liberal arts, which includes departments like English, philosophy, comparative literature, and art history. Although these courses generally do not prepare students for specific jobs when they graduate, they help develop analytic and decision-making skills that are invaluable over a lifetime. Liberal arts majors often go on to a graduate or professional school and wind up in a variety of professions including law, business management, and publishing.

Ultimately, only you can decide how important the career connection is to you. Use the following strategies as you explore what's out there.

Use resources. Visit the career center to take a career assessment or to find out what career areas currently have the best long-term prospects. Talk to people who have jobs that interest you. Read current media to keep up with where the best prospects are.

Explore the educational requirements of different careers. Your choice of a major may be more or less crucial depending on the career area. For example, pursuing a career in medicine almost always requires a major in some area of the biological sciences, whereas aspiring writers may have majored in anything from political science to philosophy.

Consider learning style. Technological and scientific careers demand strength in logical–mathematical thinking, for example, and educational careers often involve extensive interpersonal interaction.

Look at your stronger and weaker areas and see what careers are likely to make the most of what you do well.

Try hands-on exploration. Extracurricular activities and volunteering opportunities might give you particular insight into what works well for you. For example, a student interested in architecture may volunteer with a group building houses for the disadvantaged, or a student considering social work can join a service fraternity.

Keep values in mind. What you think you want in a career might not always go along with your most closely held values. Ask yourself what careers support the principles that guide your life choices. How important to you are service to others, financial security, a broad-based education, time for family? Where do you stand on political and moral issues? Think carefully about how your values are supported by any career you consider.[5] Chapter 3 has more information on exploring your values.

Finally, when exploring careers, avoid assumptions about what is available to you. Every career area has job options that aren't obvious right away. For example, a student working toward a teaching certification doesn't have to teach in a public school. This student can develop curricula, act as a consultant for businesses, develop an on-line education service, teach overseas for the Peace Corps, or create a public television program. The sky's the limit.

Explore Academic Options

Once you have a good idea of who you are and what interests you in the working world, the next step is to find out as much as you can about the academic choices open to you. This helps you narrow down possible majors until you find one that works. The following suggestions will help you explore. Some suggestions involve your contact with others. As you read, keep in mind the importance of establishing a support network early on. Advisors, instructors, tutors, classmates, RAs (resident assistants), and others can give you important advice and feedback all along the path.

Read the college catalog to learn your parameters. Every school has its own set of rules that govern the declaration (and changing) of majors. Your catalog tells you what you need to know (some schools may even have their catalogs available on-line). Right from the start, examine what your school requires of you. Find answers to these general questions first:

- When do I have to declare a major? (generally at the end of the second year for four-year programs; earlier for associate or certificate programs)
- What majors are offered at my school?

- What are my options in majoring? (double majors, minors, or inter-disciplinary majors)

Once you have this basic information, take time during your first semester to review the majors your school offers. If a major looks interesting, read the detailed course descriptions and learn the departmental requirements you have to meet. Then, for each major you want to explore further, look for answers to the following questions:

- What minimum grade point average, if any, does the department require before it will accept me as a major?
- What preparatory courses (prerequisites) are required?
- What courses (within or without the department) am I required to take? How many credits do I need to graduate in the major?
- Do I have to take courses according to a prescribed sequence—and if so, what is the recommended order of courses?
- Will I have to write a thesis to graduate in this major?
- Who are the departmental advisors?

Work closely with your advisor. Don't make decisions in a vacuum. Begin discussing your major early on with your advisor, even if you don't intend to declare right away. For any given major, your advisor may be able to tell you about the course work and career possibilities. Your advisor can help you evaluate what's available and together you can find the best options.

Visit the department. Ask the department secretary for information (in print form or on the Web) about majors offered by that department (most academic departments compile information to help students make an informed decision about requirements). Then, ask about sitting in on several classes to get a first-hand introduction to the instructors and the work. If, after this experience, you continue to be interested, consider asking an instructor for an appointment to discuss becoming a major.

Speak to people with experience in the major. This includes both current majors and alumni. Ask students who are a year or two ahead to describe their experiences with the courses, the workload, and the professors. Ask them about the link between their career goals and their major. Ask, also, if there is a special club for student majors. For example, a student attending a meeting of the Psi Chi Club for psychology majors might pick up valuable information about courses, instructors, department requirements, and career paths.

Think out of the box—look at creative options for majoring. Don't limit your choices before you have to. Schools often have one or more of the following open to you:

- *Double majors.* Say, for example, you are interested in majoring in English and philosophy. Ask your academic advisor if it is possible to meet the requirements for both departments. Double majors are encouraged for committed students capable of handling the increased workload.

- *Interdisciplinary majors.* If what you want to major in isn't listed in the college catalog, don't immediately assume it's impossible. Talk with your academic advisor. Some schools allow certain students to design their own majors with help and approval from their advisors and instructors. In such a case, you and your advisor work together to come up with a unique list of courses. An example is a course load that combines biology, chemistry, and political science for a career path into public policy medicine.

- *Minors.* A minor also involves a concentration of courses in a particular department, but has fewer requirements than a major. As a sociology major, for example, you can satisfy your career goal to become a social worker by minoring in Spanish, an important second language in the region you hope to work. Or you can use your minor to pursue a lifelong interest—to study the trombone, learn about archaeology, learn about world religions.

- *Majors involving courses outside your school.* Some schools may have study abroad programs (spending a semester or a year at an affiliated college in a different country) or opportunities to take courses at nearby schools. Such courses might apply to a major that interests you.

Plan your curriculum. Although you won't necessarily want to plan out your entire college course load at the beginning of your first semester, planning a tentative curriculum—both within and without your major—can help to give you a clearer idea of where you are heading. It can also help you avoid pitfalls, such as not being able to get into a course you need. Here are some tips:

CURRICULUM
The particular set of courses required for a degree.

- *Fulfill core requirements.* Make time for your core courses in the beginning of your college career. The sooner you complete them, the sooner you can focus your studies on the areas that interest you most. Plus, you cannot graduate without fulfilling these requirements, no matter how distinguished your performance in your major.

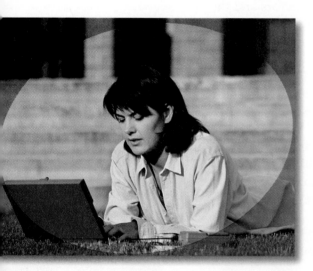

- *Use electives to branch out.* Prior to declaring your major, choose electives in your areas of interest. Enlarging the scope of your knowledge helps to improve your critical thinking, broaden your perspectives, and perhaps introduce you to career possibilities you have never considered.

- *Register early.* When students wait until the last minute to register for the following semester, some courses they want have already been filled; as a result, they may have to take courses they would not necessarily have chosen. In a worst-case scenario, you may have to delay your graduation in order to fit in a required course.

- *Stay flexible.* Even as you plan, know that your goals, available courses, and other factors may change anytime. One of the advantages of having a plan is that you have something concrete to turn to and adjust when change comes your way.

Be open to changing majors. Some students may change their minds one or more times before finding a major that fits. For example, a pre-med student taking a course in medical ethics might find that his true passion lies in philosophy and religion. You have a right to change your mind; each detour along the way helps to guide you to a path that feels like home. Just act on your new decision right away by informing your advisor and planning a schedule linked to your new choices. Some courses you've taken may even apply to your new major.

No matter what path you choose, working toward any major helps you to develop your most important skill—knowing how to use your mind. More than anything, your future success in school and career depends on your ability to contribute to the workplace through clear, effective, and creative thinking.

Follow Your Passion

It is tempting to tailor your major and career to an area that seems like a sure success. Friends or parents may have warned you against certain careers, encouraging you to stay with "safe" careers that seem socially acceptable or that pay well. In many cases, family and financial circumstances lead students to choose a major that leads directly to well-paying job opportunities and to avoid areas that don't seem to have a clear-cut path to a stable job.

> "Great minds have purposes; others have wishes."
>
> **WASHINGTON IRVING**

Prestige and money may be important—but they usually are not viable replacements for deep personal satisfaction. Furthermore, your major, important as it is, might not ultimately be strongly linked to your career. The Penn State University Web site article "Major Decisions," reports:

> Studies have shown that within ten years after graduation most people are working in careers that are not directly connected to their undergraduate majors. . . . Many jobs that exist today will be performed in very different ways five years from now or may even be obsolete by then. New types of jobs are emerging every year, and most of us have no way of knowing what those jobs will be or what type of education will be needed in order to qualify for them. Consequently, the current emphasis in career planning at the undergraduate level is on the development of general, transferable skills (writing, speaking, computer, problem-solving, team-building) that employers want and that graduates will need in order to adjust to rapidly-changing careers.[6]

Think carefully about your courses, your major, and your career. If your true passion takes you off what seems like a safer path, the choice may be very challenging. However, you are the one who has to live with your decision. Make a choice that leads you toward the life you have dreamed of. Make a choice that makes the most of the real you.

sabiduría

In Spanish, the term *sabiduría* represents the two sides of learning: knowledge and wisdom. Knowledge—building what you know about how the world works—is the first part. Wisdom—deriving meaning and significance from knowledge and deciding how to use it—is the second. As you continually learn and experience new things, the *sabiduría* you build will help you make knowledgeable and wise choices about how to lead your life.

Think of this concept as you discover more about how you receive knowledge in all aspects of your life—in school, work, and personal situations. As you learn how your unique mind works and how to use it, you can more confidently assert yourself. As you expand your ability to use your mind in different ways, you can create lifelong advantages for yourself.

Building Skills
FOR COLLEGE, CAREER, AND LIFE SUCCESS

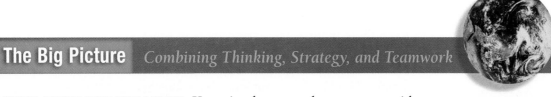

The Big Picture   *Combining Thinking, Strategy, and Teamwork*

LEARNING ABOUT HOW YOU LEARN. Knowing how you learn can provide insight that will help you make the best possible decisions about your future. List your two strongest intelligences.

_____

_____

Describe a positive experience at work or school that you can attribute to these strengths.

_____

_____

_____

_____

_____

_____

Name your two least-developed intelligences.

_____

_____

What challenge do you face that may be related to your least-developed intelligences?

_____

_____

_____

_____

_____

_____

Thinking about your strongest intelligences, name two majors that might suit you.

1. _____

2. _____

For each major, name a corresponding career area you may want to explore.

1. _____

2. _____

Keep these majors and career areas in mind as you gradually narrow your course choices in the time before you declare a major.

Finally, divide into groups according to the four types of the Personality Spectrum—Thinker-dominant students in one group, Organizer-dominant students in another, Giver-dominant students in a third, and Adventurer-dominant students in the fourth. If you have scored the same in more than one of these types, join whatever group is smaller. With your group, brainstorm four lists for your type:

> the **strengths** of this type
>
> the **struggles** it brings
>
> the **stressors** (things that cause stress) for this type
>
> **career** areas that tend to suit this type

If there is time, each group can present this information to the entire class to enable everyone to have a better understanding and acceptance of one another's intelligences. You might also brainstorm strategies for dealing with your intelligence's struggles and stressors, and present those ideas to the class as well.

Writing *Discovery Through Journaling*

To record your thoughts, use a separate journal or the lined pages at the end of the chapter.

YOUR LEARNING STYLE. Discuss the insights you have gained through exploring your multiple intelligences and personality spectrum. What strengths have come to your attention? What challenges have been clarified? Give some specific ideas of how you might use your strengths and address your challenges in the courses you are taking this semester.

SELF-PORTRAIT. A self-portrait is an important step in your career exploration because self-knowledge allows you to make the best choices about what to study and what career to pursue. Use this exercise to synthesize everything you have been exploring about yourself into one comprehensive "self-portrait." Design your portrait in "think link" style, using words and visual shapes to describe your learning style, habits, interests, abilities, and anything else you think is an important part of who you are.

A think link is a visual construction of related ideas, similar to a map or web, that represents your thought process. Ideas are written inside geometric shapes, often boxes or circles, and related ideas and facts are attached to those ideas by lines that connect the shapes. See the note-taking section in Chapter 6 for more about think links.

Use the style shown in the example in Figure 2.2 or create your own. For example, in this exercise you may want to create a "wheel" of ideas

Figure 2.2 Sample self-portrait think link.

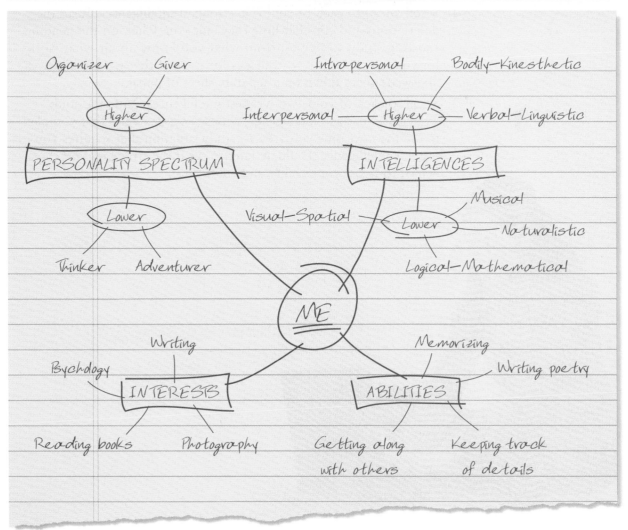

coming off your central shape, entitled "Me." Then, spreading out from each of those ideas (interests, learning style, etc.), draw lines connecting all of the thoughts that go along with that idea. Connected to "Interests," for example, might be "singing," "stock market," and "history." You don't have to use the wheel image. You might want to design a treelike think link or a line of boxes with connecting thoughts written below the boxes, or anything else you like. Let your design reflect who you are, just as the think link itself does.

Assess Yourself *Student Success Strategies*

If you have access to the CD-ROM Strategies for Success, *use the following questions to assess your thoughts and enhance your understanding of the chapter. The questions below represent only some of the activities provided on the CD for the chapter topics—try others if you have time.*

Click on the Learning Styles bookmark. From completing the Multiple Intelligences assessment in the chapter, recall your two strongest intelligences and your two weakest.

1. Scroll ahead to each of your two strongest intelligences. Read the descriptions and consider how they suit you. Click on the heading showing study strategies; from what you know about what works for you, create two new strategies for each of the two intelligences and write them down on a separate sheet of paper.

2. Scroll to each of your two weakest intelligences. Note the study strategies. For each intelligence, choose two strategies that you plan to use the next time you are in a study situation that requires you to use this intelligence. Evaluate later to see if the strategies you chose helped to boost your ability and confidence.

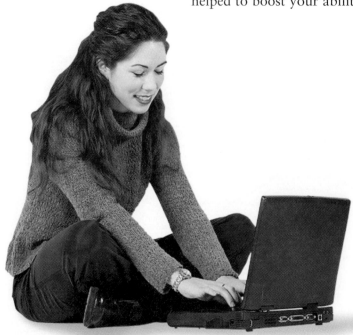

Suggested Readings

Barger, Nancy J., Linda K. Kirby, and Jean M. Kummerow. *Work Types: Understand Your Work Personality—How It Helps You and Holds You Back, and What You Can Do to Understand It.* New York: Warner Books, 1997.

College Board, ed. *The College Board Index of Majors and Graduate Degrees 2001.* New York: College Entrance Examination Board, 2000.

Gardner, Howard. *Intelligence Reframed: Multiple Intelligences for the 21st Century.* New York: Basic Books, 2000.

Harrington, Paul, et al. *The College Majors Handbook: The Actual Jobs, Earnings, and Trends for Graduates of 60 College Majors.* Indianapolis, IN: Jist Works, 1999.

Keirsey, David. *Please Understand Me II: Temperament, Character, Intelligence.* Del Mar, CA: Prometheus Nemesis Book Company, 1998.

Pearman, Roger R. and Sarah C. Albritton. *I'm Not Crazy, I'm Just Not You: The Real Meaning of the 16 Personality Types.* Palo Alto, CA: Consulting Psychologists Press, 1997.

Phifer, Paul. *College Majors and Careers: A Resource Guide for Effective Life Planning,* 4th ed. Chicago: Ferguson Publishing, 1999.

Endnotes

1. Howard Gardner, *Multiple Intelligences: The Theory in Practice.* New York: Harper-Collins, 1993, pp. 5–49.

2. Ibid, p. 7.

3. Developed by Joyce Bishop, Ph.D., Psychology faculty, Golden West College, Huntington Beach, CA. Based on Howard Gardner, *Frames of Mind: The Theory of Multiple Intelligences.* New York: Harper-Collins, 1993.

4. Randall S. Hansen, Ph.D. (January 2001). "Choosing a College Major: How to Chart Your Ideal Path" [on-line]. Available at www.quintcareers.com/choosing_major.html (March 2001).

5. Michael J. Leonard (January 1996). "Major Decisions: For Students Who Are Exploring Majors" (Division of Undergraduate Studies, The Pennsylvania State University) [on-line]. Available at www.psu.edu/dus/md/ (July 2001).

6. Ibid.

Internet Resources

Keirsey Sorter and other Myers-Briggs information: www.keirsey.com

Prentice Hall Student Success Supersite Majors Exploration: www.prenhall.com/success/MajorExp/index.html

Exploring Multiple Intelligences: www.multi-intell.com

54

JOURNAL

name   date

visit: www.prenhall.com/carter NY Times link for this chapter

IN THIS CHAPTER

In this chapter you explore answers to the following questions:

- What defines your values? • How do you set and achieve goals? • How can
you manage your time? • Why is procrastination a problem?

Goal setting and time management

PEOPLE DREAM of what they want out of life, but as Rosalia Chavez (see next page) has experienced, obstacles can interfere with those dreams. However, when you set goals, prioritize, and manage your time effectively, you can develop the kind of "big picture" vision that gets you moving. This chapter explains how defining your values and taking specific steps toward goals can help you turn your dreams into reality. The section on time management discusses how to translate your goals into daily, weekly, monthly, and yearly steps. Finally, you explore how procrastination can derail your dreams and how to avoid it.

using values to map your course

Rosalia Chavez, University of Arizona, Tucson, Arizona

Norma Seledon, Las Mujeres en Accion, Chicago, Illinois

How can I stay focused on my school goals?

Your desire to learn and grow . . . will fuel your efforts.

I married at 18 and didn't finish high school. After our two sons were born, I decided to get my G.E.D., but my husband didn't want me to. At this point, I knew I had to start making opportunities for myself. Shortly after I had begun to further my education, my husband died. I am now taking classes full-time and I work part-time in the Chicano/Hispano Student Affairs Office. I would like to empower future generations of Hispanic women to follow their dreams by telling them my story.

I have to make daily decisions about priorities, and my life situations often get in the way of my schoolwork. Recently, I had to drop a class because my children were sick and I couldn't keep up. My son, who is 11, has ADHD (attention deficit hyperactivity disorder). I can no longer afford his medicine because I was denied state medical assistance. Can you offer suggestions about how I can manage my life and stay focused on my school goals?

Your story is not atypical. Your taking control of your life is, however, exemplary. As director of an organization whose primary focus is Latina leadership and working with survivors of domestic violence, I am aware that setting and sticking to your goals is not easy, particularly when you have cultural and societal factors working against you. With many higher education programs designed for those without families, it is challenging to meet the demands of school and parenting. Your desire to learn and grow, not only for yourself but for your family and community, will fuel your efforts.

I recognize some of your challenges. In my last year of college I had a newborn, was pregnant, worked full-time, and attended school full-time. You must prioritize and pace yourself so that you find a balance. It may help to speak to professors about your situation. My daughter was due at the middle of my last semester, and some professors were flexible with my assignments. My son is also diagnosed with ADHD. I demand periodic meetings with a team of school officials so that we may approach my son's education from a team perspective.

With patience and perseverance, you will achieve your current goals and set more for yourself. Continue to develop a support system and to share your story. We must all continue to figure out how to distill the beauty and strength of our culture and traditions. Felicidades!

What defines your *values*?

VALUES

Principles or qualities that one considers important, right, or good.

Your personal **values** are the beliefs that guide your choices. As a group, they constitute your *value system*. For example, your values may include strength of family, being educated, living independently, and seeking worthwhile employment. Each person has a unique value system that sets the foundation for action.

You demonstrate your particular value system in the priorities you set, how you communicate with others, your family life, your educational and career choices, and even the material things with which you surround yourself. Take a look at yourself and your choices: What do they say about you? Going all-out to be on time to appointments and classes shows that you value punctuality. Making time for music, movies, and museums shows that you value the arts. Driving your grandfather to his doctor visits shows that you value family—and health. Fitting school into your busy life shows that you value education.

Here are some reasons why examining your values is a useful first step in goal setting.

- *Self-understanding.* You cannot create a clear picture of what you want out of life until you understand what is truly important to you. You can achieve what you value with the help of goals tailored to those values.

- *Relating to the world around you.* Understanding what you value helps you choose your relationships with people (e.g., family, friends, instructors, supervisors) and organizations (e.g., schools, companies, political or charitable groups) according to how their values compare to yours.

- *Building a personal foundation.* Having a strong set of values gives you a foundation to return to when difficulty in achieving a goal forces you to reevaluate what you want and what is possible.

Values are the foundation on which to build your goals. Start exploring your values by looking at their sources.

Sources of Values

Values are choices. People often choose values based on what others seem to value. A value system is constructed over time, using information from many different sources, including:

- parents, guardians, siblings, and other relatives
- friends and peers
- religious beliefs
- instructors, supervisors, mentors, and others

- ideas from books, newspapers and magazines, television, the Internet, and other media
- workplace and school

A particular value may come from one or more sources. For example, a student may value education (primary source: parents), sports (primary sources: media and friends), and a spiritual life (primary sources: religious organization and grandparents). Another student may have abandoned many of the values that he or she grew up with and adopted the values of a trusted mentor. Still another may find that adopting certain values became important in order to succeed in a particular career area. Being influenced by the values of others is natural, although you should use critical thinking to make sure your choices are right for you.

Choosing and Evaluating Values

Examining the sources of your values can help you define what you believe in. Sources, however, aren't as important as evaluating how your choices fit into your total value system. Your responsibility is to make value choices based on what is right for you and those involved with you. Think through the following when considering your values:

Be wary of setting goals according to other people's values. Friends or family may encourage you to strive for what they think you should value. You may, of course, share their values. If you follow advice that you don't believe in, however, you may have a hard time sticking to your path. For example, someone who attends school primarily because a parent thought it was right may have less motivation than someone who made an independent decision to become a student. Staying in tune with your own values helps you to make decisions that are right for you.

Evaluate your values carefully to determine if they are right for you. Although some values may seem positive on the surface, they may actually have a negative impact on you and others. For example, you might consider it important to keep up with the latest technologies, but continually buying computers, software, CD players, cell phones, and pagers might jeopardize your finances. Ask yourself: How will adopting this value affect my life?

Reevaluate your values periodically as you experience change. Life changes and new experiences may alter your values. For example, a student may have loved growing up in a small town where everyone shared similar backgrounds. However, starting college exposes him, for the first time, to people from different ethnic, racial, and religious backgrounds, and he realizes how much he can benefit from knowing them. This exposure creates a change in values that leads to his decision to live and work in a large, diverse city after graduation. Similarly, people who survive near-fatal car accidents often place greater value after the accident on time spent with friends and family. Your values grow and develop as you do if you continue to think them through.

The goals that you set for yourself express your values and translate them into action. You experience a strong drive to achieve if you build goals around what is most important to you.

How do you set and *achieve* goals?

A **goal** can be something as concrete as buying a health insurance plan or as abstract as working to control your temper. When you set goals and work to achieve them, you engage your intelligence, abilities, time, and energy in order to move ahead. From major life decisions to the tiniest day-to-day activities, setting goals helps you define how you want to live and what you want to achieve.

Like learning a new physical task, setting and working toward goals takes a lot of practice and repeated efforts. As long as you do all that you can to achieve a goal, you haven't failed, even if you don't achieve it completely or in the time frame you had planned. Even one step in the right direction is an achievement. For example, if you wanted to raise your course grade to a B from a D, and you ended up with a C, you have still accomplished something important.

Paul Timm, an expert in self-management, believes that focus is a key ingredient in setting and achieving goals: "Focus adds power to our actions. If somebody threw a bucket of water on you, you'd get wet. . . . But if water was shot at you through a high-pressure nozzle, you might get injured. The only difference is focus."[1] Focus your goal-setting energy by defining a personal mission, placing your goals in long-term and short-term time frames, evaluating goals in terms of your values, setting priorities, and exploring different types of goals.

GOAL

An end toward which effort is directed; an aim or intention.

Identifying Your Personal Mission

How often do you step back and look at where you are, where you've been, and where you want to be? Life moves fast, and it's easy to get caught up in just getting through each day. Not having a big-picture view, however, may leave you feeling empty, not knowing what you've done or why. You can avoid that emptiness by periodically thinking carefully about your life's mission and most far-reaching goals.

Where do you start? One helpful way to determine your general direction is to write a personal mission statement. Dr. Stephen Covey, author of *The Seven Habits of Highly Effective People,* defines a mission statement as a philosophy outlining what you want to be (character), what you want to do (contributions and achievements), and the principles by which you live (your values). Dr. Covey compares the personal mission statement to the Constitution of the United States, a statement of principles that guides the country: "A personal mission statement . . . becomes a personal constitution, the basis for making major, life-directing decisions, the basis for making daily decisions in the midst of the circumstances and emotions that affect our lives."[2]

Your personal mission shouldn't be written in stone. What you want out of life changes as you move from one phase to the next—from single person to spouse, from student to working citizen. Stay flexible and reevaluate your personal mission from time to time.

Here are some examples of mission statements. The following personal mission statement was written by Carol Carter, one of the authors of *Keys to Success*.

My mission is to use my talents and abilities to help people of all ages, stages, backgrounds, and economic levels achieve their human potential through fully developing their minds and their talents. I also aim to balance work with people in my life, understanding that my family and friends are a priority above all else.

A company, like a person, has to establish standards and principles that guide its many activities. Companies often have mission statements so that each member of the organization clearly understands what to strive for. Here is a mission statement from the company that publishes this text:

To provide the most innovative resources—books, technology, programs—to help students of all ages and stages achieve their academic and professional goals inside the classroom and out.

If you are not sure how to start formulating your mission statement, look to your values to guide you. Define your mission based on what is important to you. For example, if you value service to others, your mission statement might focus on choosing a service-oriented career path.

You have an opportunity to write your own personal mission statement at the end of this chapter. Thinking through your personal mission can help to put you in control of your life instead of allowing circumstances and events to control you. If you frame your mission statement carefully so that it truly reflects your goals, it can be your guide in everything you do.

Placing Goals in Time

Everyone has the same 24 hours in a day, but it often doesn't feel like enough. Have you ever had a busy day flash by so quickly that it seems you accomplished nothing? Have you ever felt that way about a longer period of time, like a month or even a year? Your commitments can overwhelm you unless you decide how to use time and plan your steps toward goal achievement.

"Obstacles are what people see when they take their eyes off the goal."

NEW YORK SUBWAY BULLETIN BOARD

If developing a personal mission statement establishes the big picture, placing your goals within particular time frames allows you to bring individual areas of that picture into the foreground. Planning your progress, step by step, helps you maintain your efforts over the extended time period often needed to accomplish a goal. There are two categories: long-term goals and short-term goals.

Setting Long-Term Goals

Establish first the goals that have the largest scope, the *long-term goals* that you aim to attain over a lengthy period of time, up to a few years or more. As a student, you know what long-term goals are all about. You have set yourself a goal to attend school and earn a degree or certificate. Getting an education is a significant goal that often takes years to reach.

Some long-term goals are lifelong, such as a goal to continually learn more about yourself and the world around you. Others have a more definite end, such as a goal to complete a course successfully. To determine your long-term goals, think about what you want out of your professional, educational, and personal life. Here is Carol Carter's long-term goal statement:

> To accomplish my mission through writing books, creating an Internet Web site, giving seminars, and developing programs that create opportunities for students to learn and develop. To create a personal, professional, and family environment that allows me to manifest my abilities and duly tend to each of my responsibilities.

For example, you may establish long-term goals such as these:

- I will make the effort, while in school, to develop my technological skills so that I am comfortable with computers and other technology when I graduate.
- I will use my current and future job experience to develop practical skills that will help me get a satisfying, well-paying job.

Long-term goals don't have to be lifelong goals. Think about your long-term goals for the coming year. Considering what you want to accomplish in a year's time gives you clarity, focus, and a sense of what needs to take place right away. When Carol thought about her long-term goals for the coming year, she came up with the following:

1. Develop books, Internet-based material, and programs to provide internships, scholarships, and other quality initiatives for students.
2. Allow time in my personal life to eat well, run five days a week, and spend quality time with family and friends. Allow time daily for quiet reflection and spiritual devotion.

In the same way that Carol's goals are tailored to her personality and interests, your goals should reflect who you are. Personal missions and goals are as unique as each individual. Continuing the previous example, you might adopt these goals for the coming year:

- I will learn to navigate the Internet and research topics on-line.
- I will look for a part-time job with a local newspaper or newsroom.

Setting Short-Term Goals

When you divide your long-term goals into smaller, manageable goals that you hope to accomplish within a relatively short time, you are setting *short-term goals*. Short-term goals narrow your focus, helping you to maintain your progress toward your long-term goals. Say you have set the long-term goals you just read in the previous section. To stay on track toward those goals, you may want to accomplish these short-term goals in the next six months:

- I will write an assigned paper using information found on the Internet.
- I will make an effort to ask instructors and advisors for advice on how to get into the news business.

These same goals can be broken down into even smaller parts, such as the following one-month goals:

- I will learn to do research on the Internet using search directories.
- I will have lunch with someone in the news business so that I can learn about his or her experience.

In addition to monthly goals, you may have short-term goals that extend for a week, a day, or even a couple of hours in a given day. Take the Internet research goal. Such short-term goals may include the following:

- By the end of today: Find out what the major search directories are.
- One week from now: Read an Internet guide book to learn how to use search directories effectively.
- Two weeks from now: Experiment with search directories to see which ones will be most useful to me.
- Three weeks from now: Research my topic using the two search directories that have the most helpful information.

As you consider your long- and short-term goals, notice how all of your goals are linked to one another. As Figure 3.1 shows, your long-term goals establish a context for the short-term goals. In turn, your short-term goals make the long-term goals seem clearer and more reachable.

Setting Different Kinds of Goals

People have many different goals, involving different parts of life and different values. School is currently a focus in your life; however, because you are more than just a student, you have other kinds of goals as well. As you consider these goals, remember that many of your goals are interconnected—a school goal is often a step toward a career goal and can affect a personal goal as well.

Career Goals

Consider the following factors when thinking about career goals.

Figure 3.1   Goals reinforce one another.

Long term		Earn a degree	
Year long	Declare major		Pass classes
Semester	Explore career areas	Work with study groups	Be in class and on time
One month	Meet with academic advisor	Plan group meetings	Cut down on late-night socializing
This week	Call advisor to set up appointment	Call friends from class about getting a group together	Study weeknights and go out on Friday nights

- The job you want after you graduate—duties and level of responsibility (e.g., manager, supervisor, independent contractor, business owner), hours, coworkers, salary, commuting distance, industry, company size, location.
- Career areas that reflect your strongest and most important values.
- Financial goals—how much money you are aiming for to pay your bills, live comfortably, and save for the future.

Personal Goals

Consider personal goals in terms of self, family, and lifestyle.

- Yourself—examine who you are and who you want to be (character, personality, health/fitness, values, and conduct).
- Family—whether you want to stay single, be married, be a parent, or increase a family you've already started, and what kind of relationship you want with family members.
- Lifestyle—where and with whom you want to live, in what kind of home, how you want to participate in your community, and what you want to do in your leisure time.

Even though your academic goals may seem like they take top priority at the moment, it's important to put them in the context of your goals in all life areas because goals are interconnected. You may want to graduate on a particular date—but not meeting a personal health goal may result in a problem that gets in the way. You might want to major in a particular subject—but thinking over your career goals may show you that your values and skills don't match up well with that subject. Keeping everything in mind helps you make better choices for yourself.

Achieving goals becomes easier when you are realistic about what is possible. Setting priorities helps you make that distinction.

Prioritizing Goals

When you set a **priority,** you identify what's important at any given moment. Prioritizing helps you focus on your most important goals, especially when the important ones are the most difficult. Human nature often leads people to tackle easy goals first and leave the tough ones for later. The risk is that you might never reach for goals that are crucial to your success.

Consider the following when setting priorities:

• *Your values.* Think about your values and personal mission: Which major life goals are more important than all others? Look at your school, career, and personal goals. Do one or two of these paths take priority for you right now? In any path, which goals take priority?

• *Your relationships with others.* For example, if you are a parent, your children's needs are probably a priority. You may be in school so you can give them a better life, and you may arrange your schedule so that you can spend time with them. If you are in a committed relationship, you may arrange your work shifts so that you and your partner are home together as often as possible.

• *Your time.* The next section helps you get a handle on how to map out your days so that you accomplish as much as you can. Your schedule affects your priorities because some days you just won't have enough time to do all that you want to do. Depending on how much time that day's goals take, you might prioritize based on what you can fit in.

You are a unique individual, and your priorities are yours alone. What may be top priority to someone else may not mean that much to you, and vice versa. You can see this in Figure 3.2, which compares the priorities of two very different students. Each student's priorities are listed in order, with the first priority at the top and the lowest priority at the bottom.

Figure 3.2 Different people, different priorities.

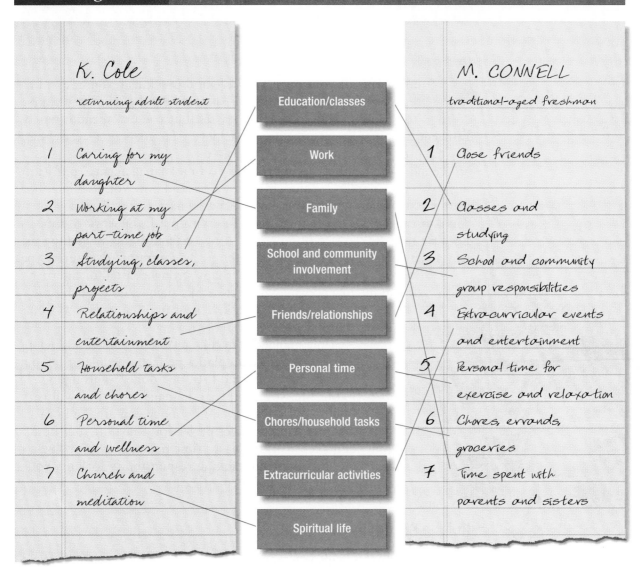

K. Cole
returning adult student

1 Caring for my daughter
2 Working at my part-time job
3 Studying, classes, projects
4 Relationships and entertainment
5 Household tasks and chores
6 Personal time and wellness
7 Church and meditation

- Education/classes
- Work
- Family
- School and community involvement
- Friends/relationships
- Personal time
- Chores/household tasks
- Extracurricular activities
- Spiritual life

M. CONNELL
traditional-aged freshman

1 Close friends
2 Classes and studying
3 School and community group responsibilities
4 Extracurricular events and entertainment
5 Personal time for exercise and relaxation
6 Chores, errands, groceries
7 Time spent with parents and sisters

Setting priorities moves you closer to accomplishing specific goals. It also helps you begin planning to achieve your goals within specific time frames. Being able to achieve your goals is directly linked to effective time management. In fact, the main goal of time management is to facilitate the achievement of your goals.

How can you *manage* your *time?*

Time is one of your most valuable and precious resources; your responsibility and potential for success lie in how you use yours. You cannot change how time passes, but you can spend it wisely. Efficient time management helps you achieve your goals in a steady, step-by-step process.

People have a variety of approaches to time management. Your learning style (see Chapter 2) can help you understand how you use time. For example, students with strong logical–mathematical intelligence and Thinker types tend to organize activities within a framework of time. Because they stay aware of how long it takes them to do something or travel somewhere, they are usually prompt. By contrast, Adventurer types and less logical learners with perhaps stronger visual or interpersonal intelligences may neglect details such as how much time they have to complete a task. They can often be late without meaning to be.

Time management, like physical fitness, is a lifelong pursuit. No one can plan a perfect schedule or build a terrific physique and then be "done." Throughout your life, your ability to manage your time will vary with your stress level, how busy you are, and other factors. Don't expect perfection—just do your best and keep working at it. Time management involves building a schedule, taking responsibility for how you spend your time, and being flexible.

Build a Schedule

Just as a road map helps you travel from place to place, a schedule is a time-and-activity map that helps you get from the beginning of the day (or week, or month) to the end as smoothly as possible. Schedules help you gain control of your life in two ways: They allocate segments of time for the fulfillment of your daily, weekly, monthly, and longer-term goals, and they serve as a concrete reminder of tasks, events, due dates, responsibilities, and deadlines.

Keep a Planner

Gather the tools of the trade: a pen or pencil and a planner (sometimes called a date book). A planner is indispensable for keeping track of your time. Some of you have planners and may have used them for years. Others may have had no luck with them or have never tried. Even if you don't feel you would benefit from one, try it. Paul Timm says, "Most time management experts agree that rule number one in a thoughtful planning process is: Use some form of a planner where you can write things down."[3]

There are two major types of planners. The day-at-a-glance version devotes a page to each day. Although it gives you ample space to write

These strategies help you find effective ways to tame your jumble of responsibilities through time management.

INTELLIGENCE	SUGGESTED STRATEGIES	WHAT WORKS FOR YOU? WRITE NEW IDEAS HERE
Verbal–Linguistic	■ Carry a small calendar and to-do list. Try carrying a small cassette recorder and dictate important scheduling. ■ Write out your main weekly priorities. Looking at what is stressful and what inspires confidence, make adjustments.	
Logical–Mathematical	■ Schedule time each day to organize and plan your tasks. Develop a logical system for indicating priority. ■ Compute how many hours a week you spend studying, working, having fun, and doing extracurricular activities. Evaluate the balance and make any necessary changes.	
Bodily–Kinesthetic	■ Schedule classes so that you have time in between to exercise or to take a long walk from one class to the next. ■ Create a schedule for the month. Take an exercise break. Come back and write your goals for this week and today.	
Visual–Spatial	■ Create your daily schedule and to-do lists using think links or other visual organizers. ■ Use wall calendars or charts to map out goals for the week and month, using different colors for different tasks/goals.	
Interpersonal	■ Involve someone in your goal achievement—make a commitment to someone to complete a step toward a goal. ■ Discuss monthly goals with friends. Ask them to evaluate whether they are too ambitious or not ambitious enough.	
Intrapersonal	■ Schedule quiet time each day to reflect on your priorities and upcoming tasks. ■ Each week, sit alone and write down that week's scheduling challenges. Brainstorm three productive ways you can deal with these challenges.	
Musical	■ Make time in your schedule for music—listen to CDs, go to a concert, play an instrument.	
Naturalistic	■ Try to schedule some time outside each day. ■ Sit outside where you feel relaxed. In this state of mind, plan out your schedule for the next week and month.	

the day's activities, it's harder to see what's ahead. The week-at-a-glance book gives you a view of the week's plans but has less room to write per day. If you write detailed daily plans, you might like the day-at-a-glance version. If you prefer to remind yourself of plans ahead of time, try the book that shows a week's schedule all at once. Some planners contain sections for monthly and yearly goals.

Another option is an electronic planner or personal digital assistant (PDA) that can hold a large amount of information. You can use it to schedule your days and weeks, make to-do lists, and create and store an address book. Electronic planners are powerful, convenient, and often fun. However, they certainly cost more than the paper version, and you can lose important data if something goes wrong with the computer inside. Evaluate your options and decide what works best for you.

Link Daily and Weekly Goals with Long-Term Goals

After you evaluate what you need to accomplish in the coming year, semester, month, week, and day to reach your long-term goals, use your schedule to record those steps. Write down the short-term goals that will enable you to stay on track. Here is how a student might map out two different goals over a year's time:

This year:	Complete enough courses to maintain class standing. Improve my physical fitness.
This semester:	Complete my biology class with a B average or higher. Lose 10 pounds and exercise regularly.
This month:	Set up biology study group schedule to coincide with quizzes. Begin walking and lifting weights.
This week:	Meet with study group; go over material for Friday's quiz. Go for a fitness walk three times; go to weight room twice.
Today:	Go over Chapter 3 in biology text. Walk for 40 minutes.

To manage your time so that you stay on top of your goals, you need to focus first on scheduling the most immediate, smaller goals—what you do on a daily and weekly basis. Scheduling daily and weekly goals, or tasks, that tie in to your long-term goals lends the following benefits:

- increased meaning for your daily activities
- a greater chance of achieving long-term goals
- a sense of order and progress

For college students, as well as working people, the week is often the easiest unit of time to consider at one shot. Weekly goal setting and planning allows you to keep track of day-to-day activities while giving you the larger perspective of what is coming up during the week. Take some time before each week starts to remind yourself of your long-term goals. Keeping long-term goals in mind helps you determine related short-term goals you can accomplish during the week to come.

Figure 3.3 Note daily and weekly tasks.

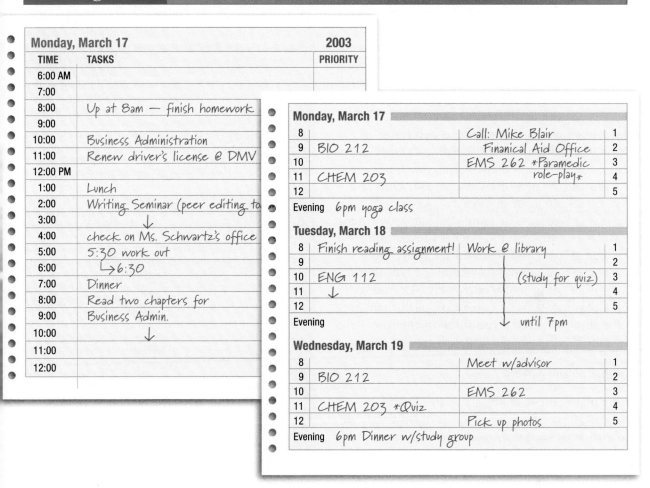

Monday, March 17		2003
TIME	**TASKS**	**PRIORITY**
6:00 AM		
7:00		
8:00	Up at 8am — finish homework	
9:00		
10:00	Business Administration	
11:00	Renew driver's license @ DMV	
12:00 PM		
1:00	Lunch	
2:00	Writing Seminar (peer editing to	
3:00	↓	
4:00	check on Ms. Schwartz's office	
5:00	5:30 work out	
6:00	↳6:30	
7:00	Dinner	
8:00	Read two chapters for	
9:00	Business Admin.	
10:00	↓	
11:00		
12:00		

Monday, March 17

8		Call: Mike Blair	1
9	BIO 212	Finanical Aid Office	2
10		EMS 262 *Paramedic	3
11	CHEM 203	role-play*	4
12			5
Evening	6pm yoga class		

Tuesday, March 18

8	Finish reading assignment!	Work @ library	1
9			2
10	ENG 112	(study for quiz)	3
11	↓		4
12			5
Evening		↓ until 7pm	

Wednesday, March 19

8		Meet w/advisor	1
9	BIO 212		2
10		EMS 262	3
11	CHEM 203 *Quiz		4
12		Pick up photos	5
Evening	6pm Dinner w/study group		

Figure 3.3 shows parts of a daily schedule and a weekly schedule.

Indicate Priority Levels

Prioritizing enables you to use your planner with maximum efficiency. On any given day, your goals have varying degrees of importance. Record your goals first, and then label them according to their level of importance using these categories: Priority 1, Priority 2, and Priority 3. Identify these categories by using any code that makes sense to you. Some people use numbers, as above. Some use letters (A, B, C). Some write activities in different colors according to priority level. Some use symbols (*, +, –).

- *Priority 1* activities are the most important and pressing things in your life. They may include attending class, completing school assignments, picking up a child from day care, and paying bills.

- *Priority 2* activities are part of your routine. Examples include a meeting of a school club, working out, a regular time you study at the library, grocery shopping, or cleaning. Priority 2 tasks are important but more flexible than Priority 1 tasks.

- *Priority 3* activities are those you would like to do but don't consider urgent, like a phone call or a night out. Many people don't enter Priority 3 tasks in their planners until they are sure they have time to get them done.

Prioritizing your activities is essential for two reasons. First, some activities are more important than others, and effective time management requires that you focus most of your energy on Priority 1 items. Second, looking at all of your priorities helps you plan when you can get things done. Often, it's not possible to get all of your Priority 1 activities done early in the day, especially if they involve scheduled classes or meetings. Prioritizing helps you set Priority 1 items and then schedule Priority 2 and 3 items around them as they fit.

Priority 3 tasks often get put off. One solution is to keep a list of Priority 3 tasks in a separate place in your planner. That way, when you have an unexpected pocket of free time, you can consult your list and see what you have time to accomplish—making a trip to the post office, returning a borrowed CD, and so on. Cross off items as you accomplish them and write in new items as you think of them. Rewrite the list when it gets too messy.

Keep Track of Events

Your planner also enables you to schedule events. Think of events in terms of how they tie in with your long-term goals, just as you would your other tasks. For example, being aware of quiz dates, due dates for assignments, and meeting dates helps reach your goals to achieve in school and become involved.

Note events in your planner so that you can stay aware of them ahead of time. Write them in daily, weekly, monthly, or even yearly sections, where a quick look will remind you that they are approaching. Writing them down also helps you see where they fit in the context of all your other activities. For example, if you have three big tests and a presentation all in one week, you'll want to take time in the weeks before to prepare for them.

Following are some kinds of events worth noting in your planner:

- due dates for papers, projects, presentations, and tests
- the details of your academic schedule, including semester and holiday breaks
- important meetings, medical appointments, or due dates for bill payments
- birthdays, anniversaries, social events, holidays, and other special occasions

PERSONAL TRIUMPH

You can't always judge a person by past academic performance. Kevin Leman was near the bottom of his high school class and dropped out of college twice. Later, with the help of inspiring people in his life, he graduated and became a nationally known writer and psychologist.

Kevin Leman was the most disinterested screwball of a student you ever met. "My high school guidance counselor told me he couldn't get me admitted to reform school, much less college," Leman admits. Growing up in western New York, he was the youngest of three siblings. His sister was the captain of the cheerleading squad; his brother was the high-school football hero. And young Kevin was, as he describes himself, "the best at being the worst." "My mother was in high school more than I was," he recalls. "I was never there. I'd cut school. She always went to those meetings they had, you know, and she'd come home with the standard story—'If only Kevin would apply himself . . .'"

Herein lay the problem: Leman really didn't know how to apply himself. He graduated near the bottom of his class with SAT scores to match. "They were in the zero percentile—which is pretty hard to do, just by the mathematics alone," he said. And he still remembers one of his college rejection letters that read, "Most regrettably, Kevin's record does not support admission, which our studies show could lead to his failure, and we must decline his application." Although he made it into another school, they threw him out a year later. Leman seemed destined for academic failure and found a job as a janitor at the local hospital.

It was here that destiny took an unexpected turn. At the hospital, he met Sande Buchheit, a nurse's assistant, who would later become his wife. Sande believed in Leman and introduced him to other people who had vision for their lives. He began to believe that there was some purpose to life and his motivation blossomed. Next, he decided to enroll at the University of Arizona.

This story has been rewritten with permission from Dan Huff, whose original article

Kevin Leman, Counselor and Public Speaker; Tucson, Arizona

"I was walking on campus," he recalls, "not really knowing where I was, and I found this guy named Robert Leonard, a professor. He sat down with me and went way beyond what you'd expect. He got the catalog out and spent two hours with me, showing me exactly what I needed to do."

To his astonishment, Leman made the dean's list that first semester. In that moment, Leman discovered one of the beauties of life: Every day offers a chance to make a new start. He decided he wanted to be a psychologist based, in part, on his earlier run-in with his high school guidance counselor who told him reform school was too high to shoot for. "I remember thinking, 'He's a counselor?'" Ironically, Leman dedicated his first book to this man.

Leman credits much of his success to the power of mentoring. When speaking about one of his professors from the U of A, Leman says, "He was a guy who changed my life. He taught me how to work with people, and he taught me that I could turn kids' behavior around, in some cases in a matter of days. I'm very grateful to him."

Kevin Leman is living proof that anyone can be a success. Today, he has a private practice as a psychologist and counselor and is a nationally known authority on family issues, having written 21 popular psychology books that have sold in the millions. He has also been a featured guest on shows like *The Today Show* and *Oprah*. "Looking back on my UA experience," he says, "I felt like I belonged. I had people there who cared about me, and that made all the difference."

Take a moment to consider . . .

- *When you've experienced a "turning point" in your life.*
- *What you might write about if you were to write books that helped and informed others.*

"The Living Proof," first appeared in *Arizona Alumnus*, Spring 2001.

- benchmarks for steps toward a goal, such as due dates for sections of a project

Take Responsibility for How You Spend Your Time

No matter what restrictions your circumstances create, you are in charge of choosing how to manage them. When you plan your activities with your most important goals in mind, you are taking responsibility for how you live. Use the following strategies:

Plan your schedule each week. Before each week starts, note events, goals, and priorities. Decide where to fit activities like studying and Priority 3 items. For example, if you have a test on Thursday, you can plan study sessions on the preceding days. If you have more free time on Tuesday and Friday than on other days, you can plan workouts or Priority 3 activities at those times. Looking at the whole week will help you avoid being surprised by something you had forgotten was coming up.

Make and use to-do lists. Use a *to-do list* to record the things you want to accomplish. If you generate a daily or weekly to-do list on a separate piece of paper, you can look at all tasks and goals at once. This helps you consider time frames and priorities. You might want to prioritize your tasks and transfer them to appropriate places in your planner. Some people create daily to-do lists right on their planner pages. You can tailor a to-do list to an important event, such as exam week, or an especially busy day. This kind of specific to-do list can help you prioritize and accomplish an unusually large task load.

Make thinking about time a priority. Take a few minutes a day to plan. Although making a schedule takes time, it can mean hours of saved time later. Say you have two errands to run, both on the other side of town; not planning ahead could result in driving across town twice in one day. Also, when you take time to write out your schedule, be sure to carry it with you and check it throughout the day. Find a planner size you like—there are books that fit into your briefcase, your bag, or even your pocket.

Post monthly and yearly calendars at home. Keeping a calendar on the wall helps you stay aware of important events. You can purchase one or draw it yourself, month by month, on plain paper. Use a yearly or a monthly version (Figure 3.4 shows a monthly calendar), and keep it where you can refer to it often. If you live with family or friends, make the calendar a group project so that you stay aware of each other's plans. Knowing each other's schedules can also help you avoid problems such as two people needing the car at the same time.

"Even if you're on the right track, you'll get run over if you just sit there."

WILL ROGERS

Schedule down time. When you're wiped out from too much activity, you don't have the energy to accomplish as much. For example, you've probably experienced one of those study sessions during which, at a certain point, you realize that you haven't absorbed anything for the last hour. Prioritize a little **down time** to refresh you and improve your attitude. Even half an hour a day helps. Fill the time with whatever relaxes you—reading, watching television, chatting on-line, playing a game or sport, walking, writing, or just doing nothing.

DOWN TIME
Quiet time set aside for relaxation and low-key activity.

Figure 3.4   **Keep track with a monthly calendar.**

APRIL

SUNDAY	MONDAY	TUESDAY	WEDNESDAY	THURSDAY	FRIDAY	SATURDAY
	1 WORK	2 Turn in English paper topic	3 Dentist 2pm	4 WORK	5	6
7 Frank's birthday	8 Psych Test 9am WORK	9	10 6:30 pm Meeting @ Student Ctr.	11 WORK	12	13 Dinner @ Ryan's
14	15 English paper due WORK	16 Western Civ paper—Library research	17	18 Library 6 p.m. WORK	19 Western Civ makeup class	20
21	22 WORK	23 2 p.m. meeting, psych group project	20 Start running program: 2 miles	25 WORK	26 Run 2 miles	27
28 Run 3 miles	29 WORK	30 Western Civ paper due	31 Run 2 miles			

Be Flexible

No matter how well you plan your time, life changes can make you feel out of control. One minute you seem to be on track, and the next minute chaos hits. Coping with changes, whether minor (a room change for a class) or major (a medical emergency), can cause stress. As your stress level rises, your sense of control dwindles.

Although you cannot always choose your circumstances, you may have some control over how you handle them. Dr. Covey says that language is important when trying to take action. Using language like "I have to" and "They made me" robs you of personal power. For example, saying that you "have to" go to school can make you feel that others control your life. However, language like "I have decided to" and "I prefer" helps energize your power to choose. Then you can turn "I have to go to school" into "I choose to go to school rather than work in a dead-end job."

Use the following ideas to cope with changes large and small.

Day-to-Day Changes

Small changes can result in priority shifts that jumble your schedule. On Monday, a homework assignment due in a week might be Priority 2; then, if you haven't gotten to it by Saturday, it becomes Priority 1.

Think of change as part of life and you will be able to more effectively solve the dilemmas that come up. For changes that occur frequently, think through a backup plan ahead of time. For sudden changes, the best you can do is to keep an open mind about possibilities and to remember to call on your resources in a pinch. Your problem-solving skills (see Chapter 4) will help you build your ability to adjust to whatever changes come your way.

Life Changes

Sometimes changes are more serious than a class schedule shift. Your car breaks down; your relationship falls apart; you fail a class; a family member develops a medical problem; you get laid off. Such changes call for more extensive problem solving. They also require an ability to look at the big picture. Although a class change affects your schedule for a day, a medical problem may affect your schedule for much longer.

When life hands you a major curve ball, sit down (ideally with someone whose opinion you trust) and lay out your options. Explore all of the potential effects before making a decision (again, the problem-solving and decision-making skills in Chapter 4 will serve you well here). Finally, make full use of your school resources. Your academic advisor, counselor, dean, financial aid advisor, and instructors may have ideas and assistance to offer you—but they can only help if you let them know what you need.

No matter how well you manage time, you will have moments when it's hard to stay in control. Knowing how to identify and avoid procrastination and other time traps helps you get back on track.

Why is *procrastination* a problem?

Procrastination occurs when you postpone tasks. People procrastinate for different reasons. Having trouble with goal setting is one reason. People may project goals too far into the future, set unrealistic goals that are too frustrating to reach, or have no goals at all. People also procrastinate because they don't believe in their ability to complete a task or don't believe in themselves in general. Procrastination is human, and not every instance of procrastination means trouble. If it is taken to the extreme, however, procrastination can develop into a habit that causes problems at school, on the job, and at home.

Jane B. Burka and Lenora M. Yuen, authors of *Procrastination: Why You Do It and What To Do About It,* say that habitual procrastinators are often perfectionists who create problems by using their ability to achieve as the only measure of their self-worth: "The performance becomes the only measure of the person; nothing else is taken into account. An outstanding performance means an outstanding person; a mediocre performance means a mediocre person."[4] For the procrastinator, the fear of failure prevents taking the risk that could bring success.

People also procrastinate in order to avoid the truth about what they are capable of achieving. "As long as you procrastinate, you never have to confront the real limits of your ability, whatever those limits are," say Burka and Yuen.[5] If you procrastinate—and fail—you can blame the failure on waiting too long or on other problems that crop up while you wait to act, not on any personal challenge or shortcoming. This might help you feel good about yourself in the short run. If you never give yourself the chance to succeed, however, you won't discover how to improve on your challenges in a lasting way—and, even more unfortunately, you will never find out how far your abilities can take you.

Anti-Procrastination Strategies

Following are some ways to fight procrastination:

Look at the effects of procrastinating versus not procrastinating. What rewards lie ahead if you get it done? What are the effects if you continue to put it off? Which situation has better effects? Chances are you will benefit more in the long term from facing the task head-on.

Set reasonable goals. Plan your goals carefully, allowing enough time to complete them. Unreasonable goals can be so intimidating that you do nothing at all. "Pay off the credit card bill next month" could throw you. However, "Pay off the credit card bill in 10 months" might inspire you to take action.

Break the task into smaller parts. Look at the task in terms of its parts. How can you approach it step by step? If you can concentrate on achieving one small goal at a time, the task may become less of a burden. In addition, setting concrete time limits for each task may help you feel more in control.

Get started whether or not you "feel like it." Going from doing nothing to doing something is often the hardest part of avoiding procrastination. The motivation techniques from Chapter 1 might help you take the first step. Once you start, you may find it easier to continue.

Ask for help. You don't always have to go it alone. For example, if you avoid a project because you dislike the student with whom you have to work, talk to your instructor about adjusting tasks or group assignments. Once you identify what's holding you up, see who can help you face the task.

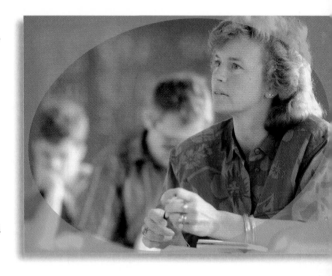

Shake off the judgments of others. A student who feels that her instructor doesn't like her, for example, might avoid studying for that course. Instead of letting judgments like these lead you to procrastinate, choose actions that put you in control. If you have trouble with an instructor, address the problem with that instructor directly and try to make the most of your time in the course.

Don't expect perfection. No one is perfect. Most people learn by starting at the beginning and wading through plenty of mistakes and confusion. It's better to try your best than to do nothing at all.

Reward yourself. The reward that lies at the end of a long road to a goal may be great, but while you are on the way, it may not always be enough to motivate you. Find ways to boost your mood when you accomplish a particular task along the way. Remind yourself—with a break, a movie, some kind of treat that you like—that you are making successful progress.

Procrastination can cause you problems if you let it get the best of you. When it does happen, take some time to think about the causes. What is it about this situation that frightens you or puts you off? Answering that question can help you address what causes lie underneath the procrastination. These causes might indicate a deeper issue that you can address.

Other Time Traps to Avoid

Procrastination isn't the only way to spend your time in less-than-productive ways. Keep an eye out for these situations too.

Saying yes when you don't have the time. First, think before you respond. Ask yourself what effects a new responsibility will have on your schedule. If it will cause you more trouble than it seems to be worth, say no graciously.

Studying at a bad time of day. When you are tired, you may need extra time to fully understand your material. If you study when you are most alert, you can take in more information in less time.

Studying in a distracting location. Find an environment that helps you maximize study time. If you need to be alone to concentrate, for example, studying near others might interfere with your focus. Conversely, people who require a busier environment to stay alert might choose a more active setting.

"I have always thought that one man of tolerable abilities may work great changes, and accomplish great affairs among mankind, if he first forms a good plan."

BENJAMIN FRANKLIN

Not thinking ahead. Forgetting important things is a big time drain. One book left at home can cost you extra time going back and forth. Five minutes of scheduling before your day starts can save you hours.

Not curbing your social time. You plan to make a quick telephone call, but the next thing you know you've been talking for an hour, losing sleep or study time. Don't cut out all socializing, but stay aware. Smart choices have results that boost your self-respect.

Taking on too many tasks and projects. You may feel overwhelmed by all that you want to accomplish in your life. See what tasks you can reasonably delegate to others. No one can take a test for you, but another day-care parent could pick up your child on a day when your time runs short.

Of course no one is going to be able to avoid all of these time traps all of the time. Do the best that you can. The first step is an awareness of your particular tendencies. Once you know how you tend to procrastinate and waste time, you can take steps to change your habits. Time is your ally—make the most of the time that you have.

In Hebrew, this word, pronounced "chai," means "life," representing all aspects of life—spiritual, emotional, family, educational, and career. Individual Hebrew characters have number values. Because the characters in the word *chai* add up to 18, the number 18 has come to be associated with good luck. The word *chai* is often worn as a good luck charm. As you plan your goals, think about your view of luck. Many people feel that a person can create his or her own luck by pursuing goals persistently and staying open to possibilities and opportunities.

Consider that your vision of life may largely determine how you live. You can prepare the way for luck by establishing a personal mission and forging ahead toward your goals. If you believe that the life you want awaits you, you will be able to recognize and make the most of luck when it comes around. *L'chaim*—to life, and good luck.

Building Skills

FOR COLLEGE, CAREER, AND LIFE SUCCESS

The Big Picture   *Combining Thinking, Strategy, and Teamwork*

DISCOVER HOW YOU SPEND YOUR TIME. Start by spending three days recording exactly what you do with your time. The chart on page 81 has blocks showing half-hour increments. As you go through the days, write in what you do each hour, indicating when you started and when you stopped. Don't forget activities that don't feel like "activities" such as sleeping, relaxing, and watching TV. Also, be honest—record your actual activities instead of how you want to spend your time or how you think you should have spent your time. There are no wrong answers.

After the three days, go through the chart to see how much time you spent on each of the categories in the following table. Tally the hours in the boxes in the table using straight tally marks; round off to half hours and use a short tally mark for each half hour. In the third column, total the hours for each activity.

Look at the totals for the different categories. What is the one biggest surprise about how you spend your time?

_____

_____

_____

_____

_____

Think about what kinds of changes might help you improve your ability to set and achieve goals. Name one change you would like to make in how you spend your time, and discuss the positive effect this change would have.

_____

_____

_____

_____

_____

ACTIVITY	TIME TALLIED OVER THREE DAYS	TOTAL TIME IN HOURS
Example: Class	ＬＨＴ ＬＨＴ Ｉǀ	11.5
Class		
Work		
Studying		
Sleeping		
Eating		
Family time/child care		
Commuting/traveling		
Chores and personal business		
Friends and important relationships		
Telephone time		
Leisure/entertainment		
Spiritual life		
Other		

Now that you have a better idea of how you spend your time, think about the goals that you feel deserve the bulk of that time. In a group of three or four people, brainstorm long-term goals and have one member of the group write them down. From that list, pick out five goals that everyone can relate to most. Each group member should then take five minutes alone to evaluate the relative importance of the five goals and rank them in the order that he or she prefers, using a 1 to 5 scale with 1 being the highest priority and 5 the lowest.

Display the rankings of each group member side by side. How many different orders are there? Discuss why each person has a different set of priorities and be open to different views. What factors in different people's lives have caused them to select particular rankings? If you have time, discuss how priorities have changed for each group member over the course of a year, perhaps by having each person re-rank the goals according to his or her needs a year ago.

Day One		Day Two		Day Three	
TIME	ACTIVITY	TIME	ACTIVITY	TIME	ACTIVITY
5:00 AM		5:00 AM		5:00 AM	
5:30 AM		5:30 AM		5:30 AM	
6:00 AM		6:00 AM		6:00 AM	
6:30 AM		6:30 AM		6:30 AM	
7:00 AM		7:00 AM		7:00 AM	
7:30 AM		7:30 AM		7:30 AM	
8:00 AM		8:00 AM		8:00 AM	
8:30 AM		8:30 AM		8:30 AM	
9:00 AM		9:00 AM		9:00 AM	
9:30 AM		9:30 AM		9:30 AM	
10:00 AM		10:00 AM		10:00 AM	
10:30 AM		10:30 AM		10:30 AM	
11:00 AM		11:00 AM		11:00 AM	
11:30 AM		11:30 AM		11:30 AM	
12:00 PM		12:00 PM		12:00 PM	
12:30 PM		12:30 PM		12:30 PM	
1:00 PM		1:00 PM		1:00 PM	
1:30 PM		1:30 PM		1:30 PM	
2:00 PM		2:00 PM		2:00 PM	
2:30 PM		2:30 PM		2:30 PM	
3:00 PM		3:00 PM		3:00 PM	
3:30 PM		3:30 PM		3:30 PM	
4:00 PM		4:00 PM		4:00 PM	
4:30 PM		4:30 PM		4:30 PM	
5:00 PM		5:00 PM		5:00 PM	
5:30 PM		5:30 PM		5:30 PM	
6:00 PM		6:00 PM		6:00 PM	
6:30 PM		6:30 PM		6:30 PM	
7:00 PM		7:00 PM		7:00 PM	
7:30 PM		7:30 PM		7:30 PM	
8:00 PM		8:00 PM		8:00 PM	
8:30 PM		8:30 PM		8:30 PM	
9:00 PM		9:00 PM		9:00 PM	
9:30 PM		9:30 PM		9:30 PM	
10:00 PM		10:00 PM		10:00 PM	
10:30 PM		10:30 PM		10:30 PM	
11:00 PM		11:00 PM		11:00 PM	
11:30 PM		11:30 PM		11:30 PM	

To record your thoughts, use a separate journal
or the lined pages at the end of the chapter.

PERSONAL MISSION STATEMENT. Using the personal mission statement
examples in the chapter as a guide, consider what you want out of your
life and create your own personal mission statement. You can write it in
paragraph form, in a list of long-term goals, or in a visual format such as
a think link (see Chapter 6 for information on think links). Take as much
time as you need in order to be as complete as possible. Draft your statement on a separate sheet of paper and take time to revise it. If it is in
written form, rewrite the final version on the journal page.

Career Portfolio *Charting Your Course*

CAREER GOALS AND PRIORITIES. The most reasonable and reachable
career goals are ones that are linked with your school and life goals. First,
name a personal long-term career goal.

_____

_____

_____

Then, imagine that you will begin working toward it. Indicate a series of
smaller goals—from short-term to long-term—that you feel will help you
achieve this goal. Write what you hope to accomplish in the next year, the
next six months, and the next month.

_____

_____

_____

Now, explore your job priorities. How do you want your job to benefit
you? On a separate sheet of paper, note your requirements in each of the
following areas.

- Duties and responsibilities
- Salary and benefits
- Hours (part-time vs. full-time)
- Job requirements (e.g., travel, location)
- Industry or field
- Flexibility
- Affiliation with school or financial aid program

What kind of job, in the career area for which you listed your goals, might fit all or most of your requirements? List two possibilities here.

1. _____

2. _____

If you have access to the CD-ROM Strategies for Success, *use the following questions to assess your thoughts and enhance your understanding of the chapter. The questions below represent only some of the activities provided on the CD for the chapter topics—try others if you have time.*

Click on the Goal Setting and Time Management bookmark. Use the following activities to hone your goal setting and time management skills:

1. Take the pre-assessment to see how you perceive yourself as a goal setter and time manager.

2. Click on Activity One: Your Personal Mission Statement. Making sure your computer is on-line, click on the Franklin Covey link and read the material. In the field provided, write—or revise, if you have already created one—your own personal mission statement based on what you have learned.

3. Click on Activity Two: Prioritizing. Complete your priority list and then analyze it on the next screen. Think about whether your priorities reflect the goals that you consider most important.

4. Click on Activity Three: Journal Reflections. Think about, and type your response to, journal question number two—procrastination.

S uggested Readings

Covey, Stephen. *The Seven Habits of Highly Effective People*. New York: Simon & Schuster, 1995.

Emmett, Rita. *The Procrastinator's Handbook: Mastering the Art of Doing It Now*. New York: Walker & Co., 2000.

Gleeson, Kerry. *The Personal Efficiency Program: How To Get Organized to Do More Work in Less Time, 2nd ed*. New York: John Wiley & Sons, 2000.

Lakein, Alan. *How to Get Control of Your Time and Your Life*. New York: New American Library, 1996.

McGee-Cooper, Ann with Duane Trammell. *Time Management for Unmanageable People*. New York: Bantam Books, 1994.

Sapadin, Linda and Jack Maguire. *Beat Procrastination and Make the Grade: The Six Styles of Procrastination and How Students Can Overcome Them*. New York: Penguin USA, 1999.

Timm, Paul R. *Successful Self-Management: A Psychologically Sound Approach to Personal Effectiveness*. Los Altos, CA: Crisp Publications, 1996.

I nternet Resources

Mind Tools (section on time management): www.mindtools.com/page5.html

Top Achievement—goal setting and self-improvement resources: www.topachievement.com

E ndnotes

1. Paul R. Timm, Ph.D., *Successful Self-Management: A Psychologically Sound Approach to Personal Effectiveness*. Los Altos, CA: Crisp Publications, 1987, pp. 22–41.

2. Stephen Covey, *The Seven Habits of Highly Effective People*. New York: Simon & Schuster, 1989, pp. 70–144, 309–318.

3. Timm, pp. 22–41.

4. Jane B. Burka, Ph.D. and Lenora M. Yuen, Ph.D., *Procrastination*. Reading, MA: Perseus Books, 1983, pp. 21–22.

5. Ibid.

JOURNAL

name _____   date _____

visit: www.prenhall.com/carter NY Times link for this chapter

PART TWO

II

Developing Your Learning Skills

In this chapter you explore answers to the following questions: • What is critical thinking? • How does critical thinking help you solve problems and make decisions? • How do you reason? • How can you open your mind to new perspectives? • Why plan strategically?

IN THIS CHAPTER

Critical and creative thinking

THE PROBLEM of getting the classes you need is just one of many faced by Edhilvia Campos (see next page) and college students everywhere. Solving that problem requires thinking through the situation and taking the steps that will bring the most positive effects— an excellent example of critical thinking.

Through the essential task of asking important questions about ideas and information, critical thinking enables your mind to process, store, and create. This chapter shows you that you think critically every day, helps you learn how your mind works when you think critically, and gives you the power to use critical-thinking processes to help you manage whatever life brings.

becoming an active learner

Edhilvia Campos, Parkland Community College, Champaign, Illinois

Shera Chantel Caviness,
Graduate, University of Memphis

How do I decide which classes I need?

Find an academic counselor in your field who can guide you . . .

Every semester it's a challenge to figure out the classes I need. I am majoring in microbiology, but the science courses I need aren't always available. Also, I eventually want to transfer to the University of Illinois. The processes for registering and figuring out what credits will transfer seem complicated.

When I came to the States for college, only a few of my math credits transferred because the math classes I had taken in high school in Venezuela were not acceptable. My freshman year I took two algebra classes and later found out that they couldn't be applied to my major. I may want to go back to Venezuela during the summers. I've considered taking classes then, but the Venezuelan universities don't really offer my major. Do you have suggestions for what I can do to make this process more efficient?

First and foremost, hang in there. I know that things seem hard now, but your efforts will pay off. Attending college is similar to a "micro" real world. Throughout college, you will have to face problems that must be solved. I understand that you feel you wasted time and money taking certain classes. But some classes are not always transferable, and unfortunately money has to be spent to take certain courses before entering a degree program.

To prepare to transfer, find an academic counselor at the University of Illinois (preferably one in your major) who can tell you what will transfer so that you will not have to repeat or take unnecessary classes. While at Parkland, find an academic counselor in your field who can guide you toward appropriate courses for that degree, and use the undergraduate catalog to stay informed of the necessary classes for your major. Get to know the professors in your field because they can help. If some classes are not available for one semester, gather at least 8 to 10 students to voice concern about opening a section. Professors are often unaware of the demand for certain courses because students do not speak up.

If you do plan to return to Venezuela for the summer, only take courses that will apply to your degree or take some general lower-division classes that are transferable. Make sure you check with the counselors at Parkland and the University of Illinois before signing up. All in all, keep your determination alive and do not let things discourage you. Always find something valuable within each course you take because this will help you become more well rounded. Remember to think positive; this is only a "micro" real-world experience, helping to prepare you for the R-E-A-L world.

What is *critical thinking?*

Y ou may have heard the term "critical thinking" before. The meaning of "thinking" seems clear—so what, exactly, could "critical thinking" mean? Although you might assume that the word *critical* implies something difficult and negative, as it is used here it actually means "indispensable" and "important." *Critical thinking means finding that which is important.*

Consider the following definition of critical thinking:

When you think critically, you take in information, examine its important aspects by asking questions about it, and then put what you have learned to use through thinking processes such as problem solving, decision making, reasoning, opening your mind to new perspectives, and planning strategically.

Questioning is at the heart of critical thinking because it allows you to go *beyond the basic recall of information.* When you think critically, you examine important aspects by asking questions.

Critical thinking brings you countless advantages, including:

- *Being able to apply knowledge.* Critical thinking moves you beyond repeating back what you know. For instance, it won't mean much for elementary education students to quote child development facts on an exam unless they can evaluate real children's needs in the classroom.
- *Being an innovator.* In class or on the job, you are valued if you look for ways to spur positive change and implement new ideas.
- *Building brain power.* Critical thinkers understand how their minds work—and they actively use their minds. Because thinking is a skill, the more you use it, the better you become.

You think critically now, in all kinds of ways—when you decide between two different courses by reading course descriptions and talking to your advisor, for example, or when you see that you need extra income and look for a job that fits your needs. You make these decisions by asking questions—What is the best course for me? What kind of job fits into my schedule?—and seeking answers.

The Path of Critical Thinking

Look at Figure 4.1 to see a visual representation of critical thinking. The critical-thinking path involves taking in information, examining it by asking questions, and then using it.

Taking in Information

Although most of this chapter focuses on questioning and using information, this first step is just as crucial. The information you receive and recall is your raw material. When you take in information accurately and without judgment, you have the best material with which to work as you think. Once you have clear, complete information, examine it through questioning.

Figure 4.1 **The critical-thinking path.**

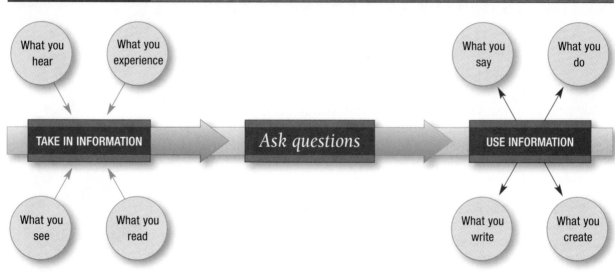

Questioning Information

A critical thinker asks many kinds of questions about a given piece of information, such as:

> Where did it come from? What could explain it? In what ways is it true or false? Do I consider it good or bad, and why? How is this information similar to or different from what I already know? What effects does it have?

Critical thinkers also ask whether information can help them solve a problem, for example, or make a decision. Questioning is the key to learning and to linking what you learn to other information.

Using Information

After taking in information, examining it by questioning, and transforming it into something they can use, critical thinkers put the information to work. Now comes the actual work of solving the problem, making the strategic plan, and so on. This last stage of the critical-thinking path is where new knowledge—inventions, ideas, creations—is born out of the mix of what you already know, what you have newly acquired, and the power of your mind.

Creativity and Critical Thinking

CREATIVITY

The ability to produce something new through imaginative skill.

Critical thinking, especially the third stage of using information, is inherently creative because it involves the creation of something new from given information. Creativity goes beyond art and music; a creation can be a novel solution, idea, approach, tangible product, work of art, system, or program. Innovations created by all kinds of people continually expand and change the world. Here are some examples of creative innovations that have had an impact:

- Jody Williams and the group she founded, International Campaign to Ban Landmines, have convinced nearly 100 countries to support a treaty that would end land mine production and sales.
- Art Fry and Spencer Silver invented the Post-it™ in 1980, enabling people to save paper and protect documents by using removable notes.
- Rosa Parks refused to give up her seat on the bus to a white person, setting off a chain of events that gave rise to the civil rights movement.
- Jim Henson revolutionized children's television, and the way children learn about the world, through his invention of the Muppets and development of *Sesame Street*.

Creativity is part of every thinking process. When you brainstorm potential problem solutions or possible decisions, you are being creative. When you come up with unique ways to challenge an assumption or achieve a strategic goal over time, you are being creative.

"The world of reality has its limits. The world of imagination is boundless."

JEAN-JACQUES ROUSSEAU

Creative and critical thinkers combine ideas and information in ways that form new solutions, ideas, processes, or products. "The hallmark of creative people is their mental flexibility," says creativity expert Roger von Oech. "Like race-car drivers who shift in and out of different gears depending on where they are on the course, creative people are able to shift in and out of different types of thinking depending on the needs of the situation at hand."[1] Figure 4.2 lists some primary characteristics of creative people. As you build critical-thinking skills, you will have opportunities to put these characteristics into play.

Figure 4.2	Characteristics of creative people.
CHARACTERISTIC	**EXAMPLE**
Willingness to take risks	Taking a difficult, high-level course.
Tendency to break away from limitations	Entering a marathon race.
Tendency to seek new challenges & experiences	Taking on an internship in a high-pressure workplace.
Broad range of interests	Inventing new moves on the basketball court and playing guitar at an open-mike night.
Ability to make new things out of available materials	Making curtains out of bedsheets.
Tendency to question norms & assumptions	Adopting a child of different ethnic background than the family's.
Willingness to deviate from popular opinion	Working for a small, relatively unknown political party.
Curiosity and inquisitiveness	Wanting to know how a computer program works.

Source: Adapted from T. Z. Tardif and R. J. Sternberg, "What Do We Know About Creativity?" in *The Nature of Creativity,* ed., R. J. Sternberg (London: Cambridge University Press, 1988).

| | | RIGID, NON-QUESTIONING | CREATIVE, QUESTIONING |
YOUR ROLE	SITUATION	RESPONSE	RESPONSE
Student	Instructor is lecturing on the causes of the Vietnam war.	You assume everything your instructor says is true.	You consider what the instructor says, write questions about issues you want to clarify and discuss them with the instructor or classmates.
Spouse/Partner	Your partner feels he/she does not have enough quality time with you.	You think he/she is wrong and defend yourself.	You ask your partner why he/she thinks this is happening, and together you come up with ways to improve the situation.
Employee	Your supervisor is angry with you about something that happened.	You avoid your supervisor or deny responsibility for the incident.	You determine what caused your supervisor to blame you; you talk with your supervisor about what happened and agree on a different approach in the future.

Table 4.1 Critical thinking involves a creative response.

A creative, critical thinker is also an open-minded thinker, one who remains receptive to possibilities rather than accepting or rejecting information or ideas without examination. Table 4.1 illustrates this concept by comparing how critical and non-critical thinkers might respond to particular situations.

Think about responses you or others have had to different situations. Consider when you have seen people take the time to question, and when you haven't, and what resulted from each way of responding. This will help you begin to see what kind of an effect critical thinking can have on the way you live.

Learning How Your Mind Works

Start to put critical thinking into real-world perspective by imagining a specific scenario. You have an opening in your schedule and are trying to decide between two science courses—biology and biomedical ethics. As you work toward a decision, you might ask questions like the following:

- Do these courses have any prerequisites—and if so, what are they?
- What are the similarities in the subject matter between biology and biomedical ethics?
- How do the workloads for these two courses differ?
- How would the biology course fit into my existing schedule?
- Would biology or biomedical ethics fit a major or career that interests me? If so, how?

- How do I investigate the rumor that the biomedical ethics instructor is too tough on students?
- Which course is the best fit for me considering all that I have discovered?

When you ask important questions like these, your mind performs basic *actions*. Sometimes it uses one action by itself, but most often it uses two or more in combination. To know these actions is to have a fundamental understanding of thinking. These actions are the building blocks with which you construct the critical-thinking processes described later in the chapter.

Identify your mind's actions using a system originally derived by educators Frank Lyman, Arlene Mindus, and Charlene Lopez[2] and developed by numerous other instructors. Based on their studies of how people think, they named seven basic types of thought. These types, referred to here as actions, are not new to you, although some of their names may be. They represent the ways in which you think all the time.

Through exploring these actions, you go beyond just thinking in order to learn *how* you think. In a way, you are studying an instruction manual for your mind. Following are explanations of each of the mind actions, including examples (some from the questions you just read). Write your own examples in the blank spaces. Icons representing each action help you visualize and remember them.

The Mind Actions

Recall: *Facts, sequence, and description.* This is the simplest action, representing the simplest level of thinking. When you **recall,** you name or describe previously learned ideas, facts, objects, or events, or put them into sequence. *Examples:*

- Identifying the prerequisites for biology and biomedical ethics (you discover there are none).
- Naming the steps of a geometry proof, in order.

Your example: Recall two school-related events scheduled this month.

_____

_____

_____

The icon: Capital R stands for *recall* or *remembering.*

Similarity: *Analogy, likeness, comparison.* This action examines what is **similar** about one or more elements—situations, ideas, people, stories, events, or objects. *Examples:*

- Examining similarities in the subject matter between biology and biomedical ethics (both are based in the sciences, both involve biology-related material).
- Comparing class notes with another student to see what facts and ideas you both consider important.

Your example: State how your two favorite classes are similar.

_____

_____

_____

The icon: The Venn diagram illustrates the idea of similarity. The two circles represent the elements being compared, and the shaded area of intersection indicates that they have some degree of similarity.

Difference: *Distinction, contrast.* This action examines what is **different** about one or more elements. *Examples:*

- Looking at how the workloads for biology and biomedical ethics differ (biology has more assignments plus a lab component; biomedical ethics has less scientific work but more papers).
- Looking at differences between two of your instructors—one divides the class into discussion groups; the other keeps desks in place and always lectures.

Your example: Explain how one of your favorite courses differs from a course you don't like as much.

_____

_____

_____

The icon: Here the Venn diagram is used again to show difference. The nonintersecting parts of the circles are shaded, indicating that the focus is on what is not in common.

Cause and Effect: *Reasons, consequences, prediction.* Using this action, you look at what has **caused** a fact, situation, or event and what **effects** come from it. In other words, you look at why something happened and the consequence of its occurrence. *Examples:*

- Thinking through how taking the biology course would affect your existing schedule (it means moving or changing another class you've already registered for because it comes right after that class and is located across campus).
- Seeing how staying up too late causes you to oversleep, which causes you to be late to class, which results in missing material, which causes you to feel confused about course topics.

Your example: Write what causes you to become motivated in a class.

_____

_____

_____

The icon: The arrows, pointing toward each other in a circular pattern, show how a cause leads to an effect.

Example to Idea: *Generalization, classification.* From one or more known **examples** (facts or events), you develop a general **idea** or ideas. Grouping facts or events into patterns may allow you to make a general statement about several of them at once. This mind action moves from the known to the previously unknown and from the specific to the general. *Examples:*

- Exploring whether biology or biomedical ethics fits a major or career interest. (You start with the examples. You like biology; you aren't sure about a career in the sciences; you are intrigued by medicine; you have an interest in law; you are fascinated by ethics. These examples lead you to the idea—biomedical ethics would probably be a better fit.)

- From several successful experiences in classes where the instructor uses visuals to illustrate ideas, you conclude that your learning style has a strong visual component.

Your example: Name activities you enjoy. Using them, derive an idea of a class you want to take.

_____

_____

_____

The icon: The arrow and "Ex" pointing to a light bulb on their right indicate how an example or examples lead to the idea (the light bulb lit up).

Idea to Example: *Analysis, substantiation, proof.* In a reverse of the previous action, you take a known **idea** or ideas and think of **examples** (events or facts) that support or prove that idea. This mind action moves from the general to the specific, the reverse of example to idea. *Examples:*

- Investigating the rumor that the biomedical ethics instructor is too tough on students. (Starting with the idea that the instructor is too tough on students, you talk to five different students who have taken the class. Examples they give you lead you to believe that the instructor is indeed demanding.)

- You present an argument to your advisor regarding a change of major. (You start with the idea—you are a good candidate for a change of major—and support it with examples—you have worked in the field you want to change to, you have already fulfilled some of the requirements for the new major.)

Your example: Name an idea of a career path you would like to follow, and support this idea with examples of your interests and skills.

_____

_____

_____

The icon: In a reverse of the previous icon, this one starts with the light bulb and has an arrow pointing to "Ex." This indicates that you start with the idea and then move to the supporting examples.

Evaluation: *Value, judgment, rating.* Here you **judge** whether something is useful or not useful, important or unimportant, good or bad, or right or wrong by identifying and weighing its positive and negative effects (pros and cons). Be sure to consider the specific situation at hand (a cold drink might be good on the beach in August but not so good in the snowdrifts in January). With the facts you have gathered, you determine the value of something in terms of the predicted effects on you and others. Cause-and-effect analysis almost always accompanies evaluation. *Examples:*

- Looking at all that you have discovered—scheduling, relation to interests, difficulty, prerequisites, subject matter—about the potential effects of taking one of the two courses you are considering, you evaluate that biomedical ethics is your best bet.

- Someone offers you a chance to cheat on a test. You evaluate the potential effects if you are caught. You also evaluate the long-term effects of not actually learning the material and of doing something ethically wrong. You decide that it isn't right or worthwhile to cheat.

Your example: Evaluate your mode of transportation to school.

_____

_____

The icon: A set of scales out of balance indicates how you weigh positive and negative effects to arrive at an evaluation.

You may want to use a mnemonic device—a memory tool, as explained in Chapter 6—to remember the seven mind actions. You can make a sentence of words that each start with a mind action's first letter, such as "Really Smart Dogs Cook Eggs In Enchiladas."

Putting Mind Actions to Work

When you first learned to write, someone taught you how to create the shape of each letter or character. You slowly practiced each curve and line. Later you carefully put letters or characters together to form words. Now, much later, you write without thinking consciously about the individual units that make up your written thoughts. You focus primarily on how to express your ideas, not on creating proper letters; your words appear on paper as you work toward that goal.

The process of learning and using mind actions is similar. If you take time now to consciously think through the specific actions your mind uses when you think, they will eventually become second nature to you, a solid foundation for your thinking on which you can build productive skills.

Because you have been using these actions for a long time, developing a working understanding of your mind will take you far less time than it took to learn to write. As you work through the actions themselves and see how they combine to form thinking processes, you will build this crucial understanding. During the semester, as you work through other chapters in the book, you will see icons marking where particular mind actions are taking place. These will help you to more easily identify how your mind is working.

You rarely use the mind actions one at a time as they are presented here. Usually you combine them and repeat them. Sometimes they overlap. When you combine them in working toward a goal (a problem to solve, a decision to make), you are performing a *thinking process*. Following are explorations of several important critical-thinking processes: solving problems, making decisions, reasoning, opening your mind to new perspectives, and planning strategically. These thinking processes are similar in that they involve the steps of gathering, evaluating, and using information. As you will see, however, the sequence or combination of mind actions may vary considerably. Figure 4.7 on page 116 reminds you that the mind actions form the core of the thinking processes.

How does *critical thinking* help you solve problems and make decisions?

P roblem solving and decision making are probably the two most crucial and common thinking processes. Each one requires various mind actions. The processes overlap somewhat because every problem that needs solving requires you to make a decision. However, not every decision requires that you solve a problem (e.g., not many people would say that deciding what to order for lunch is a problem).

Although both of these processes have multiple steps, you do not always have to work through each step. As you become more comfortable solving problems and making decisions, your mind automatically clicks through the steps. Also, you become more adept at evaluating which problems and decisions require serious consideration and which can be taken care of quickly and simply.

Problem Solving

Life constantly presents problems to be solved, ranging from common daily problems (how to manage study time) to life-altering situations (how to design a child-custody plan during a divorce). Choosing a solution without thinking critically may have negative effects. If you move through the steps of a problem-solving process, however, you have a good chance of coming up with a favorable solution.

Brainstorming

Brainstorming is a crucial element of problem solving. You are brainstorming when you approach a problem by letting your mind free-associate, coming up with as many possible ideas, examples, or solutions as you can

BRAINSTORMING

The spontaneous, rapid generation of ideas, examples, or solutions, undertaken by a group or an individual, often as part of a problem-solving process.

without immediately evaluating them as good or bad. **Brainstorming** is also referred to as divergent thinking; you start with the issue or problem and then let your mind diverge, or go in many different directions, in search of ideas or solutions.

Following are some general guidelines for creative and successful brainstorming:[3]

Don't evaluate or criticize an idea right away. Write down your ideas so that you remember them. Evaluate them later, after you have had a chance to think about them. Try to avoid criticizing other people's ideas as well. Students often become stifled when their ideas are evaluated during brainstorming.

Focus on quantity; don't worry about quality until later. Generate as many ideas or examples as you can without worrying about which one is "right." The more thoughts you generate, the better the chance that one may be useful. Brainstorming works well in groups. Group members can become inspired by, and make creative use of, one another's ideas.

Let yourself play. People often hit on their most creative ideas when they are exercising or just relaxing. Often when your mind switches into play mode, it can more freely generate new thoughts. A thought that seems crazy might be a brilliant discovery. For example, the idea for Velcro came from examining how a burr sticks to clothing. Dreams can also be a source.[4]

Use analogy. Think of similar situations and write down what you remember; what ideas or strategies have worked before? *Analogy* puts the similarity mind action to work recalling potentially helpful ideas and examples and stimulating your mind to come up with new ones. For example, the Velcro discovery is a product of analogy: When trying to figure out how two pieces of fabric could stick to each other, the inventor thought of the similar situation of a burr sticking to clothing.

Don't fear failure. Even Michael Jordan got cut from the basketball team as a high school sophomore in Wilmington, North Carolina. If you insist on getting it right all the time, you may miss out on the creative path—often paved with failures—leading to the best possible solution.[5]

The Problem-Solving Process

When you have a problem to solve, taking the following steps will maximize the number of possible solutions and will allow you to explore each one carefully. Figure 4.3 demonstrates a way to visualize the flow of problem solving.

1. *Identify the problem accurately.* What are the facts? *Recall* the details of the situation. To define a problem correctly, focus on its *causes* rather than its *effects*. Consider the Chinese saying: "Give a man a fish, and he will eat for a day. Teach a man to fish, and he will eat for a lifetime." You may state the problem first as "The man is hungry." If you stay with this statement, giving him a fish seems like a good solution. Unfortunate-

Figure 4.3   Problem-solving plan.

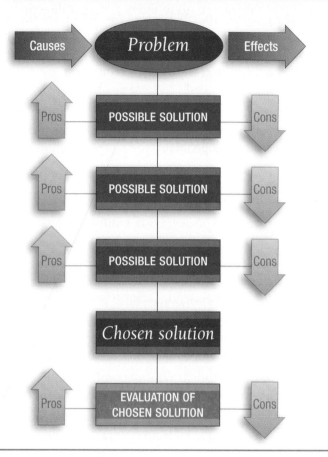

Source: © 1983 George Eley and Frank Lyman, University of Maryland.

ly, the problem returns—because hunger is an effect. Focusing on the probable cause brings a new definition: "The man does not know how to find food." Given that his lack of knowledge is the true cause, teaching him to fish truly solves the problem.

2. *Analyze the problem.* Analyze, or break down into understandable pieces, what surrounds the problem. What *effects* of the situation concern you? What *causes* these effects? Which causes are most powerful or significant? Are there hidden causes? Look at the causes and effects that surround the problem.

3. *Brainstorm possible solutions.* Brainstorming helps you to think of examples of how you solved similar problems, consider what is different about this problem, and come up with new possible solutions. Remember that to get to the heart of a problem, you must base possible solutions on the most significant causes instead of putting a bandage on the effects.

4. *Explore each solution.* Why might your solution work or not work? Might a solution work partially or in a particular situation? *Evaluate* ahead of time the pros and cons (positive and negative effects) of each proposed solution. Create a chain of causes and effects in your head, as far into the future as you can, to see where this solution might lead.

5. *Choose and implement the solution you decide is best.* Decide how you will put your solution to work. Then, carry out your plan.

6. *Evaluate the solution that you acted on.* What are the positive and negative *effects* of what you did? In terms of your needs and those of others, was it a useful solution or not? Could the solution use any adjustments to be more useful? In evaluating, you are collecting data.

7. *Refine the solution.* Problem solving is a process. You may have opportunities to apply the same solution again. Evaluate repeatedly, making changes that you decide make the solution better (i.e., more closely related to the causes of the problem).

The following example illustrates one way to use this plan to solve a problem.

- *Step 1: Identify.* A student is having trouble understanding course material.
- *Step 2: Analyze.* If some effects of not understanding include poor grades and lack of interest, some causes may include poor study habits, not listening in class, or lack of sleep.
- *Step 3: Brainstorm.* Seeing the most significant cause as being poor study habits, the student comes up with ideas such as seeking help from his instructor or working with a study group.
- *Step 4: Explore.* The student considers individually the effects of different solutions: improved study habits, more sleep, tutoring, or dropping the class.
- *Step 5: Choose.* The student decides on a combination of improved study habits and tutoring.
- *Step 6: Evaluate.* Evaluating his choice, the student may decide that the effects are good but that his fatigue still causes problems in understanding the material.
- *Step 7: Refine the solution.* The student may decide to continue to study more regularly but, after a few weeks of tutoring, could opt to trade in the tutoring time for some extra sleep. He may decide to take what he has learned from the tutor so far and apply it to his increased study efforts.

Using this process enables you to solve school, work, and personal problems in a thoughtful, comprehensive way. Figures 4.4 and 4.5 show two examples of how to use this plan to solve a problem. They represent the same plan as Figure 4.3, but include writing space for use during the problem-solving process.

Decision Making

Decisions are choices. Making a choice, or decision, requires thinking critically through the possible choices and evaluating which will work best for you, considering the situation.

Before you begin the process, evaluate what kind of decision you have to make. Some decisions, such as what books to bring to class, are little day-to-day considerations that you can take care of quickly. Others, such

CAUSES OF PROBLEM	STATE PROBLEM HERE:	EFFECTS OF PROBLEM
Lost financial aid due to slipping grades Part-time job doesn't bring in much money	I don't have enough money to cover tuition next semester	Need to find money from a different source Might be unable to continue school right now

Use boxes below to list possible solutions:

POTENTIAL POSITIVE EFFECTS	SOLUTION #1	POTENTIAL NEGATIVE EFFECTS
List for each solution: Ability to stay on planned school schedule Ability to stay in school	Find new source of financial aid	*List for each solution:* Money might not be renewable like current grant Time and effort spent to find and qualify for new aid
More money to pay for college More on-the-job experience	**SOLUTION #2** Find full-time, better-paying job	Less time for college May have to take classes part-time, graduate later
More time to study More ability to focus	**SOLUTION #3** Take classes part-time next semester	Extends how long I'll be in college Could make me ineligible for certain kinds of aid

Now choose the solution you think is best—and try it.

ACTUAL POSITIVE EFFECTS	CHOSEN SOLUTION	ACTUAL NEGATIVE EFFECTS
List for chosen solution: More money earned More study time and ability to focus resulted in better grades	For next semester, take classes part-time and work full-time	*List for chosen solution:* Had to put off planned graduation date Ineligible this semester for most aid, had to use my own money for tuition

FINAL EVALUATION: Was it a good or bad choice?

It was tough but it worked out well. Even though I had to pay for classes myself, the full-time job and fewer classes allowed me to do that. Then, with better focus, I was able to raise my GPA back up so that next semester I'll requalify for aid and can go back to being a full-time student.

CAUSES OF PROBLEM	STATE PROBLEM HERE:	EFFECTS OF PROBLEM
We have radically different views and personality types I don't feel listened to in class or respected	I don't like my instructor for a particular course	Dampened interest in the class material No motivation to work on assignments Grades are suffering.

Use boxes below to list possible solutions:

POTENTIAL POSITIVE EFFECTS	SOLUTION #1	POTENTIAL NEGATIVE EFFECTS
List for each solution: Don't have to deal with that instructor Less stress	Drop the course	*List for each solution:* Grade gets entered on my transcript I'll have to take the course eventually; it's required for my major

	SOLUTION #2	
Getting credit for the course Feeling like I've honored a commitment	Put up with it until the end of the semester	Stress every time I'm there Lowered motivation Probably not such a good final grade

	SOLUTION #3	
A chance to express myself Could get good advice An opportunity to ask direct questions of the instructor	Schedule meetings with advisor and instructor	Have to face instructor one-on-one Might just make things worse

Now choose the solution you think is best—and try it.

ACTUAL POSITIVE EFFECTS	CHOSEN SOLUTION	ACTUAL NEGATIVE EFFECTS
List for chosen solution: Got some helpful advice from advisor Talking in person with the instructor actually promoted a fairly honest discussion I won't have to take the course again	Schedule meetings with both advisor and instructor, and stick with the course	*List for chosen solution:* The discussion was difficult and sometimes tense I still don't know how much learning I'll retain from this course

FINAL EVALUATION: Was it a good or bad choice?

The solution has improved things. I'll finish the course, and even though the instructor and I aren't the best of friends, we have a mutual understanding now. I feel more respected and more willing to put my time into the course.

as what to major in or whether to quit your part-time job, require thoughtful evaluation, time, and perhaps the input of others you trust. The following is a list of steps for thinking critically through the more complex kind of decision.

1. *Identify a goal.* Why is this decision necessary? What result do you want from this decision, and what is its value? Considering the desired *effects* can help you formulate your goal.

2. *Establish needs. Recall* the needs of everyone involved in the decision. Consider all who will be affected.

3. *Name, investigate, and evaluate available options.* Brainstorm possible choices, and then look at the facts surrounding each. *Evaluate* the good and bad effects of each possibility. Weigh these effects in light of the needs you have established and judge which is the best course of action.

4. *Decide on a plan and take action.* Make a choice based on your evaluation, and act on it.

5. *Evaluate the result.* Was it useful? Not useful? Some of both? Weigh the positive and negative effects.

Look at this example to see one way of using the decision-making plan.

- *Step 1: Identify a goal.* A student currently attends a small private college. Her goal is to become a physical therapist. The school has a good program, but her father has changed jobs and the family can no longer pay the tuition and fees.

- *Step 2: Establish needs.* The student needs a school with a full physical therapy program; she and her parents need to cut costs; she needs to be able to transfer credits.

- *Step 3: Evaluate options.* Here are some possible decisions that the student might consider:

  a. *Continue at the current college.* **Positive effects:** No need to adjust to a new place or to new people; ability to continue course work as planned. **Negative effects:** Need to finance most of my tuition and costs on my own, such as through loans, grants, or work; may be difficult to find time to work as much as I would need to; might not qualify for aid.

  b. *Transfer to the state college.* **Positive effects:** Opportunity to reconnect with people there that I know from high school; cheaper tuition and room costs; ability to transfer credits. **Negative effects:** Need to earn some money or get financial aid; physical therapy program is small and not very strong.

  c. *Transfer to the community college.* **Positive effects:** Many of the courses I need to continue with the physical therapy curriculum are available; school is close so I could live at home and avoid paying housing costs; credits will transfer; tuition is reasonable. **Negative effects:** No personal contacts; less independence; no bachelor's degree offered.

- *Step 4: Decide.* In this case, the student might decide to go to the community college for two years and then transfer back to a four-year school to earn a bachelor's degree in physical therapy. Although she

Apply techniques in both your stronger and weaker intelligences to become a more versatile critical thinker.

INTELLIGENCE	SUGGESTED STRATEGIES	WHAT WORKS FOR YOU? WRITE NEW IDEAS HERE
Verbal–Linguistic	▪ When a problem bothers you, write it out. Challenge yourself to come up with at least 10 possible solutions. ▪ Discuss new ideas or problems with other people. Write down any useful ideas they come up with.	
Logical–Mathematical	▪ Outline all possible outcomes to various possible actions. ▪ Analyze each possible solution to a problem. What effects might occur? What is the best choice and why?	
Bodily–Kinesthetic	▪ Pace while you brainstorm—have a tape recorder running and record your ideas as they come up. ▪ Think about solutions to a problem while you are running or doing any other type of exercise.	
Visual–Spatial	▪ Use a problem-solving flow chart like the one in Figure 4.4 and complete all the areas. ▪ Brainstorm ideas about, and solutions to, a problem by drawing a think link about the problem.	
Interpersonal	▪ When you are stuck on a problem, ask one of your friends to discuss it with you. Consider any new ideas or solutions the friend may offer. ▪ Discuss new creative ideas with one or more people and analyze the feedback.	
Intrapersonal	▪ Take time alone to think through a problem. Freewrite your thoughts about the problem in a journal. ▪ Sit quietly and think about your ability to evaluate solutions to a problem. Write three ways you can improve.	
Musical	▪ When you are stuck on a problem, shut down your brain for a while and listen to music you love. Come back to the problem later to see if new ideas have surfaced.	
Naturalistic	▪ Take a long walk in nature to inspire creative ideas or to think of solutions to a problem. ▪ Think about your favorite place in nature before concentrating on brainstorming about a problem.	

might lose some independence and contact with friends, the positive effects are money saved, opportunity to spend time on studies rather than working to earn tuition, and the availability of classes that match the physical therapy program requirements.

- *Step 5: Evaluate.* If the student decides to transfer, she may find that it can be hard being back at home, although her parents are adjusting to her independence and she is trying to respect their concerns. Fewer social distractions result in her getting more work done. The financial situation is favorable. All things considered, she evaluates that this decision is a good one.

Making important decisions can take time. Think through your decisions thoroughly, considering your own ideas as well as those of others you trust, but don't hesitate to act once you have your plan. You cannot benefit from your decision until you follow through on it.

How do you *reason?*

R easoning refers to using one's ability to connect idea to example and draw cause-and-effect conclusions. One aspect of reasoning that affects your ability to be a good critical thinker is determining the accuracy of information by distinguishing fact from opinion. Another important aspect—evaluating arguments—is addressed in Chapter 5 in the context of reading.

Before you can distinguish fact from opinion, you must be able to define both. A *statement of fact,* according to the dictionary, is information presented as objectively real and verifiable—something that can be proven. A *statement of opinion* is defined as a belief, conclusion, or judgment and is inherently difficult, and sometimes impossible, to verify. Being able to distinguish fact from opinion is crucial to your ability to evaluate the credibility of what you read, hear, and experience.

Table 4.2 has some examples of factual statements versus statements of opinion; note that facts refer to the observable or measurable, while opinions usually involve cause-and-effect exploration. Use the blank lines to add your own examples.

Characteristics of Facts and Opinions

The following information will help you determine what is fact and what is opinion.[6]

Characteristics of fact are:

- *Statements that deal with actual people, places, objects, events.* If the existence of the elements involved can be verified through observation or record, chances are that the statement itself can also be proven true or false. "Jimmy Carter was a peanut farmer in Georgia before becoming president" is a fact, for example.

Table 4.2	How facts differ from opinions.	
TOPIC	**FACTUAL STATEMENT**	**STATEMENT OF OPINION**
Stock market	In 1999, the Dow Jones Industrial average rose above 10,000 for the first time.	The Dow Jones Industrial average will continue to grow throughout the first decade of the 21st century.
Weather	It's raining outside.	This is the worst rainstorm yet this year.
Cataloging systems	Computer databases have replaced card catalogs in most college libraries.	Computer databases are an improvement over card catalogs.

- *Statements that use concrete words or measurable statistics.* Any statement that uses concrete, measurable terms and avoids the abstract is likely to be a fact. Examples include "Thirty-six inches equal a yard" and "There are 2,512 full-time students enrolled this semester."

Characteristics of opinions include:

- *Statements that show evaluation.* Any statement of value, such as "Television is bad for children," indicates an opinion. Words such as *bad, good, pointless,* and *beneficial* indicate value judgments.
- *Statements that predict future events.* Nothing that will happen in the future can be definitively proven in the present. Most statements that discuss something that may happen in the future are opinions.
- *Statements that use abstract words.* Although "one gallon" can be defined, "love" has no specific definition. Abstract words—*strength, misery, success*—usually indicate an opinion.
- *Statements that use emotional words.* Emotions are by nature unverifiable. Chances are that statements using such words as *delightful, nasty, miserable,* or *wonderful* express an opinion.
- *Statements that use absolutes.* Absolute qualifiers, such as *all, none, never,* and *always,* point to an opinion. For example, "All students need to have a job while in school" is an opinion.

When you find yourself feeling that an opinion is fact, it may be because you agree strongly with the opinion. Don't discount your feelings; "not verifiable" is not the same as "inaccurate." Opinions are not necessarily wrong even if you cannot prove them. Also, when you think that an apparent statement of fact is an opinion, it may be because you don't trust the source.

Handwritten margin notes:

ABSTRACT
Theoretical; disassociated from any specific instance.

QUALIFIER
A word, such as always, never, or often, that changes the meaning of another word or word group.

Investigating Truth and Accuracy

Once you label a statement as a fact or opinion, ask questions to explore its degree of truth. Because both stated facts and opinions can be true or false—for example, "There are 25 hours in a day" is a false factual statement—both require investigation through questioning. Critical-thinking experts Sylvan Barnet and Hugo Bedau state that when you test for the truth of a statement, you "determine whether what it asserts corresponds with reality; if it does, then it is true, and if it doesn't, then it is false."[7] In order to determine to what degree a statement "corresponds with reality," ask questions such as the following:

- What facts or examples provide evidence of truth?
- Is there another fact that disproves this statement or information or shows it to be an opinion?
- How reliable are the sources of information?
- What about this statement is similar to or different from other information I consider fact?
- Are these truly the causes and effects?

Distinguishing fact from opinion by asking important questions helps you to approach a variety of situations with an open mind. Supporting your opinions with indisputable facts increases your credibility; recognizing whether others support their opinions likewise helps you avoid responding in a reactionary, unsubstantiated way to issues that arise in school, work, or at home. The creative part of this process comes in the choice to be proactive—you consider what's possible instead of getting caught in your own tendencies to see the world a certain way, resting on certain assumptions.

How can you *open your mind* to new perspectives?

PERSPECTIVE
A cluster of related assumptions and opinions that incorporate values, interests, and knowledge.

Perspective is complex and unique to each individual. You have your own way of looking at everything that you encounter. Perspective is the big-picture point of view that forms the basis for and guides your thoughts on ideas, activities, people, places, and so on. Consider the classic question: Do you generally see the glass as half full or half empty? Either view is an example of perspective.

A given perspective shapes various opinions and assumptions that in turn reflect the overall perspective of the thinker. For instance, your perspective on public education may lead you to specific opinions and assumptions about schools, teachers, and government involvement. Here is a set of examples to further explain:

ASSUMPTION
An idea or statement accepted as true without examination or proof; a hardened opinion.

Perspective: Education is essential; everyone has the right to an education.

A related assumption: The amount of money school systems spend per student has a major impact on the quality of education.

A related opinion: State funding should attempt to equalize per-student spending so that all schools can deliver a quality education.

When your opinion clashes with someone else's, it often reflects a difference in perspective. If a friend has a negative opinion of your choosing to live with a significant other, for example, that friend might have a different perspective from yours on relationships, with accompanying different opinions and assumptions about how they should progress.

You probably know how difficult it can be when someone cannot understand your perspective on something. Perhaps an instructor thinks students should never miss class and can't understand an absence you had, or a parent can't understand why you would date someone of a different race. However, it is just as important for you to try to understand other perspectives as it is for others to try to understand yours. Seeing the world only from your point of view—and resisting any challenges to that perspective—can be inflexible, limiting, and frustrating to both you and others. Opening your mind to other perspectives both educates you and helps you to evaluate and refine your own views and behavior.

Evaluating Perspectives

Using an evaluation system based on the critical-thinking path (Figure 4.1) allows you to think more broadly about the world around you, introducing you to new ideas, improving your communication with others, and encouraging mutual respect.

Step 1: Take in New Information

The first step is to take in new perspectives and simply acknowledge that they exist without immediately judging, rejecting, or even accepting them. It's easy to feel so strongly about a topic—for example, whether capital punishment is morally defensible—that you don't even consider any other view. If someone offers an opposing view, hold back your opinions while you *listen*. Critical thinkers are able to allow for the existence of perspectives that differ from, and even completely negate, their own.

Step 2: Evaluate the Perspective

Asking questions helps you maintain flexibility and openness.

- What is similar and different about this perspective and mine? What personal experiences have led to our particular perspectives?
- What examples, evidence, or reasons could be used to support or justify this perspective? Do some reasons provide good support even if I don't agree with the reasons?
- What effects may come from this way of being, acting, or believing? Are the effects different on different people and in different situations?

Even if this perspective seems to have negative effects for me, how might it have positive effects for others and therefore have value?

- What can I learn from this different perspective? Is there anything I could adopt that would improve my life? Is there anything I wouldn't agree with but that I can still respect and learn from?

Step 3: Accept—and Perhaps Adopt

On the one hand, perhaps your evaluation leads you simply to recognize and appreciate the other perspective, even if you decide that it is not right for you. On the other hand, thinking through the new perspective may lead you to feel that you want to try it out or to adopt it as your own. You may feel that what you have learned has led you to a new way of seeing yourself, your life, or the world around you.

"We do not live to think, but, on the contrary, we think in order that we may succeed in surviving."

JOSÉ ORTEGA Y GASSET

Perspectives are made up of many different assumptions. Challenging assumptions is an important part of opening your mind to other perspectives. When you question the assumptions that you and others hold, you do the critical thinker's job of looking carefully at the validity of perspectives.

Identifying and Evaluating Assumptions

"A more expensive car is a better car." "Students get more work done in a library." These statements reveal assumptions—evaluations or generalizations influenced by values and based on observing *cause* and *effect*—that can often hide within seemingly truthful statements. An assumption can influence choices—you may assume that you should earn a certain degree or own a car. Many people don't question whether their assumptions make sense, nor do they challenge the assumptions of others.

Assumptions come from sources such as parents or relatives, television and other media, friends, and personal experiences. As much as you think such assumptions work for you, it's just as possible that they can close your mind to opportunities and even cause harm. Investigate each assumption as you would any statement of fact or opinion, questioning the truth of the supposed causes and effects.

The first step in uncovering the assumptions that underlie an opinion or perspective is to look at the cause-and-effect pattern, seeing whether the way reasons move to conclusions, or causes are connected to effects, is supported by evidence or involves a hidden assumption. Figure 4.6 has examples of questions you can ask to uncover and evaluate an assumption.

For example, here's how you might use these questions to investigate the following statement: "The most productive schedule involves getting

Figure 4.6 **Questioning an assumption.**

What is the source of this assumption? How reliable is the source—can it be counted on to have investigated this assumption?

What positive and negative effects has this assumption had on me or others?

What harm could be done by always taking this assumption as fact?

In what cases is this assumption valid or invalid? What examples prove or disprove it?

started early in the day." First of all, a cause-and-effect evaluation shows that this statement reveals the following assumption: "The morning is when people have the most energy and are most able to get things done." Here's how you might question the assumption:

- This assumption may be true for people who have good energy in the morning hours. Does it work for people who are at their best in the afternoon or evening hours?

- Society's basic standard of daytime classes and 8:00 A.M. to 5:00 P.M. working hours supports this assumption. Therefore, the assumption may work for people who have early jobs and classes. How does it work for people who work other shifts or who take evening classes?

- Were people who believe this assumption raised to start their days early, or do they just go along with what seems to be society's standard? Aren't there people who operate on a different schedule and yet enjoy successful, productive lives?

- What effect would taking this assumption as fact have on people who don't operate at their peak in the earlier hours? In situations that favor their particular characteristics—later classes and jobs, career areas that don't require early morning work—don't such people have as much potential to succeed as anyone else?

Be careful to question all assumptions, not just those that seem problematic from the start. Form your opinion after investigating the positive and negative effects of making the assumption.

The Value of Seeing Other Perspectives

Seeing beyond one's own perspective can be difficult. Why put in the effort? Here are some of the benefits of being able to see and consider other perspectives.

Improved communication. When you consider another person's perspective, you open the lines of communication. For example, if you want to add or drop a course and your advisor says it's impossible before listening to you, you might not feel much like explaining. But if your advisor asks to hear your underlying reasons, you may sense that your needs are respected and be ready to talk.

Mutual respect. When someone takes the time and energy to understand how you feel about something, you probably feel respected and, in return, offer respect to the person who made the effort. When people respect one another, relationships become stronger and more productive, whether they are personal, work-related, or educational.

Continued learning. Every time you open your mind to a different perspective, you can learn something new. There are worlds of knowledge and possibilities outside your experience. You may find different yet equally valid ways of getting an education, living as a family, or relating to others. Above all else, you may see that each person is entitled to his or her own perspective, no matter how foreign it may be to you.

By being able to recognize perspectives, the connection that you foster with others may mean the difference between success and failure in today's world. This becomes more significant as the Information Age introduces you to an increasing number of perspectives every day. This

"The best way to escape from a problem is to solve it."

ALAN SAPORTA

dynamic global environment requires that you broaden your perspectives, continually evaluate choices as objectively as possible, and push yourself to embrace new and innovative ideas. The more creative you are in terms of combining known elements to create new ideas or perspectives, the better your chances for success.

Why plan *strategically?*

f you've ever played a game of chess, participated in a martial arts match, or made a detailed plan of how to reach a particular goal, you have had experience with *strategy*. Strategy is the plan of action, the method or the "how," behind achieving any goal.

Strategic planning means looking at the next week, month, year, or 10 years and exploring the future positive and negative effects that current choices and actions may have. As a student, you have planned strategically by deciding that the effort of school is a legitimate price to pay for the skills and opportunities you will receive. Being strategic

113

means using decision-making skills to choose how to accomplish tasks. It means asking questions. It sometimes means delaying immediate gratification for future gain.

Strategy and Critical Thinking

In situations that demand strategy, think critically by asking questions like these:

- If you aim for a certain goal, what actions may cause you to achieve that goal?
- What are the potential effects, positive or negative, of different actions or choices?
- What can you learn from previous experiences that may inspire similar or different actions?
- What could cause you to fail—what barriers stand in the way?
- What can you recall about what others have done in similar situations?
- Which set of effects are most helpful or desirable to you?

For any situation that would benefit from strategic planning, from getting ready for a study session to aiming for a career, the steps in this variation on the decision-making plan on page 105 will help you make choices that bring about the most positive effects. Throughout the process of achieving your goal, remember to be flexible. Because you never know what may happen to turn your plan upside down, the concept of flexibility is critical to landing on your feet.

1. *Establish a goal.* What do you want to achieve, and when? Why do you want to achieve it?

2. *Brainstorm possible plans.* What are some ways that you can get where you want to go? What steps toward your goal do you need to take today, 1 year, 5 years, 10 years, or 20 years from now?

3. *Anticipate as many potential effects of each plan as possible.* What positive and negative effects may occur, both soon and in the long term? What approach may best help you to overcome barriers and achieve your goal? Talk to people who are where you want to

PERSONAL TRIUMPH

*d*iscovering personal power can turn a life around. As mentors and activities helped Susie Ivy deal with her past and learn of her strength and creativity, she found ways to achieve that she never would have imagined.

People tell me I'm motivated and that I take initiative to make good things happen. It's funny because I see myself as a pretty laid-back person. But I do believe having someone who believes in you can make a difference. Everyone needs to be lifted up, at least once in a while.

I am the youngest of five children. My mother suffered from schizophrenia, and she was addicted to drugs. When my aunt called the Department of Child and Family Services and reported our situation, my brothers and sisters and I were placed in foster care. I was five years old.

We all were placed in the same home, where at times there were as many as 10 foster children living. Although we weren't physically abused, we didn't get the emotional support we needed. We didn't receive counseling, and no one ever explained how long we would be in foster care or what to expect. For years I fantasized that our mother would get her life together and bring us home. But that never happened.

When I was eight years old, we started attending a church youth group. I really enjoyed the activities and the youth leaders. I participated in the weekly meetings and went to summer camp. One of the youth leaders is still my mentor today. As I think back, I realize that this is when my positive childhood memories began to form.

During my teen years, many girls at my high school got pregnant and left school. Although I wasn't happy at home, I knew I didn't want that to be my fate. Instead, I joined the track and swim teams. I swam all four years and won most valuable player

Susie Ivy, Fashion Design major;
Dominican University, River Forest, Illinois

each year. Discovering something I was good at had a profound impact on the way I saw myself. I set out to prove that I was smart and talented.

Before graduation, I made plans to attend college, thinking I wanted to be a surgical nurse. In my senior year, I changed my mind. I was talking with a few friends about the prom and decided to make my own dress. I couldn't draw well, so I described the dress to my foster dad, and he drew it for me. I was so pleased with how the dress turned out! Right then and there I decided to major in fashion design, and I began applying to colleges that offered fashion design programs.

I love my major. I like exploring the creative process and pushing myself to do my best. Every year, my school sponsors a spring fashion show, and my clothes are modeled in front of an audience. Last year, I was selected from my school to go to New York City for a fashion tour, where I saw new designs and visited other colleges. These are the highlights of my college experience.

I've also discovered that competition is a motivating force in my life, especially when it comes to my designs. For example, a girl in one of my classes comes from a rich family. She can afford the nicest fabrics for her projects, and she doesn't have to work like I do to pay for school. But I remind myself that money can't buy talent. Everybody who is famous didn't start with a lot of money. When I think about where I've been, I'm happy about who I'm becoming.

Take a moment to consider . . .

- *What you consider to be the most motivating factor in your life.*
- *How you consider yourself creative, and what you are proud to have created.*

be—professionally or personally—and ask them what you should anticipate.

4. *Put your plan into action.* Act on the decision you have made.

5. *Evaluate continually.* Because a long-term goal lies in the future, the evaluation period could be long. Check regularly to see whether your strategies are having the effects you predicted. If you discover that events are not going the way you planned, for any reason, reevaluate and change your strategy.

The most important critical-thinking question for successful strategic planning begins with "how." How do you remember what you learn? How do you develop a productive idea at work? The process of strategic planning helps you find the best answer.

Benefits of Strategic Planning

Strategic planning has many positive effects, including the following:

Keeping up with technology. Technological developments have increased the pace of workplace change. Thinking strategically about job opportunities may lead you to a broader range of courses or a major and career in a growing career area, making it more likely that your skills will be in demand when you graduate.

Successful goal setting. Thinking strategically improves your ability to work through and achieve goals over time. For example, a student might have a goal of paying tuition; this student could plan a strategy of part-time jobs and cutting back on spending in order to achieve that goal. Strategy keeps you headed toward the target.

School and work success. A student who wants to do well in a course needs to plan study sessions. A lawyer needs to anticipate how to respond to points raised in court. Strategic planning creates a vision into the future that allows the planner to anticipate possibilities and to be prepared for them.

Strategic planning entails using critical thinking to develop a vision of your future.

Figure 4.7 **The wheel of thinking.**

THINKING PROCESSES

Solving Problems

Making Decisions

mind actions

Recall

Similarity

Cause & effect

R

Difference

Evaluation

Seeing New Perspectives

Planning Strategically

EX

EX

Example to idea   Idea to example

Reasoning

Although you can't predict with certainty what will happen, you can ask questions about the potential effects of your actions. With what you learn, you can make plans that bring the best possible effects for you and others.

κριvειv

The word *critical* is derived from the Greek word *krinein,* which means to separate in order to choose or select. To be a mindful, aware critical thinker, you need to be able to separate, evaluate, and select ideas, opinions, and facts.

Think of this concept as you apply critical thinking to your reading, writing, and interaction with others. Be aware of the information you absorb and how your mind works. Be selective in the thinking processes you use, and separate out and select the best solutions, decisions, perspectives, plans, arguments, and opinions. Critical thinking gives you the power to make sense of life by deliberately selecting how to respond to the information, people, and events that you encounter.

Building Skills

FOR COLLEGE, CAREER, AND LIFE SUCCESS

The Big Picture — *Combining Thinking, Strategy, and Teamwork*

GROUP PROBLEM SOLVING. As a class, brainstorm a list of problems in your lives. Write the problems on the board or on a large piece of paper attached to an easel. Include any problems you feel comfortable discussing with others. Such problems may involve academics, relationships, jobs, discrimination, parenting, housing, procrastination, and others. Divide into groups of two to four with each group choosing or being assigned one problem to work on. Use the empty problem-solving flowchart (Figure 4.8) on the next page to fill in your work.

1. *Identify the problem.* As a group, state your problem specifically, without causes ("I'm not attending all of my classes" is better than "lack of motivation"). Then, explore and record the causes and effects that surround it. Remember to look for "hidden" causes (you may perceive that traffic makes you late to school, but getting up too late might be the hidden cause).

2. *Brainstorm possible solutions.* Determine the most likely causes of the problem; from those causes, derive possible solutions. Record all the ideas that group members offer. After 10 minutes or so, each group member should choose one possible solution to explore independently.

3. *Explore each solution.* In thinking independently through the assigned solution, each group member should (a) weigh the positive and negative effects, (b) consider similar problems, and (c) describe how the solution affects the causes of the problem. Evaluate your assigned solution. Is it a good one? Will it work?

4. *Choose your top solution(s).* Come together again as a group. Take turns sharing your observations and recommendations, and then take a vote: Which solution is the best? You may have a tie or may want to combine two different solutions. Either way is fine. Different solutions suit different people and situations. Although it's not always possible to reach agreement, try to find the solution that works for most of the group.

Figure 4.8 Walking through a problem . . . .

| CAUSES OF PROBLEM | STATE PROBLEM HERE: | EFFECTS OF PROBLEM |

Use boxes below to list possible solutions:

| POTENTIAL POSITIVE EFFECTS | SOLUTION #1 | POTENTIAL NEGATIVE EFFECTS |

List for each solution:

List for each solution:

SOLUTION #2

SOLUTION #3

Now choose the solution you think is best—and try it.

| ACTUAL POSITIVE EFFECTS | CHOSEN SOLUTION | ACTUAL NEGATIVE EFFECTS |

List for chosen solution:

List for chosen solution:

FINAL EVALUATION: Was it a good or bad choice?

5. *Evaluate the solution you decide is best.* When you decide on your top solution or solutions, discuss what would happen if you went through with it. What do you predict would be the positive and negative effects of this solution? Would it turn out to be a truly good solution for everyone?

Writing *Discovery Through Journaling*

To record your thoughts, use a separate journal or the lined pages at the end of the chapter.

PERSPECTIVES. Write about a perspective that has a great deal of influence on your life. How did you develop this perspective—what are its sources? What effects, positive or negative, does it have on how you think and how you live? If it has some significant negative effects, do you want to change it? How do you plan to do so?

Career Portfolio *Charting Your Course*

INVESTIGATE A CAREER. Choose one career that interests you. Use your critical-thinking processes to think through all aspects of this career strategically. Be an investigator. Find out as many facts as you can, and evaluate all opinions based on what you already know.

- What are the different kinds of jobs available in this career?
- What is the condition of the industry—growing, lagging, or holding steady?
- Does this career require you to live in a certain area of the country or world?
- Whom can you consult to find out more information about this career?
- What are the pros and cons (positive and negative effects) of working in this area?
- What types of people tend to succeed in this career, and what types tend not to do well?
- What are the opinions of those around you about this career?
- What preparation—in school or on the job—does this career require?

Then, write up your findings in a report. You may want to use each question as a separate heading. Keep your research in your portfolio with your other Career Portfolio work. Write below a brief conclusion about your prospects in this career area based on what you learned in your investigation.

_____

_____

_____

_____

If you have access to the CD-ROM Strategies for Success, use the following questions to assess your thoughts and enhance your understanding of the chapter. The questions below represent only some of the activities provided on the CD for the chapter topics—try others if you have time.

Click on the Creative Thinking bookmark. Use the following activities to expand your ability to think creatively:

1. Take the pre-assessment to determine your view of the role of creativity in your life.

2. Watch the video and think about the impact of creativity on your career. In the field provided, write about how you plan to use creative thinking on the job—or how you use it right now, if you currently have a job—and give specific examples.

3. Click on Activity Three: Journal Reflections. Scroll to the third question, which asks you to brainstorm a creative way to solve a school-related problem of yours, and type your answer.

4. Take the post-assessment to see how these activities have expanded your perspective on creativity.

Suggested Readings

Cameron, Julia with Mark Bryan. *The Artist's Way: A Spiritual Path to Higher Creativity.* New York: G.P. Putnam's Sons, 1995.

deBono, Edward. *Lateral Thinking: Creativity Step by Step.* New York: Perennial Library, 1990.

Noone, Donald J., Ph.D. *Creative Problem Solving.* New York: Barron's, 1998.

Sark. *Living Juicy: Daily Morsels for Your Creative Soul.* Berkeley, CA: Celestial Arts, 1994.

von Oech, Roger. *A Kick in the Seat of the Pants.* New York: Harper & Row Publishers, 1986.

von Oech, Roger. *A Whack on the Side of the Head.* New York: Warner Books, 1998.

Internet Resources

Roger von Oech's Creative Think Web site: www.creativethink.com

Endnotes

1. Roger von Oech, *A Kick in the Seat of the Pants.* New York: Harper & Row Publishers, 1986, pp. 5–21.

2. Frank T. Lyman, Jr., Ph.D., "Think-Pair-Share, Thinktrix, Thinklinks, and Weird Facts: An Interactive System for Cooperative Thinking." In *Enhancing Thinking Through Cooperative Learning,* Neil Davidson and Toni Worsham, eds. New York: Teachers College Press, 1992, pp. 169–181.

3. Dennis Coon, *Introduction to Psychology: Exploration and Application,* 6th ed. St. Paul: West Publishing Company, 1992, p. 295.

4. Roger von Oech, *A Whack on the Side of the Head.* New York: Warner Books, 1990, pp. 11–168.

5. Ibid.

6. Ben E. Johnson, *Stirring Up Thinking.* New York: Houghton Mifflin Company, 1998, pp. 268–270.

7. Sylvan Barnet and Hugo Bedau, *Critical Thinking, Reading, and Writing: A Brief Guide to Argument,* 2nd ed. Boston: Bedford Books of St. Martin's Press, 1996, p. 43.

JOURNAL

name   date

visit: www.prenhall.com/carter NY Times link for this chapter

UNDERSTAND

5

reading and studying

In this chapter you explore answers to the following questions:

- What will help you understand what you read?
- How can you set the stage for reading?
- How can SQ3R help you own what you read?
- How can you respond critically to what you read?
- How and why should you study with others?

IT ISN'T JUST students with learning disabilities, like Darrin Estepp (see next page), who find college reading challenging. Your reading background—your past as a reader—may not necessarily prepare you for reading that often requires deep-level understanding. You may also experience an overload of assignments.

College reading and studying require a step-by-step approach aimed at the construction of meaning and knowledge. This chapter presents techniques that help you read and study efficiently, while still having time left over for other responsibilities and activities.

focusing on content

Darrin Estepp, Ohio State
University, Columbus, Ohio

Morgan Paar, Graduate Student,
Academy of Art College, San Francisco, California

How can I cope with learning disabilities?

One thing I learned in college was that there is more than one way to succeed . . .

In elementary school, I needed extra help with reading. By high school, I was having a hard time keeping up, and a test I took showed I had dyslexia. Study assistance helped, but I attended high school for an extra year to improve my record. Then, I enrolled in community college and worked part-time as a nursing home cook. I transferred to Ohio State after two years. Recently I was also diagnosed with attention deficit hyperactivity disorder (ADHD).

I learn best by hearing, seeing, and doing all at once. If I just hear something, it doesn't sink in very well. It seems no matter how hard I try, it's never enough. I keep hanging in there though. Eventually, I would like to help others in my career—I can see myself being on the lookout for the early signs of disabilities like mine. What suggestions do you have for how I can cope with my learning disabilities?

My reading-related disability was discovered in the fourth grade. I remember dreading to read out loud to my class; students would laugh. One thing I learned in college was that there is more than one way to succeed, even if I couldn't keep up with the reading. First, I attended every single class without exception. Second, if I got behind in my note taking (and I often did), I would borrow a friend's notes and rewrite mine, combining them with theirs. Third, I made friends with my teachers, and they would help me during their office hours.

One incident showed me that anything was possible. A friend worked for a newspaper and asked me to write a story. I laughed— I said I could barely spell my name, never mind write an article. He said, "Come on, computers have spell checkers." I labored through it; my friend loved the writing (though he did say that I had used some very creative grammar), and it appeared as a two-part story in the travel section. I have since had 17 articles published.

It never gets easy—but one route to success is to do something you love. I write travel stories because I love traveling and sharing stories. I am now a filmmaker, and I am studying film in graduate school so I can someday teach it. Darrin, you already know the skills you need to achieve your goals, though maybe they are deep in your subconscious mind. I was 27 years old before I knew what I really wanted to do. Just keep following your passions, never give up, figure out what you need to do to achieve your goals, and know that there is more than one path to your destination.

What will *help you understand* what you read?

More than anything else, reading is a process that requires you, the reader, to *make meaning* from written words. When you make meaning, you connect yourself to the concepts being communicated. Your prior knowledge or familiarity with a subject, culture and home environment, life experiences, and even personal interpretation of words and phrases affect your understanding. Because these factors are different for every person, your reading experiences are uniquely your own.

Reading *comprehension* refers to your ability to understand what you read. True comprehension goes beyond just knowing facts and figures—a student can parrot back a pile of economics statistics on a test, for example, without understanding what they mean. Only when you thoroughly comprehend the information you read can you make the most effective use of that information.

All reading strategies help you to achieve a greater understanding of what you read. Therefore, every section in this chapter will in some way help you maximize your comprehension. Following are some general comprehension boosters to keep in mind as you work through the chapter and as you tackle individual reading assignments.

Build knowledge through reading and studying. More than any other factor, what you already know before you read a passage influences your ability to understand and remember important ideas. Previous knowledge gives you a context for what you read.

> CONTEXT
>
> *Written or spoken knowledge that can help to illuminate the meaning of a word or passage.*

Think positively. Instead of telling yourself that you cannot understand, think positively. Tell yourself: *I can learn this material. I am a good reader.*

Think critically. Ask yourself questions. Do you understand the sentence, paragraph, or chapter you just read? Are ideas and supporting examples clear? Could you explain the material to someone else? Later in this chapter, you will learn strategies for responding critically to what you read.

Build vocabulary. Lifelong learners consider their vocabulary a work in progress. They never stop learning new words. The more you know, the more material you can understand without stopping to wonder what new words mean.

Look for order and meaning in seemingly chaotic reading materials. The information in this chapter on the SQ3R reading technique and on critical reading will help you discover patterns and achieve a depth of understanding. Finding order within chaos is an important skill, not just in the mastery of reading, but also in life. This skill gives you power by helping you "read" (think through) work dilemmas, personal problems, and educational situations.

How can you *set the stage* for reading?

On any given day during your college career, you may be faced with reading assignments like these:

- A textbook chapter on the history of South African apartheid (world history)
- An original research study on the relationship between sleep deprivation and the development of memory problems (psychology)
- Chapters 4–6 in John Steinbeck's classic novel *The Grapes of Wrath* (American literature)
- A technical manual on the design of computer antivirus programs (computer science—software design)

This material is rigorous by anyone's standards. To get through it—and master its contents—you need a systematic approach. The following strategies help you set the stage for reading success.

If you have a reading disability, if English is not your primary language, or if you have limited reading skills, you may need additional support (see "Quick Start to College" for more on learning disabilities and support services). Most colleges provide services for students through a reading center or tutoring program. Take the initiative to seek help if you need it. Many accomplished learners benefit from help in specific areas. Remember: The ability to succeed is often linked to the ability to ask for help.

Take an Active Approach to Difficult Texts

Because texts are often written to challenge the intellect, even well-written, useful texts may be difficult to read. Some textbook authors may not explain information in the friendliest manner for nonexperts. And, as every student knows, some textbooks are poorly written and organized.

Generally, the further you advance in your education, the more complex your required reading. You may encounter new concepts, words, and terms that seem like a foreign language. Assignments can also be difficult when the required reading is from *primary sources*—original documents rather than another writer's interpretation of these documents—or from academic journal articles and scientific studies that don't define basic terms or supply a wealth of examples. Primary sources include:

- historical documents
- works of literature (e.g., novels, poems, and plays)
- scientific studies, including lab reports and accounts of experiments
- journal articles

The following strategies may help you approach difficult material actively and positively:

Approach your reading assignments with an open mind. Be careful not to prejudge them as impossible or boring before you even start.

Know that some texts may require some extra work and concentration. Set a goal to make your way through the material and learn. Do whatever it takes.

Define concepts that your material does not explain. Consult resources—instructors, students, reference materials—for help.

To help with your make-meaning-of-textbooks mission, you may want to create your own mini-library at home. Collect reference materials that you use often, such as a dictionary, a thesaurus, a writer's style handbook, and maybe an atlas or computer manual (many of these are available as computer software or CD-ROMs). You may also benefit from owning reference materials in your particular areas of study. "If you find yourself going to the library to look up the same reference again and again, consider purchasing that book for your personal or office library," advises library expert Sherwood Harris.[1]

Choose the Right Setting

Finding a place and time that minimize distractions helps you achieve the focus and discipline that your reading requires. Here are some suggestions.

Select the right company (or lack thereof). If you prefer to read alone, establish a relatively interruption-proof place and time such as an out-of-the-way spot at the library or an after-class hour in an empty classroom. Even if you don't mind activity nearby, try to minimize distraction.

Select the right location. Many students study at a library desk. Others prefer an easy chair at the library or at home, or even the floor. Choose a spot that's comfortable but not so cushy that you fall asleep. Make sure that you have adequate lighting and aren't too hot or cold. You may also want to avoid the distraction of studying in a room where people are talking or a television is on.

"No barrier of the senses shuts me out from the sweet, gracious discourse of my book friends. They talk to me without embarrassment or awkwardness."

HELEN KELLER

Select the right time. Choose a time when you feel alert and focused. Try reading just before or after the class for which the reading is assigned, if you can. Eventually, you will associate preferred places and times with focused reading.

Deal with internal distractions. Although a noisy environment can get in the way of your work, so can internal distractions—for example, personal worries, anticipation of an event, or even hunger. Different strategies may help. You may want to take a break and tend to one of the issues that worries you. Physical exercise may relax and refocus you. For some people, studying while listening to music quiets a busy mind. For others, silence may do the trick. If you're hungry, take a snack break and come back to your work.

Students with families have an additional factor involved when deciding when, where, and how to read. Figure 5.1 explores some ways that parents or others caring for children may be able to maximize their study efforts. These techniques will also help after college if you choose to telecommute—work from home through an Internet-linked computer—while your children are still at home under your care.

Figure 5.1 **Managing children while studying.**

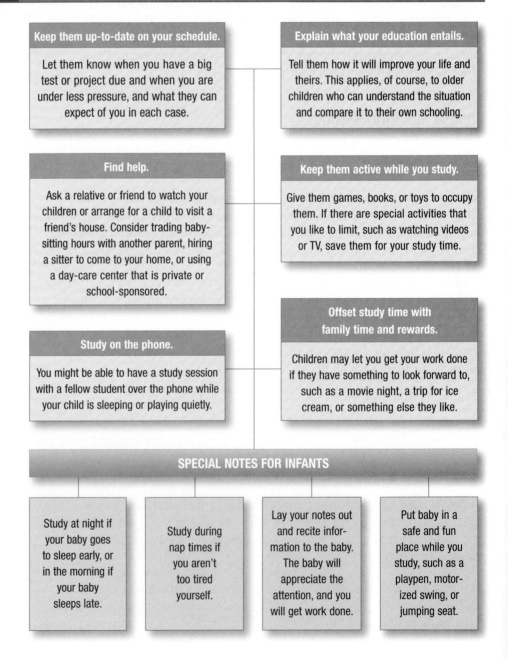

Keep them up-to-date on your schedule.

Let them know when you have a big test or project due and when you are under less pressure, and what they can expect of you in each case.

Explain what your education entails.

Tell them how it will improve your life and theirs. This applies, of course, to older children who can understand the situation and compare it to their own schooling.

Find help.

Ask a relative or friend to watch your children or arrange for a child to visit a friend's house. Consider trading baby-sitting hours with another parent, hiring a sitter to come to your home, or using a day-care center that is private or school-sponsored.

Keep them active while you study.

Give them games, books, or toys to occupy them. If there are special activities that you like to limit, such as watching videos or TV, save them for your study time.

Offset study time with family time and rewards.

Children may let you get your work done if they have something to look forward to, such as a movie night, a trip for ice cream, or something else they like.

Study on the phone.

You might be able to have a study session with a fellow student over the phone while your child is sleeping or playing quietly.

SPECIAL NOTES FOR INFANTS

Study at night if your baby goes to sleep early, or in the morning if your baby sleeps late.

Study during nap times if you aren't too tired yourself.

Lay your notes out and recite information to the baby. The baby will appreciate the attention, and you will get work done.

Put baby in a safe and fun place while you study, such as a playpen, motorized swing, or jumping seat.

Define Your Purpose for Reading

When you define your purpose, you ask yourself *why* you are reading a particular piece of material. One way to do this is by completing this sentence: "In reading this material, I intend to define/learn/ answer/achieve . . ." With a clear purpose in mind, you can decide how much time and what kind of effort to expend on various reading assignments.

Achieving your reading purpose requires adapting to different types of reading materials. Being a flexible reader—adjusting your reading strategies and pace—helps you to adapt successfully.

Purpose Determines Reading Strategy

With purpose comes direction; with direction comes a strategy. Following are four reading purposes. You may have one or more for any "reading event."

Purpose 1: Read for understanding. In college, studying means reading to comprehend the material. The two main components of comprehension are *general ideas* and *specific facts or examples*. Facts and examples help to explain or support ideas, and ideas provide a framework that helps the reader to remember facts and examples.

- *General ideas.* Reading for a general idea is rapid reading that seeks an overview of the material. You search for general ideas by focusing on headings, subheadings, and summary statements.

- *Specific facts or examples.* At times, readers may focus on locating specific pieces of information—for example, the stages of intellectual development in children. Often, a reader may search for examples that support or explain general ideas—for example, the causes of economic recession.

Purpose 2: Read to evaluate critically. Critical evaluation involves understanding. It means approaching the material with an open mind, examining causes and effects, evaluating ideas, and asking questions that test the writer's argument and search for assumptions. Critical reading brings an understanding of the material that goes beyond basic information recall (see page 146 for more on critical reading).

Purpose 3: Read for practical application. A third purpose for reading is to gather usable information that you can apply toward a specific goal. When you read a computer manual or an instruction sheet for assembling a gas grill, your goal is to learn how to do something. Reading and action usually go hand in hand. Remembering the specifics requires a certain degree of general comprehension.

Purpose 4: Read for pleasure. Some materials you read for entertainment, such as *Sports Illustrated* magazine or the latest John Grisham courtroom thriller. Recreational reading may also go beyond materials that seem obviously designed to entertain. Whereas some people may read a Jane Austen novel for comprehension, as in a class assignment, others may read her books for pleasure.

Use selected reading techniques in Multiple Intelligence areas to strengthen your ability to read for meaning and retention.

INTELLIGENCE	SUGGESTED STRATEGIES	WHAT WORKS FOR YOU? WRITE NEW IDEAS HERE
Verbal–Linguistic	■ Mark up your text with marginal notes while you read. ■ When tackling a chapter, use every stage of SQ3R, taking advantage of each writing opportunity (writing Q stage questions, writing summaries, and so on).	
Logical–Mathematical	■ Read material in sequence. ■ Think about the logical connections between what you are reading and the world at large; consider similarities, differences, and cause-and-effect relationships.	
Bodily–Kinesthetic	■ Take physical breaks during reading sessions—walk, stretch, exercise. ■ Pace while reciting important ideas.	
Visual–Spatial	■ As you read, take particular note of photos, tables, figures, and other visual aids. ■ Make charts, diagrams, or think links illustrating difficult concepts you encounter in your reading.	
Interpersonal	■ With a friend, have a joint reading session. One should read a section silently and then summarize aloud the important concepts for the other. Reverse the order of summarizer and listener for each section. ■ Discuss reading material and clarify important concepts in a study group.	
Intrapersonal	■ Read in a solitary setting and allow time for reflection. ■ Think about how a particular reading assignment makes you feel, and evaluate your reaction by considering the material in light of what you already know.	
Musical	■ Play music while you read. ■ Recite important concepts in your reading to rhythms or write a song to depict those concepts.	
Naturalistic	■ Read and study in a natural environment. ■ Before reading indoors, imagine your favorite place in nature in order to create a relaxed frame of mind.	

Match Strategies to Different Areas of Study

Different subject matter presents different reading challenges. This is due in part to essential differences between the subjects (a calculus text and history of world religions text have very little in common), and in part to reader learning style and preferences (you are most likely more comfortable with some subjects than you are with others).

When you have a good idea of the kind of reading that is tough for you, you can choose the strategies that seem to help you the most. Although the information in this chapter will help with any academic subject, math and science often present unique challenges. You may benefit from using some of these specific techniques when reading math or science.

Interact with the material critically as you go. Math and science texts tend to move sequentially (later chapters build on concepts and information introduced in previous chapters) and are often problem-and-solution-based. Keep a pad of paper nearby and take notes of examples. Work steps out on your pad. Draw sketches to help visualize the material. Try not to move on until you understand the example and how it relates to the central ideas. Write down questions to ask your instructor or fellow students.

Note formulas. Evaluate the importance of formulas and recall whether the instructor emphasized them. Make sure you understand the principle behind the formula—why it works—rather than just memorizing the formula itself. Read the assigned material to prepare for any homework.

FORMULA

A general fact, rule, or principle usually expressed in mathematical symbols.

Use memory techniques. Science textbooks are often packed with vocabulary specific to that particular science (e.g., a chapter in a psychobiology course may give medical names for the parts of the brain). Put your memory skills to use when reading science texts—use mnemonic devices, test yourself using flash cards, and rehearse aloud or silently (see Chapter 6). Selective highlighting and writing summaries of your readings, in table format for example, also helps.

In this chapter's exercise set, you will see excerpts from textbooks treating three different subject areas. As you read them, notice the differences—and notice which seem easier or harder to you. This will give you some clues as to how you might approach longer reading assignments.

Build Reading Speed

Many students balance heavy academic loads with other important responsibilities. It's difficult to make time to study at all, let alone handle all of your reading assignments. If you can increase your reading speed, you will save valuable time and effort—as long as you don't sacrifice comprehension. Greater comprehension is the primary goal and actually promotes faster reading.

The average American adult reads between 150 and 350 words per minute, and faster readers can be capable of speeds up to 1,000 words per minute.[2] However, the human eye can only move so fast; reading speeds in excess of 350 words per minute involve "skimming" and "scanning" (see page 137). The following suggestions will help increase your reading speed:

- Try to read groups of words rather than single words.
- Avoid pointing your finger to guide your reading; use an index card to move quickly down the page.
- When reading narrow columns, focus your eyes in the middle of the column. With practice, you'll be able to read the entire column width as you read down the page.
- Avoid *vocalization*—speaking the words or moving your lips—when reading.

The key to building reading speed is practice and more practice, says reading expert Steve Moidel. To achieve your goal of reading between 500 and 1,000 words per minute, Moidel suggests that you start practicing at three times the rate you want to achieve, a rate that is much faster than you can comprehend.[3] For example, if your goal is 500 words per minute, speed up to 1,500 words per minute. Reading at such an accelerated rate pushes your eyes and mind to adjust to the faster pace. When you slow down to 500 words per minute—the pace at which you can read and comprehend—your reading rate will feel comfortable even though it is much faster than your original speed. You may even want to check into self-paced computer software that helps you improve reading speed.

Expand Your Vocabulary

As your reading materials at school and at work become more complex, how much you comprehend—and how readily you do it—depends on your vocabulary. A strong vocabulary increases reading speed and comprehension; when you understand the words in your reading material, you don't have to stop as often to think about what they mean.

The best way to build your vocabulary is to commit yourself to learning new and unfamiliar words as you encounter them. This involves certain steps.

Analyze Word Parts

Often, if you understand part of a word, you can figure out what the entire word means. This is true because many English words are made up of a combination of Greek and Latin prefixes, roots, and suffixes. *Prefixes* are word parts that are added to the beginning of a root. *Suffixes* are added to the end of the root. Table 5.1 contains just a few of the prefixes, roots, and suffixes you will encounter as you read. Knowing these verbal building blocks dramatically increases your vocabulary.

Figure 5.2 shows how one root can be the stem of many different words.

Using prefixes, roots, and suffixes, you can piece together the meaning of many new words you encounter. To use a simple example, the word *prologue* is made up of the prefix *pro* (before) and the root *logue* (to speak). Thus, *prologue* refers to words spoken or written before the main text.

ROOT

The central part or basis of a word, around which prefixes and suffixes can be added to produce different words.

Table 5.1 — Common prefixes, roots, and suffixes.

Prefix	Primary Meaning	Example
a-, ab-	from	abstain, avert
con-, cor-, com-	with, together	convene, correlate, compare
il-	not	illegal, illegible
sub-, sup-	under	subordinate, suppose

Root	Primary Meaning	Example
-chron	time	synchronize
-ann	year	biannual
-sper	hope	desperate
-voc	speak, talk	convocation

Suffix	Primary Meaning	Example
-able	able	recyclable
-meter	measure	thermometer
-ness	state of	carelessness
-y	inclined to	sleepy

Figure 5.2 — Building words from a single root.

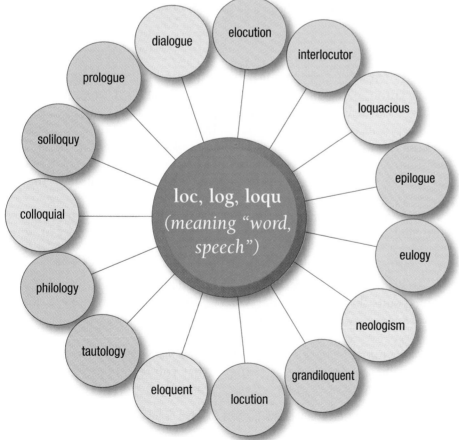

loc, log, loqu (meaning "word, speech")

dialogue, elocution, interlocutor, loquacious, epilogue, eulogy, neologism, grandiloquent, locution, eloquent, tautology, philology, colloquial, soliloquy, prologue

Use Words in Context

Most people learn words best when they read and use them in written or spoken language. Although a definition tells you what a word means, it may not include a context. Using a word in context after defining it helps to anchor the information so that you can remember it and continue to build on it. Here are some strategies for using context to solidify new vocabulary words.

Use new words in a sentence or two right away. Do this immediately after reading their definitions while everything is still fresh in your mind.

Reread the sentence where you originally saw the word. Go over it a few times to make sure that you understand how the word is used.

Use the word over the next few days whenever it may apply. Try it while talking with friends, writing letters or notes, or in your own thoughts.

Consider where you may have seen or heard the word before. When you learn a word, going back to sentences you previously didn't "get" may solidify your understanding. For example, most children learn the Pledge of Allegiance by rote without understanding what "allegiance" means. Later, when they learn the definition of "allegiance," the pledge provides a context that helps them better understand the word.

Seek knowledgeable advice. If after looking up a word you still have trouble with its meaning, ask an instructor or friend to help you figure it out.

Use a Dictionary

Standard dictionaries provide broad information such as word origin, pronunciation, part of speech, and multiple meanings. Using a dictionary whenever you read increases your comprehension. Buy a standard dictionary, keep it nearby, and consult it for help in understanding passages that contain unfamiliar words. Some textbooks also have a text-specific "dictionary" called a *glossary* that defines terms found in the text. Such definitions are often limited to the meaning of the term as used in that particular textbook.

You may not always have time to use the following suggestions, but when you can use them, they will help you make the most of your dictionary.

Read every meaning of a word, not just the first. Think critically about which meaning suits the context of the word in question, and choose the one that makes the most sense to you.

Substitute a word or phrase from the definition for the word. Use the definition you have chosen. Imagine, for example, that you read the following sentence and do not know the word *indoctrinated:*

The cult indoctrinated its members to reject society's values.

In the dictionary, you find several definitions, including *brainwashed* and *instructed*. You decide that the one closest to the correct meaning is brainwashed. With this term, the sentence reads as follows:

The cult brainwashed its members to reject society's values.

So far, this chapter has focused on reading as a deliberate, purposeful process of meaning construction. Recognizing obstacles and defining reading purposes lay the groundwork for effective studying—the process of mastering the concepts and skills contained in your texts.

How can SQ3R help you *own* what you read?

When you study, you take ownership of the material you read, meaning that you learn it well enough to apply it to what you do. For example, by the time students studying to be computer hardware technicians complete their course work, they should be able to analyze hardware problems that lead to malfunctions. On-the-job computer technicians use the same study technique to keep up with changing technology. Studying to understand and learn also gives you mastery over concepts. For example, a dental hygiene student learns the causes of gum disease, and a business student learns about marketing.

SQ3R is a technique that will help you grasp ideas quickly, remember more, and review effectively for tests. SQ3R stands for *Survey, Question, Read, Recite,* and *Review*—all steps in the studying process. Developed more than 55 years ago by Francis Robinson, the technique is still used today because it works.[4]

Moving through the stages of SQ3R requires that you know how to skim and scan. Skimming involves the rapid reading of chapter elements, including introductions, conclusions, and summaries; the first and last lines of paragraphs; boldfaced or italicized terms; and pictures, charts, and diagrams. The goal of skimming is a quick construction of the main ideas. In contrast, scanning involves the careful search for specific facts and examples. You might use scanning during the review phase of SQ3R when you need to locate particular information (such a formula in a chemistry text).

Approach SQ3R as a framework on which you build your house, not as a tower of stone. In other words, instead of following each step by rote, bring your personal learning styles and study preferences to the system. For example, you and another classmate may focus on elements in a different order when you survey, write different types of questions, or favor different sets of review strategies. Explore the strategies, evaluate what works, and then make the system your own.

SKIMMING

Rapid, superficial reading of material that involves glancing through to determine central ideas and main elements.

SCANNING

Reading material in an investigative way, searching for specific information.

Survey

Surveying refers to the process of previewing, or pre-reading, a book before you actually study it. Compare it to looking at a map before you drive somewhere—those few minutes taking a look at your surroundings and where you intend to go will save you a lot of time and trouble once you are on the road.

Most textbooks include devices that give students an overview of the whole text as well as of the contents of individual chapters. When you survey, pay attention to the following elements.

The front matter. Before you even get to page 1, most textbooks have a table of contents, a preface, and other materials. The table of contents gives you an overview with clues about coverage, topic order, and features. The preface, in particular, can point out the book's unique approach. For example, the preface for the American history text *Out of Many* states that it highlights "the experiences of diverse communities of Americans in the unfolding story of our country."[5] This tells you that cultural diversity is a central theme.

The chapter elements. Generally, each chapter has devices that help you make meaning out of the material. Among these are:

- The chapter title, which establishes the topic and perhaps author perspective
- The chapter introduction, outline, list of objectives, or list of key topics
- Within the chapter, headings, tables and figures, quotes, marginal notes, and photographs that help you perceive structure and important concepts
- Special chapter features, often presented in boxes set off from the main text, that point you to ideas connected to themes that run through the text
- Particular styles or arrangements of type (**boldface**, *italics,* underline, larger fonts, bullet points, boxed text) that call your attention to new words or important concepts

At the end of a chapter, a summary may help you tie concepts together. Review questions and exercises help you review and think critically about the material. Skimming these *before* reading the chapter gives you clues about what's important.

The back matter. Here some texts include a glossary. You may also find an *index* to help you locate individual topics and a *bibliography* that lists additional reading on particular topics covered in the text.

Figure 5.3 shows the many devices that books employ. Think about how many of these devices you already use, and which you can start using now to boost your comprehension.

Figure 5.3   **Text and chapter previewing devices.**

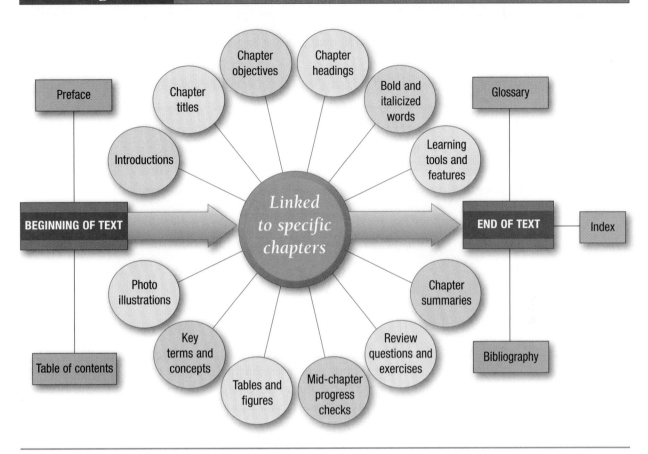

Question

Your next step is to examine the chapter headings and, on a separate piece of paper or in the margins, to write *questions* linked to them. If your reading material has no headings, develop questions as you read. These questions focus your attention and increase your interest, helping you build comprehension and relate new ideas to what you already know. You can take questions from the textbook or from your lecture notes, or come up with them on your own when you survey, based on what ideas you think are most important.

The table at the top of the next page shows how this works. The column on the left contains primary- and secondary-level headings from a section of *Out of Many.* The column on the right rephrases these headings in question form.

There is no "correct" set of questions. Given the same headings, you could create your own particular set of questions. The more useful kinds of questions engage the critical-thinking mind actions and processes discussed in Chapter 4.

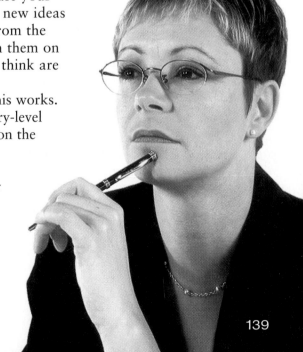

The Meaning of Freedom	What did freedom mean for both slaves and citizens in the United States?
Moving About	Where did African Americans go after they were freed from slavery?
The African American Family	How did freedom change the structure of the African American family?
African American Churches and Schools	What effect did freedom have on the formation of African American churches and schools?
Land and Labor after Slavery	How was land farmed and maintained after slaves were freed?
The Origins of African American Politics	How did the end of slavery bring about the beginning of African American political life?

Read

Your questions give you a starting point for *reading,* the first R in SQ3R. Learning from textbooks requires that you read *actively.* Active reading means engaging with the material through questioning, writing, note taking, and other activities. As you can see in Figure 5.4, the activities of SQ3R promote active reading. Following are some specific strategies that will keep you active when you read.

Focus on your Q-stage questions. Read the material with the purpose of answering each question. As you come on ideas and examples that relate to your question, write them down or note them in the text.

Look for important concepts. As you read, record key words, phrases, and concepts in your notebook. Some students divide the notebook into two columns, writing questions on the left and answers on the right. This method is called the Cornell note-taking system (see Chapter 6).

Mark up your textbook. Being able to make notations will help you to make sense of the material; for this reason, owning your textbooks is an enormous advantage. You may want to write notes in the margins, circle key ideas, or highlight key points. Figure 5.5 shows how this is done on a marketing textbook section that introduces the concept of markets. Some people prefer to underline, although underlining adds more ink to the lines of text and may overwhelm your eyes. Bracketing an entire key passage is a good alternative to underlining.

Selective highlighting may help you pinpoint material to review before an exam, although excessive highlighting may actually interfere with comprehension. Here are some tips on how to strike a balance.

- Mark the text *after* you read the material once through. If you do it on the first reading, you may mark less important passages.

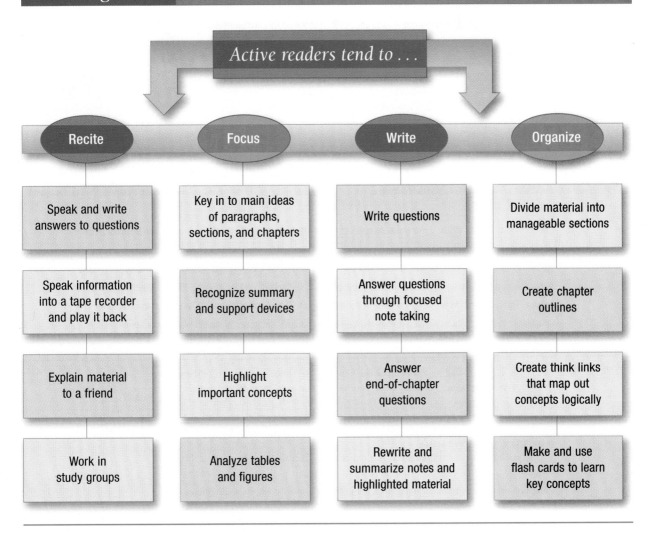

Figure 5.4 Use SQ3R to become an active reader.

Active readers tend to . . .

Recite	Focus	Write	Organize
Speak and write answers to questions	Key in to main ideas of paragraphs, sections, and chapters	Write questions	Divide material into manageable sections
Speak information into a tape recorder and play it back	Recognize summary and support devices	Answer questions through focused note taking	Create chapter outlines
Explain material to a friend	Highlight important concepts	Answer end-of-chapter questions	Create think links that map out concepts logically
Work in study groups	Analyze tables and figures	Rewrite and summarize notes and highlighted material	Make and use flash cards to learn key concepts

- Highlight key terms and concepts. Mark the examples that explain and support important ideas.
- Avoid overmarking. A phrase or two in any paragraph is usually enough. Set off long passages with brackets rather than marking every line.
- Don't mistake highlighting for learning. You will not learn what you highlight unless you interact with it through careful review—questioning, writing, and reciting.

Be sure to divide your reading into digestible segments, pacing yourself so that you understand as you go. If you find you are losing the thread of the ideas, you may want to try smaller segments or take a break and come back to it later. Try to avoid reading in mere sets of time—such as, "I'll read for 30 minutes and then quit"—or you may short-circuit your understanding by stopping in the middle of a key explanation.

Figure 5.5   Effective highlighting and marginal notes aid memory.

Markets

The term *market* has acquired many meanings over the years. In its original meaning, a market is a physical place where buyers and sellers gather to exchange goods and services. Medieval towns had market squares where sellers brought their goods and buyers shopped for goods. In today's cities, buying and selling occur in shopping areas rather than markets. To an economist, a market describes all the buyers and sellers who transact over some good or service. Thus, the soft-drink market consists of sellers such as Coca-Cola and PepsiCo, and of all the consumers who buy soft drinks. To a marketer, a market is the set of all actual and potential buyers of a product or service.

O rganizations that sell to consumer and business markets recognize that they cannot appeal to all buyers in those markets, or at least not to all buyers in the same way. Buyers are too numerous, too widely scattered, and too varied in their needs and buying practices. And different companies vary widely in their abilities to serve different segments of the market. Rather than trying to compete in an entire market, sometimes against superior competitors, each company must identify the parts of the market that it can serve best.

Definition of a market

Companies can't appeal to everyone

Sellers have not always practiced this philisophy. Their thinking has passed through three stages:

One-size-fits-all approach

- *Mass marketing.* In mass marketing, the seller mass produces, mass distributes, and mass promotes one product to all buyers. At one time, Coca-Cola produced only one drink for the whole market, hoping it would appeal to everyone. The argument for mass marketing is that it should lead to the lowest costs and prices and create the largest potential market.

Offer variety to buyers

- *Product-variety marketing.* Here, the seller produces two or more products that have different features, styles, quality, sizes, and so on. Later, Coca-Cola produced several soft drinks packaged in different sizes and containers that were designed to offer variety to buyers rather than to appeal to different market segments. The argument for product-variety marketing is that consumers have different tastes that change over time. Consumers seek variety and change.

A tailored approach to specific market segments

- *Target marketing.* Here, the seller identifies market segments, selects one or more of them, and develops products and marketing mixes tailored to each. For example, Coca-Cola now produces soft drinks for the sugared-cola segment (Coca-Cola Classic and Cherry Coke), the diet segment (Diet Coke and Tab), the no-caffeine segment (Caffeine-Free Coke), and the noncola segment (Minute Maid sodas).

Current approach is usually TARGET MARKETING

Today's companies are moving away from mass marketing and product-variety marketing toward target marketing. Target marketing can better help sellers find their marketing opportunities. Sellers can develop the right product for each target market and adjust their prices, distribution channels, and advertising to reach the target market efficiently. Instead of scattering their marketing efforts (the "shotgun" approach), they can focus on the buyers who have greater purchase interest (the "rifle" approach).

87

Source: Marketing: An Introduction, 4/E by Kotler/Armstrong, © 1997. Reprinted with permission of Pearson Education, Inc., Upper Saddle River, NJ.

Finding the Main Idea

One crucial skill in textbook reading is finding the main, or central, idea of a piece of writing (e.g., a book, a chapter, an article, a paragraph). The *main idea* refers to the thoughts that are at the heart of the writing, the idea that creates its essential meaning. Comprehension depends on your ability to recognize main ideas and to link the author's other thoughts to them.

Where do you find the main idea? As an example, consider a paragraph. The main idea may be:

- In a *topic sentence* at the very beginning of the paragraph, stating the topic of the paragraph and what about that topic the author wants to communicate, and followed by sentences adding support.
- At the end of the paragraph, following supporting details that lead up to it.
- Buried in the middle of the paragraph, sandwiched between supporting details.
- In a compilation of ideas from various sentences, each of which contains a critical element. It is up to the reader to piece these elements together to create the essence of meaning.
- Never explicitly stated, but implied by the information presented in the paragraph.

How, then, do you decide just what the main idea is? Ophelia H. Hancock, a specialist in improving reading skills for college students, takes a three-step approach:[6]

1. *Search for the topic of the paragraph.* The topic of the paragraph is not the same thing as the main idea. Rather, it is the broad subject being discussed—for example, former President John F. Kennedy, hate crimes on campus, or the World Wide Web.

2. *Identify the aspect of the topic that is the paragraph's focus.* If the general topic is former President John F. Kennedy, the writer may choose to focus on any of literally thousands of aspects of that topic. Here are just a few: his health problems, his civil rights policies, key events in his early adult years, the people he chose as cabinet members, his effectiveness as a public speaker, his relationship with family.

3. *Find what the author wants you to know about the specific aspect being discussed, which is the main idea.* The main idea of a paragraph dealing with President Kennedy as a public speaker may be this:

> President Kennedy was a gifted, charismatic speaker who used his humor, charm, and intelligence to make the presidency accessible to all Americans during regularly televised presidential news conferences.

You can use this three-step approach to find the main idea of the following paragraph:

> Tone relates not so much to what you say as to how you say it. The tone of your writing has a major impact on what you are trying to communicate to your audience. Tone involves your choice of words interacting

with your message. Have you ever reacted to someone's understanding of what you wrote with "That's not what I meant to say"? Your tone can be what has thrown your readers off track, although you can only be misunderstood if your writing is unclear or imprecise.[7]

Q: What is the topic of the paragraph?
A: The tone of your writing
Q: What aspect of tone is being discussed?
A: The meaning of tone and its impact on readers
Q: What main idea is being communicated about this aspect?
A: The tone of your writing has a major impact on what you are trying to communicate to your audience. In this paragraph, the second sentence completely states the main idea.

Recite

Once you finish reading a topic, stop and answer the questions you raised in the Q-stage of SQ3R. You may decide to *recite* each answer aloud, silently speak the answers to yourself, tell or teach the answers to another person, or write your ideas and answers in brief notes. Writing is often the most effective way to solidify what you have read because writing from memory checks your understanding.

"The best effect of any book is that it excites the reader to self-activity."

THOMAS CARLYLE

Keep your learning styles (Chapter 2) in mind when you explore different strategies. For example, an intrapersonal learner may prefer writing, while an interpersonal learner might want to recite answers aloud to a classmate. A logical–mathematical learner may benefit from organizing material into detailed outlines, while a musical learner might want to chant information aloud to a rhythm.

After you finish one section, read the next. Repeat the question–read–recite cycle until you complete the entire chapter. If you find yourself fumbling for thoughts, you may not yet "own" the ideas. Reread the section that's giving you trouble until you master its contents. Understanding each section as you go is crucial because the material in one section often forms a foundation for the next.

Review

Review soon after you finish a chapter. Reviewing, both immediately and periodically in the days and weeks after you read, is the step that solidifies your understanding. Chances are good that if you close the book after you read, much of your focused reading work will slip away from memory. Here are some techniques for reviewing—try many and use what works best for you.

- Skim and reread your notes. Then, try summarizing them from memory.

- Answer the text's end-of-chapter review, discussion, and application questions.

- Quiz yourself, using the questions you raised in the Q stage. If you can't answer one of your own or one of the text's questions, go back and scan the material for answers.

- Review and summarize in writing the material you have highlighted or bracketed.

- Create a chapter outline in standard outline form or think link form.

- Reread the preface, headings, tables, and summary.

- Recite important concepts to yourself, or record important information on a cassette tape and play it on your car's tape deck or your portable cassette player.

- Make flash cards that have an idea or word on one side and examples, a definition, or other related information on the other. Test yourself.

- Think critically: Break ideas down into examples, consider similar or different concepts, recall important terms, evaluate ideas, and explore causes and effects (see the next section for details).

- Discuss the concepts with a classmate or in a study group. Trying to teach study partners what you learned will pinpoint the material you know and what still needs work.

- Make think links that show how important concepts relate to one another.

If you need help clarifying your reading material, ask your instructor. Pinpoint the material you want to discuss, schedule a meeting during office hours, and bring a list of questions.

Refreshing your knowledge is easier and faster than learning it the first time. Set up regular review sessions; for example, once a week. Reviewing in as many different ways as possible increases the likelihood of retention. Critical reading may be the most important of these ways.

How can you *respond critically* to what you read?

Textbook features often highlight important ideas and help you determine study questions. As you advance in your education, however, many reading assignments—especially primary sources—will not be so clearly marked. You need critical-reading skills to select important ideas, identify examples that support them, and ask questions about the text without the aid of any special features.

Critical reading enables you to develop a thorough understanding of reading material. A critical reader is able to discern the central idea of a piece of reading material, as well as identify what in that piece is true or accurate, such as when choosing material as a source for an essay. A critical reader can also compare one piece of material to another and evaluate which makes more sense, which proves its thesis more successfully, or which is more useful for the reader's purposes.

Engage your critical-thinking processes by using the following suggestions for critical reading.

Use SQ3R to "Taste" Reading Material

Sylvan Barnet and Hugo Bedau, authors of *Critical Thinking, Reading, and Writing: A Brief Guide to Argument,* suggest that the active reading of SQ3R helps you form an initial idea of what a piece of reading material is all about. Through surveying, skimming for ideas and examples, highlighting and writing comments and questions in the margins, and reviewing, you can develop a basic understanding of its central ideas and contents.[8]

Summarizing, part of the SQ3R review process, is one of the best ways to develop an understanding of a piece of reading material. To construct a summary, focus on the central ideas of the piece and the main examples that support them. A summary does not contain any of your own ideas or your evaluation of the material. It simply condenses the material, making it easier to focus on the structure and central ideas of the piece. At that point, you can begin asking questions, evaluating the piece, and introducing your own ideas. Using the mind actions described in Chapter 4 helps you.

SUMMARY

A concise restatement of the material, in your own words, that covers the main points.

Ask Questions Based on the Mind Actions

The essence of critical reading, as with critical thinking, is asking questions. Instead of simply accepting what you read, seek a more thorough understanding by questioning the material as you go along. Using the mind actions to formulate your questions helps you understand the material.

What parts of the material you focus on depends on your purpose for reading. For example, if you are writing a paper on the causes of World War II, you might look at how certain causes fit your thesis. If you are comparing two pieces of writing that contain opposing arguments, you may focus on picking out their central ideas and evaluating how well the writers use examples to support them.

You can question any of the following components of reading material:

- the central idea of the entire piece
- a particular idea or statement
- the examples that support an idea or statement
- the proof of a fact
- the definition of a concept

Following are some ways to critically question reading material. Apply them to any component you want to question by substituting the component for the words *it* and *this*.

Similarity:	What does this remind me of or how is it similar to something else I know?
Difference:	What different conclusions are possible?
	How is this different from my experience?
Cause and effect:	Why did this happen or what caused this?
	What are the effects or consequences of this?
	What effect does the author intend or what is the purpose of this material?
	What effects support a stated cause?
Example to idea:	How do I classify this or what is the best idea to fit this example?
	How do I summarize this or what are the key ideas?
	What is the thesis or central idea?
Idea to example:	What evidence supports this or what examples fit this idea?
Evaluation:	How do I evaluate this? Is it useful or well constructed?
	Does this example support my thesis or central idea?
	Is this information or point of view important to my work? If so, why?

Engage Critical-Thinking Processes

Certain thinking processes from Chapter 4, *reasoning* and *opening your mind to new perspectives,* can help to deepen your analysis and evaluation of what you read. Within these processes you ask questions that use the mind actions.

Reasoning

With what you know about how to reason, you can evaluate any statement in your reading material, identifying it as fact or opinion and challenging how it is supported. Evaluate statements using questions such as the following:

- Is this fact? Is the factual statement true? How does the writer know?
- Is this opinion? How could I test its validity?
- What else do I know that is similar to or different from this?
- What examples that I already know support or disprove this?

Your reasoning ability also helps you evaluate any argument you find in your reading material. In this case, *argument* refers to a persuasive case—a set of connected ideas supported by examples—that a writer makes to prove or disprove a point.

It's easy—and common—to accept or reject an argument outright, according to whether it fits with one's own opinions and views. If you ask questions about an argument, however, you can determine its validity and learn more from it. Furthermore, critical thinking helps you avoid accepting premises that are not supported by evidence.

Reasoning through an argument involves two kinds of evaluations:

- evaluating the quality of the evidence
- evaluating whether the evidence adequately supports the premise (whether the examples fit the idea)

Together, these evaluations help you see whether an argument works. If quality evidence (accurate input) combines with quality use of evidence (valid reasoning), you get a solid argument.

Evidence quality. Ask the following questions in order to see whether the evidence itself is accurate:

- What type of evidence is it—fact or opinion? Do the facts seem accurate?
- How is the evidence similar to, or different from, what I already believe to be true?
- Where is the evidence from? Are those sources reliable and free of bias?

PERSONAL TRIUMPH

h *aving a particular drive to make something of yourself when deciding to attend college can make the experience that much more meaningful. Dani Day's determination led her through family strife and financial aid difficulties into a stimulating educational experience.*

I was living in a subsidized apartment complex with an abusive husband and was pregnant with my third child. I decided I didn't want to put my kids through this anymore so I left him. I went through the pregnancy by myself and got my G.E.D. Even though I had few resources and low self-esteem, I had the will to survive.

In 1993, I became a home owner through Habitat for Humanity.* I put in 500 hours of manual labor, which Habitat calls "sweat equity." Getting my own home was the catalyst for change; it was the first step toward a new life for me and my family. My house was the first in the Denver area built entirely by women, so it brought a lot of publicity. I became a spokesperson for the organization and found I was comfortable in front of a camera speaking to groups of people.

The most significant decision I made was to attend college, but trying to come up with the money to pay for school became discouraging. Because I owned a house, I didn't qualify for financial assistance, and government agencies didn't want to pay for child care. Some financial aid representatives said they turned me down because I was "self-initiated." I rebelled at this, and my personal motto became "I'm going to school with or without any help."

Six months after moving in, I explored my desire to be in front of the camera by enrolling in a communications program. I also landed two internships, which helped me pay for college. I did on-camera pieces for public broadcasting networks, and I even tried stand-up comedy, but these jobs didn't pay the bills. Also, my schedule was crazy. I grew weary from the constant strain of trying to juggle my

Dani E. Day, Communication Studies;
Community College of Denver, Denver, Colorado

children's needs with work. I knew something had to change.

I found that opportunities for permanent jobs were in the technical fields, and I turned toward management for the normal work hours. Technical work wasn't my inclination, but I thought if nothing else it's a good opportunity to learn the other side of the business. To my surprise, I found that I had a knack for television engineering.

I'm still interested in being on television, maybe as a news anchor or as the host of a public television station. I won't let go of that desire, but right now I have three kids to feed and my oldest son has special needs. I need to make time for him and focus on being the most productive I can for my family.

I enjoy learning, and I try to apply what I need from each step and use that for my next step. Fear does not paralyze me; it actually motivates me to work harder. My children have seen the constant drive that it takes to succeed. Watching me is helping them embrace life's challenges. They want college, and they want to make something of their lives.

In every situation, I do the best I can to adapt. Negative situations will hold you back if you let them. One person insinuated that I would never be qualified to do more than minimum wage work. If I had believed that, I wouldn't be where I am today. It's not what other people believe about you that matters but what you believe about yourself.

*Habitat for Humanity International is a nonprofit organization that lends no-profit, no-interest mortgages to people in need. Since 1976, they have built more than 100,000 houses around the world.

Take a moment to consider . . .

- *How you think college will help you "make something of your life."*

- *A book you have read or a course you have taken that surprised you by showing you an interest you didn't know you had.*

Support quality. Ask these questions to determine whether you think the evidence successfully makes the argument:

- Do examples and ideas, and causes and effects, logically connect to one another?
- Do I believe this argument? How is the writer trying to persuade me?
- Are there enough pieces of evidence to adequately support the central idea?
- What different and perhaps opposing arguments seem just as valid?
- Has the argument evaluated all of the positive and negative effects involved? Are there any negative effects to the conclusion that haven't been considered?

Don't rule out the possibility that you may agree wholeheartedly with an argument. However, use critical thinking to make an informed decision rather than accepting the argument outright.

For example, imagine that you are reading an article whose main argument is, "The dissolving of the family unit is the main cause of society's ills." You might examine the facts and examples the writer uses to support this statement, looking carefully at the cause-and-effect structure of the argument. You might question the writer's sources. You might think of examples you know of that support the statement. You might find examples that disprove this argument, such as successful families that don't fit the traditional definition of family used by the writer. Finally, you might think your way through a couple of opposing arguments, thinking of the ideas and examples you would use to support those arguments.

Opening Your Mind to New Perspectives

This critical-thinking process helps you understand that many reading materials are written from a particular perspective. For example, if both a recording artist and a music censorship advocate were to write a piece about a controversial song created by that artist, their different perspectives would result in two very different pieces of writing.

To analyze perspective, ask questions like the following:

- What perspective is guiding this?

- Who wrote this and with what intent?
- How does the material's source affect its perspective?
- How is this perspective supported?
- What assumptions underlie this?
- What examples do not fit this assumption?

Think again about the example—the piece of writing claiming that "the dissolving of the family unit is the main cause of society's ills." Considering perspective, you might ask questions like these:

- How do I define the perspective of this piece? What are the central opinions that influence this material?
- Who wrote this and why? Is it designed to communicate statistics as objectively as possible, or does the author intend to promote a particular message?
- What is the source, and how does that affect the piece? (For example, a piece appearing in the *New York Times* may differ from one appearing in a magazine that promotes a particular way of living.)
- What examples and evidence does the author use to support the claim? Is the support valid? After reading it, do I feel comfortable with the perspective?
- What assumptions underlie this statement (e.g., assumptions about the definition of "family" or about what constitutes "society's ills")?
- Can I think of examples of families or success stories that do not fit these assumptions?

Seek Understanding

The fundamental purpose of all college reading is to understand the material. Think of your reading process as an archaeological dig. The first step is to excavate a site and uncover the artifacts, which corresponds to your initial survey and reading of the material. As important as the excavation is, the process is incomplete if you stop there. The second half of the process is to investigate each item, evaluate what they all mean, and derive new knowledge and ideas from what you discover. Critical reading allows you to complete that crucial second half of the process.

Critical reading takes time and focus. Give yourself a chance at success by finding a time, place, and purpose for reading. Learn from others by working in pairs or groups whenever you can.

Why and how should you *study with others?*

Much of what you know and will learn comes from your interaction with the outside world. Often this interaction takes place between you and one or more people. You listen to instructors and other students, you read materials that people have written, and you try out the behavior and ideas of those whom you most trust and respect. You often work in a *team*—a group of fellow students, coworkers, family members, or others who strive together to reach an objective.

Learning takes place the same way in your career and personal life. Today's workplace puts the emphasis on work done through team effort. Companies value the ideas, energy, and cooperation that result from a well-coordinated team.

Leaders and Participants

Study groups and other teams rely on both leaders and participants to accomplish goals. Becoming aware of the roles each plays will increase your effectiveness.[9] Keep in mind that participants sometimes perform leadership tasks and vice versa. In addition, some teams shift leadership frequently during a project.

Being an Effective Participant

Some people are most comfortable when participating in a group that someone else leads. However, even when they are not leading, participants are "part owners" of the team process with a responsibility for, and a stake in, the outcome. The following strategies will help you become more effective in this role.

- *Get involved.* Let people know your views on decisions.
- *Be organized.* The more focused your ideas, the more other group members will take them seriously.
- *Be willing to discuss.* Be open to the opinions of others, even if they differ from your own.
- *Keep your word.* Carry out whatever tasks you promise to do.
- *Play fairly.* Give everyone a chance to participate and always be respectful.

Being an Effective Leader

Some people prefer to initiate the action, make decisions, and control how things proceed. Leaders often have a "big-picture" perspective that allows them to envision how different aspects of a group project will come together. In any group, the following strategies help a leader succeed.

- *Define and limit projects.* The leader should define the group's purpose (e.g., brainstorming, decision making, or project collaboration) and limit tasks so that the effort remains focused.

- *Assign work and set a schedule.* A group functions best when everyone has a particular contribution to make and when deadlines are clear.

- *Set meeting and project agendas.* The leader should, with advice from other group members, establish and communicate goals and define how the work will proceed.

- *Focus progress.* It is the leader's job to keep everyone on target and headed in the right direction.

- *Set the tone.* If the leader is fair, respectful, encouraging, and hard working, group members are likely to follow the example.

- *Evaluate results.* The leader should determine whether the team is accomplishing its goals on schedule. If the team is not moving ahead, the leader should make changes.

Strategies for Study Group Success

Every study group is unique. The way a group operates may depend on the members' personalities, the subject you study, the location of the group, and the size of the group. No matter what your particular group's situation, though, certain general strategies will help.

Choose a leader for each meeting. Rotating the leadership, among members willing to lead, helps all members take ownership of the group. If a leader has to miss class for any reason, choose another leader for that meeting.

Set long-term and short-term goals. At your first meeting, determine what the group wants to accomplish over the semester. At the start of each meeting, have one person compile a list of questions to address.

Adjust to different personalities. Respect and communicate with members. The art of getting along will serve you well in the workplace, where you don't often choose your coworkers.

Share the workload. The most important factor is a willingness to work, not a particular level of knowledge.

Set a regular meeting schedule. Try every week, every two weeks, or whatever the group can manage.

Create study materials for one another. Give each group member the task of finding a piece of information to compile, photocopy, and review for the other group members.

Help each other learn. One of the best ways to solidify knowledge is to teach it. Have group members teach pieces of information; make up quizzes for each other; go through flash cards together.

Pool your note-taking resources. Compare notes with your group members and fill in any information you don't have. Try other note-taking styles: For example, if you generally use outlines, rewrite your notes in a think link. If you tend to map out ideas in a think link, try the Cornell System (see Chapter 6 for more on note taking).

Benefits of Working with Others

If you apply this information to your schoolwork, you will see that studying with a partner or in a group can enhance your learning in many ways. You benefit from shared knowledge, solidified knowledge, increased motivation, and increased teamwork ability.

"The wise person learns from everyone."

ETHICS OF THE FATHERS

Shared knowledge. Each student has a unique body of knowledge and individual strengths. Students can learn from one another. To have individual students pass on their knowledge to each other in a study group requires less time and energy than for each of those students to learn all of the material alone.

Solidified knowledge. When you discuss concepts or teach them to others, you reinforce what you know and strengthen your critical thinking. Part of the benefit comes from simply repeating information aloud and rewriting it on paper, and part comes from how you think through information in your mind before you pass it on to someone else.

Increased motivation. When you study by yourself, you are accountable to yourself alone. In a study group, however, others see your level of work and preparation, which may increase your motivation.

Increased teamwork ability. The more you understand the dynamics of working with a group and the more experience you have at it, the more you build your ability to work well with others. This is an invaluable skill for the workplace, and it contributes to your personal marketability.

читать

This word may look completely unfamiliar to you, but anyone who can read the Russian language and knows the alphabet will know that it means "read." People who read languages that use different kinds of characters, such as Russian, Japanese, or Greek, learn to process those characters as easily as you process the letters of your native alphabet. Your mind learns to process individually each letter or character you see. This ability enables you to move to the next level of understanding—making sense of those letters or characters when they are grouped to form words, phrases, and sentences.

Think of this concept when you read. Remember that your mind processes immeasurable amounts of information so that you can understand the concepts on the page. Give yourself the opportunity to succeed by reading often and by focusing on the elements that help you read to the best of your ability.

Building Skills
FOR COLLEGE, CAREER, AND LIFE SUCCESS

The Big Picture *Combining Thinking, Strategy, and Teamwork*

Studying a Text Page

The following page is from the chapter "Groups and Organizations" in the sixth edition of John J. Macionis's *Sociology*.[10] Survey the excerpt using what you know about the S stage of SQ3R; then, complete the questions that follow.

1. Identify the headings on the page and the relationship between them. Mark primary-level headings with a #1, secondary headings with a #2, and tertiary (third-level heads) with a #3. Which heading serves as an umbrella for the rest?

2. What do the headings tell you about the content of the page?

3. After reading the chapter headings, write three study questions.
    a.

    b.

    c.

Divide into small groups of three or four. As a group, discuss the study questions you wrote. Each person should select one question to focus on while reading (no two people should have the same question). Group members should then read the material on their own, using critical-thinking skills to explore their particular questions as they read, and finally, they should write down answers to their questions.

SOCIAL GROUPS

Virtually everyone moves through life with a sense of belonging; this is the experience of group life. A **social group** refers to *two or more people who identify and interact with one another.* Human beings continually come together to form couples, families, circles of friends, neighborhoods, churches, businesses, clubs, and numerous large organizations. Whatever the form, groups encompass people with shared experiences, loyalties, and interests. In short, while maintaining their individuality, the members of social groups also think of themselves as a special "we."

Groups, Categories, and Crowds

People often use the term "group" imprecisely. We now distinguish the group from the similar concepts of category and crowd.

Category. A *category* refers to people who have some status in common. Women, single fathers, military recruits, homeowners, and Roman Catholics are all examples of categories.

Why are categories not considered groups? Simply because, while the individuals involved are aware that they are not the only ones to hold that particular status, the vast majority are strangers to one another.

Crowd. A *crowd* refers to a temporary cluster of individuals who may or may not interact at all. Students sitting in a lecture hall do engage one another and share some common identity as college classmates; thus, such a crowd might be called a loosely formed group. By contrast, riders hurtling along on a subway train or

bathers enjoying a summer day at the beach pay little attention to one another and amount to an anonymous aggregate of people. In general, then, crowds are too transitory and impersonal to qualify as social groups.

The right circumstances, however, could turn a crowd into a group. People riding in a subway train that crashes under the city streets generally become keenly aware of their common plight and begin to help one another. Sometimes such extraordinary experiences become the basis for lasting relationships.

Primary and Secondary Groups

Acquaintances commonly greet one another with a smile and the simple phrase, "Hi! How are you?" The response is usually a well scripted, "Just fine, thanks, how about you?" This answer, of course, is often more formal than truthful. In most cases, providing a detailed account of how you are *really* doing would prompt the other person to beat a hasty and awkward exit.

Sociologists classify social groups by measuring them against two ideal types based on members' genuine level of personal concern. This variation is the key to distinguishing *primary* from *secondary* groups.

According to Charles Horton Cooley (1864–1929), a **primary group** is a *small social group whose members share personal and enduring relationships.* Bound together by primary relationships, individuals in primary groups typically spend a great deal of time together, engage in a wide range of common activities, and feel that they know one another well. Although not without periodic conflict, members of primary groups display sincere concern for each other's welfare. The family is every society's most important primary group.

Cooley characterized these personal and tightly integrated groups as *primary* because they are among the first groups we experience in life. In addition, the family and early play groups also hold primary importance in the socialization process, shaping attitudes, behavior, and social identity.

Source: Sociology 6/E by Macionis, © 1997. Reprinted by permission of Pearson Education, Inc., Upper Saddle River, NJ.

When you answer your question, focus on finding ideas that help to answer the question and examples that support them. Consider other information you know, relevant to your question, that may be similar to or different from the material in the passage. If your questions look for causes or effects, scan for them in the passage. Be sure to make notes as you read.

When you have finished reading critically, gather as a group. Each person should take a turn presenting the question, the response or answer that was derived through critical reading, and any other ideas that came up while reading. The group then has an opportunity to present any other ideas to add to the discussion. Continue until all group members have had a chance to present what they worked on.

Writing *Discovery Through Journaling*

To record your thoughts, use a separate journal or the lined pages at the end of the chapter.

READING CHALLENGES. What is your most difficult college reading challenge? A challenge might be a particular kind of reading material, a reading situation, or the achievement of a reading goal. Considering the tools that this chapter presents, make a plan that addresses this challenge. What techniques might be able to help, and how will you test them? What positive effects do you anticipate they may have?

Career Portfolio *Charting Your Course*

READING SKILLS ON THE JOB. The society you live and work in revolves around the written word. Although the growth of computer technology may seem to have made technical knowledge more important than reading, the focus on word processing and computer handling of documents has actually increased the need for literate employees. As a 1996 Condition of Education report states, "In recent years, literacy has been viewed as one of the fundamental tools necessary for successful economic performance in industrialized societies. Literacy is no longer defined merely as a basic threshold of reading ability, but rather as the ability to understand and use printed information in daily activities, at home, at work, and in the community."[11]

On a separate sheet of paper, do the following: For each of the skill areas listed, indicate all of the ways you know of in which you use that skill on the job or know you will need to use it in your future career. Then, also for each skill, rate your ability on a scale from 1 to 10, with 10 being highest. Finally, on the same sheet of paper, circle the two skills that you think will be most important for your career.

- Ability to define your reading purpose
- Reading speed

- Reading comprehension
- Vocabulary building
- Identification and use of text-surveying devices
- Evaluating reading material with others
- Ability to understand and use visual aids

For the two skill areas in which you rated yourself lowest, think about how you can improve your abilities. Make a problem-solving plan for each (use a flowchart like the one on page 118).

Assess Yourself *Student Success Strategies*

If you have access to the CD-ROM Strategies for Success, *use the following questions to assess your thoughts and enhance your understanding of the chapter. The questions below represent only some of the activities provided on the CD for the chapter topics—try others if you have time.*

Click on the **Reading Effectively** bookmark. Use the following activities to further boost your reading powers:

1. Take the pre-assessment to clarify your perspective on reading.
2. Click on **Activity One: Surveying Skills.** Read the passage, type in what you believe are the most important key words and phrases, and then compare them to the ideal list.
3. Click on **Activity Two: Surveying Technical Material.** Complete the exercise to assess your competence with technical material and to see what improvements you may have made based on your experience with Activity One.
4. Click on **Activity Three: Journal Reflections.** Scroll to the second question, which asks you to compare the reading strategies you use for classes with varying levels of difficulty. Type your answer in the field provided.

Suggested Readings

Armstrong, William H. and M. Willard Lampe II. *Barron's Pocket Guide to Study Tips: How to Study Effectively and Get Better Grades.* New York: Barron's Educational Series, 1990.

Chesla, Elizabeth. *Reading Comprehension Success: In 20 Minutes a Day, 2nd ed.* Garden Grove, CA: Learning Express, 1998.

Frank, Steven. *The Everything Study Book.* Holbrook, MA: Adams Media, 1996.

Luckie, William R., Wood Smethurst, and Sarah Beth Huntley. *Study Power Workbook: Exercises in Study Skills to Improve Your Learning and Your Grades.* Cambridge, MA: Brookline Books, 1999.

Silver, Theodore. *The Princeton Review Study Smart: Hands-on, Nuts and Bolts Techniques for Earning Higher Grades.* New York: Villard Books, 1996.

Internet Resources

SQ3R Method: www.u.arizona.edu/ic/wrightr/other/sq3r.html

Prentice Hall Student Success Supersite—Study Skills: www.prenhall.com/success/StudySkl/index.html

Endnotes

1. Sherwood Harris, *The New York Public Library Book of How and Where to Look It Up.* Englewood Cliffs, NJ: Prentice Hall, 1991, p. 13.

2. Steve Moidel, *Speed Reading.* Hauppauge, NY: Barron's Educational Series, 1994, p. 18.

3. Ibid.

4. Francis P. Robinson, *Effective Behavior.* New York: Harper & Row, 1941.

5. John Mack Faragher, et al., *Out of Many, 3rd ed.* Upper Saddle River, NJ: Prentice Hall, p. xxxvii.

6. Ophelia H. Hancock, *Reading Skills for College Students, 5th ed.* Upper Saddle River, NJ: Prentice Hall, 2001, pp. 54–59.

7. Excerpted from Lynn Quitman Troyka, *Simon & Schuster Handbook for Writers, 5th ed.* Upper Saddle River, NJ: Prentice Hall, 1999, p. 12.

8. Sylvan Barnet and Hugo Bedau, *Critical Thinking, Reading, and Writing: A Brief Guide to Argument, 2nd ed.* Boston, MA: Bedford Books of St. Martin's Press, 1996, pp. 15–21.

9. Louis E. Boone, David L. Kurtz, and Judy R. Block, *Contemporary Business Communication.* Englewood Cliffs, NJ: Prentice Hall, 1994, pp. 489–499.

10. John J. Macionis, *Sociology, 6th ed.* Upper Saddle River, NJ: Prentice Hall, 1997, p. 174.

11. U.S. Department of Education, National Center for Education Statistics, *The Condition of Education 1996,* NCES 96–304, by Thomas M. Smith. Washington, DC: U.S. Government Printing Office, 1996, p. 84.

JOURNAL

name   date

visit: www.prenhall.com/carter NY Times link for this chapter

*L*istening, note taking, and memory

In this chapter
you explore
answers to the
following questions: •
How can you become a
better listener? • How
can you make the most
of note taking? • Which
note-taking system should
you use? • How can you
write faster when taking
notes? • How does
memory work? • How
can you improve your
memory?

COLLEGE exposes you daily to facts, opinions, and ideas—and, as Litzka Stark is discovering (see next page), your job as a student is to find a way to retain what you learn. This chapter shows you how to do just that through listening (taking in information), note taking (recording what's important), and memory skills (remembering information). Compare your skills to using a camera: You start by locating an image through the viewfinder, then you carefully focus the lens (listening), record the image on film (note taking), and produce a print (remembering). The chapter also shows you how better retention leads to the ability to apply your new knowledge to new situations.

taking in, recording, and retaining information

Litzka Stark, Sarah Lawrence
College, Bronxville, New York

How can I improve my memory?

I learn best when I study themes, understand concepts, and try to integrate the material into my life. At my college, most of our exams are essay. I haven't had to expend much effort memorizing facts. When I do, though, I use the standard mnemonic devices and write the information on index cards.

The greatest difficulty I have with memorization is being able to retain what I've learned. In a very short time, the information is gone unless it's somehow reinforced. My question is, how do I retain the material or formulas I'm asked to remember and not forget all of it down the road? I know that in particular subjects I just can't accomplish learning without memorization.

Carlos Vela Shimano,
ITESM Campus, Queretaro, Mexico

I learned to link random ideas together in a chain.

When I was in junior high, I took an alternative class that taught memorization skills. I learned to link random ideas together in a chain. That way, I could visualize numerous concepts that were not necessarily related.

Today, in my classes, I create mind maps during lectures. I draw a circle in the middle of the page representing the main theme. Then, I link smaller circles off to one side or the other with related themes. Each one of those has circles of material or ideas relating to it. This really helps me keep the information visually organized. I think for me that is probably the best way to remember things.

I also have another method that helps me to remember dates, phone numbers, combination numbers, and PIN numbers. I link the number with something else in my life. For instance, I play on a soccer team. My PIN number for one of my accounts is the number of my jersey, plus the numbers of my two friends' jerseys who also play on the team. Because I love sports, I link numbers I need to remember with the shirts of famous athletes. My locker combination number has the same numbers as the ones Michael Jordan and Magic Johnson wear.

Finally, if you learn to build ideas from the simplest to the most complex—really understanding the reasons behind the concept and where and why the concepts were developed in the first place—it will truly help you retain more of what you study.

How can you become a
better listener?

T he act of hearing isn't quite the same as the act of listening. While *hearing* refers to sensing spoken messages from their source, *listening* involves a complex process of communication. Successful listening occurs when the speaker's intended message reaches the listener. In school and at home, poor listening may cause communication breakdowns and mistakes. Skilled listening, however, promotes progress and success. Listening is a teachable—and learnable—skill.

Ralph G. Nichols, a pioneer in listening research, studied 200 students at the University of Minnesota over a nine-month period. His findings demonstrate that effective listening depends as much on a positive attitude as on specific skills.[1] Just as understanding the mind actions involved in critical thinking helps you work out problems, understanding the listening process helps you become a better listener.

LISTENING

A process that involves sensing, interpreting, evaluating, and reacting to spoken messages.

Know the Stages of Listening

Listening is made up of four stages that build on one another: sensing, interpreting, evaluating, and reacting. These stages take the message from the speaker to the listener and back to the speaker (see Figure 6.1).

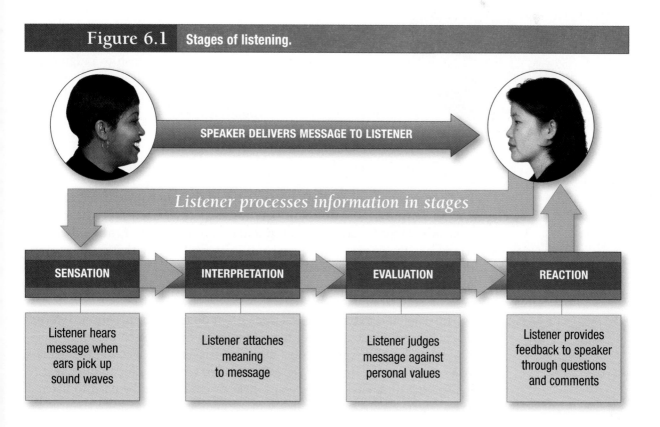

Figure 6.1 **Stages of listening.**

SPEAKER DELIVERS MESSAGE TO LISTENER

Listener processes information in stages

SENSATION	INTERPRETATION	EVALUATION	REACTION
Listener hears message when ears pick up sound waves	Listener attaches meaning to message	Listener judges message against personal values	Listener provides feedback to speaker through questions and comments

- During the *sensation* stage (also known as hearing), your ears pick up sound waves and transmit them to the brain. For example, you are sitting in class and hear your instructor say, "The only opportunity to make up last week's test is Tuesday at 5:00 P.M."

- In the *interpretation* stage, listeners attach meaning to a message. This involves understanding what is being said and relating it to what you already know. For example, you relate this message to your knowledge of the test, whether you need to make it up, and what you are doing on Tuesday at 5:00 P.M.

- In the *evaluation* stage of listening, you decide what you think or how you feel about the message—whether, for example, you like it or agree with it. This involves considering the message as it relates to your needs and values. In this example, if you do need to make up the test but have to work Tuesday at 5:00 P.M., you may evaluate the message as less than satisfactory.

- The final stage of listening involves a *reaction* to the message in the form of direct feedback. Your reaction, in this example, may be to ask the instructor for an alternative to the scheduled makeup test time.

Improving your listening skills involves two primary actions: managing listening challenges and becoming an active listener. Although becoming a better listener will help in every class, it is especially important in subjects that are challenging for you.

Manage Listening Challenges

Communication barriers can interfere with listening at every stage. In fact, classic studies have shown that immediately after listening, students are likely to recall only half of what was said. This is partly due to particular listening challenges such as divided attention and distractions, the tendency to shut out the message, the inclination to rush to judgment, and partial hearing loss or learning disabilities.[2]

To help create a positive listening environment in both your mind and your surroundings, explore how to manage these challenges.

Divided Attention and Distractions

Imagine you are talking with a coworker in the company cafeteria when you hear your name mentioned across the room. You strain to hear what someone might be saying about you and, in the process, hear neither your friend nor the person across the room very well. This situation illustrates the consequences of divided attention. Although you are capable of listening to more than one message at the same time, you may not completely hear or understand any of them.

Internal and external distractions often divide your attention. *Internal distractions* include anything from hunger to headache to personal worries. Something the speaker says may also trigger a recollection that causes your mind to drift. In contrast, *external distractions* include noises (e.g., whispering or sirens) and excessive heat or cold. It can be hard to listen in an overheated room in which you are falling asleep.

Your goal is to reduce distractions so that you can focus on what you're hearing. Sitting near the front where you can clearly see and hear helps you to listen. To avoid distracting activity, you may want to sit away from people who might chat or make noise. Dress comfortably, paying attention to the temperature of the classroom, and try not to go to class hungry or thirsty. Work to concentrate on class when you're in class and worry about personal problems later.

Shutting Out the Message

Instead of paying attention to everything the speaker says, many students fall into the trap of focusing on specific points and shutting out the rest of the message. If you perceive that a subject is too difficult or uninteresting, you may tune out. Shutting out the message makes listening harder from that point on because the information you miss may be the foundation for future class discussions.

"No one cares to speak to an unwilling listener. An arrow never lodges in a stone; often it recoils upon the sender of it."

ST. JEROME

Creating a positive listening environment includes accepting responsibility for listening. Although the instructor is responsible for communicating information to you, he or she cannot force you to listen. You are responsible for taking in that information. Instructors often cover material from outside the textbook during class and then test on that material. If you work to take in the whole message in class, you can read over your notes later and think critically about what is most important.

The Rush to Judgment

People tend to stop listening when they hear something they don't like. If you rush to judge what you've heard, making a quick uncritical assumption about it, your focus turns to your personal reaction rather than the content of the message. Judgments also involve reactions to the speakers themselves. If you do not like your instructors or if you have preconceived notions about their ideas or background, you may assume that their words have little value.

Work to recognize and control your judgments by listening first without jumping to conclusions. Ask critical-thinking questions about assumptions (see page 112). Stay aware of what you tend to judge so that you can avoid rejecting messages that clash with your opinions. Consider education as a continuing search for evidence, regardless of whether that evidence supports or negates your perspective.

Partial Hearing Loss and Learning Disabilities

Good listening techniques don't solve every listening problem. If you have some level of hearing loss, seek out special services that can help you listen in class. For example, you may be able to tape record the lecture and play it back at a louder-than-normal volume after class, have special tutoring, or arrange for a classmate to take notes for you. In addition, you may be able to arrange to meet with your instructor outside of class to clarify your notes.

Other disabilities, such as attention deficit disorder (ADD) or a problem with processing spoken language, can make it hard to focus on and understand oral messages. If you have one of these disabilities, don't blame yourself for your difficulty. Visit your school's counseling or student health center, or talk with your advisor or instructors about getting the help you need to meet your challenges.

Become an Active Listener

On the surface, listening seems like a passive activity; you sit back and listen as someone else speaks. Effective listening, however, is really an active process that involves setting a purpose for listening, paying attention to verbal signposts, and asking questions.

Set purposes for listening. Active listening is possible only if you know (and care) why you are listening. In any situation, establish what you want to achieve through listening, such as greater understanding of the material or better note taking. Having a purpose gives you a goal that motivates you to listen.

Pay attention to verbal signposts. You can identify important facts and ideas and predict test questions by paying attention to the speaker's specific choice of words. Verbal signposts often involve transition words and phrases that help organize information, connect ideas, and indicate what is and is not important. Let phrases like those in Table 6.1 direct your attention to the material that follows them.

Ask questions. Successful listening is closely linked to asking questions. A willingness to ask questions shows a desire to learn and is the mark of a critical thinker. Asking questions has two benefits. First of all, it helps

VERBAL SIGNPOSTS

Spoken words or phrases that call your attention to the information that follows.

Table 6.1	Verbal signposts point out important information.

Signals Pointing to Key Concepts	Signals of Support
There are two reasons for this . . .	For example, . . .
A critical point in the process involves . . .	Specifically, . . .
Most important, . . .	For instance, . . .
The result is . . .	Similarly, . . .
Signals Pointing to Differences	**Signals that Summarize**
On the contrary, . . .	Finally, . . .
On the other hand, . . .	Recapping this idea, . . .
By contrast, . . .	In conclusion, . . .
However, . . .	As a result, . . .

you to deepen your understanding of what you hear. This happens when you ask either informational or clarifying questions. *Informational* questions, such as any questions beginning with "Can you explain . . ." seek information that you haven't yet heard or acquired. *Clarifying* questions ask if your understanding of something you just heard is correct, such as "So some learning disabilities can be improved with treatment?" Second, of all, questions help to solidify your memory of what you are hearing. As you think of the question, raise your hand, speak, and listen to the answer, brain activity and physical activity combine to reinforce the information you are taking in.

Listening in order to acquire knowledge is only the first step. Once you hone your listening skills, you need to make a record of what you've heard by taking effective notes.

How can you *make the most* of note taking?

Notes help you learn when you are in class, doing research, or studying. Because it is virtually impossible to take notes on everything you hear or read, the act of note taking encourages you to decide what is worth remembering, and involves you in the learning process in many important ways:

- Your notes provide material that helps you study and prepare for tests.
- When you take notes, you listen better and become more involved in class.
- Notes help you think critically and organize ideas.
- The information you learn in class may not appear in any text; you will have no way to study it without writing it down.
- If it is difficult for you to process information while in class, having notes to read can help you process and learn the information.
- Note taking is a skill that you will use on the job, in community activities, and in your personal life.

Good note taking demands good listening. The listening skills you just explored are what allow you to hear what you will be evaluating and writing down. Listening and note taking depend on one another.

Recording Information in Class

Your notes have two purposes: First, they should reflect what you heard in class, and second, they should be a resource for studying, writing, or comparing with your text material. If lectures include material that is not in your text or if your instructor talks about specific test questions, your class notes become even more important as a study tool.

Preparing to Take Class Notes

Taking good class notes depends on good preparation.

Preview your reading material. Survey the text (or any other assigned reading material) to become familiar with the topic and any new concepts that it introduces. Visual familiarity helps note taking during lectures.

Gather your supplies. Use separate pieces of 8.5 × 11 inch paper for each class. If you use a three-ring binder, punch holes in handouts and insert them immediately following your notes for that day. Make sure your pencils are sharp and your pens aren't about to run out.

Location, location, location. Find a comfortable seat where you can easily see and hear—sitting near the front, where you minimize distraction and maximize access to the lecture or discussion, might be your best bet. Be ready to write as soon as the instructor begins speaking.

Choose the best note-taking system. Select a system that is most appropriate for the situation. Later in the chapter, you will learn about different note-taking systems. Take the following factors into account when choosing one to use in any class:

- *The instructor's style* (you'll be able to determine this style after a few classes). Whereas one instructor may deliver organized lectures at a normal speaking rate, another may jump from topic to topic or talk very quickly.
- *The course material.* After experimenting for a few class meetings, you may decide that an informal outline works best for your philosophy course, but that a think link works for your sociology course.
- *Your learning style.* Choose strategies that make the most of your strong points and help boost weaker areas. A visual–spatial learner might prefer think links or the Cornell system (see page 178), for example, while a Thinker type might stick to outlines; an interpersonal learner might use the Cornell system and fill in the cue column in a study group setting (see Chapter 2 for a complete discussion of learning styles).

Gather support. For each class, set up a support system with two students. That way, when you are absent, you can get the notes you missed from one or the other.

What to Do During Class

Because no one has time to write down everything he or she hears, the following strategies will help you choose and record what you feel is important in a format that you can read and understand later. This is not

Note taking is a critical learning tool. The tips below will help you retain information for both the short and long term.

INTELLIGENCE	SUGGESTED STRATEGIES	WHAT WORKS FOR YOU? WRITE NEW IDEAS HERE
Verbal–Linguistic	■ Rewrite important ideas and concepts in class notes from memory. ■ Write summaries of your notes in your own words.	
Logical–Mathematical	■ Organize the main points of a lecture or reading using outline form. ■ Make charts and diagrams to clarify ideas and examples.	
Bodily–Kinesthetic	■ Make note taking as physical as possible—use large pieces of paper and different colored pens. ■ When in class, choose a comfortable spot where you have room to spread out your materials and shift body position when you need to.	
Visual–Spatial	■ Take notes using colored markers. ■ Rewrite lecture notes in think link format, focusing on the most important and difficult points from the lecture.	
Interpersonal	■ Whenever possible, schedule a study group right after a lecture to discuss class notes. ■ Review class notes with a study buddy. See what you wrote that he or she missed and vice versa.	
Intrapersonal	■ Schedule some quiet time as soon as possible after a lecture to reread and think about your notes. If no class is meeting in the same room after yours and you have free time, stay in the room and review there.	
Musical	■ Play music while you read your notes. ■ Write a song that incorporates material from one class period's notes or one particular topic. Use the refrain to emphasize the most important concepts.	
Naturalistic	■ Read or rewrite your notes outside. ■ Review notes while listening to a nature CD—running water, rain, forest sounds.	

a list of "musts." Rather, it is a list of ideas to try as you work to find the note-taking strategies that work best for you. Experiment until you feel that you have found a successful combination.

Remember that the first step in note taking is to listen actively; you can't write down something that you don't hear. Use the listening strategies you read earlier in the chapter to make sure you are prepared to take in the information that comes your way.

- Date and identify each page. When you take several pages of notes during a lecture, add an identifying letter or number to the date on each page; for example, 11/27 A, 11/27 B, or 11/27—1 of 3, 11/27—2 of 3. This helps you keep track of the order of your pages. Add the specific topic of the lecture at the top of the page. For example: 11/27—U.S. Immigration Policy After World War II.
- If your instructor jumps from topic to topic during class, try starting a new page for each new topic.
- Ask yourself critical-thinking questions: Do I need this information? Is the information important or just a digression? Is the information fact or opinion? If it is opinion, is it worth remembering? (Chapter 4 discusses how to distinguish between fact and opinion.)
- Record whatever an instructor emphasizes—key terms, definitions, ideas, and examples (see Figure 6.2 for specifics on how an instructor might call attention to particular information).
- Continue to take notes during class discussions and question-and-answer periods. What your fellow students ask about may help you as well.

Figure 6.2   How to pick up on instructors' cues.

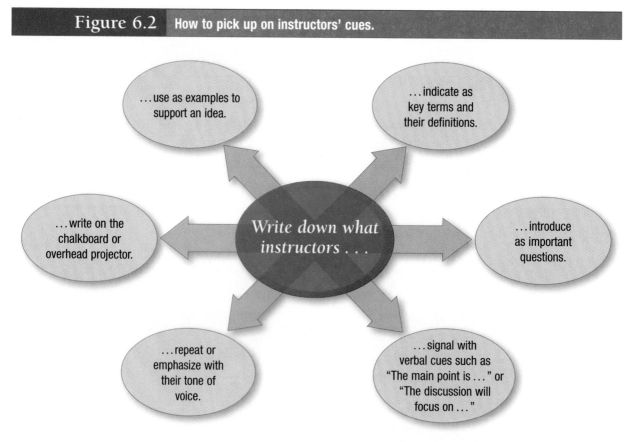

- Leave one or more blank spaces between points. This white space helps you review your notes because information appears in self-contained sections.

- Draw pictures and diagrams that help illustrate ideas.

- Indicate material that is especially important with a star, with underlining, with a highlighting marker, or by writing words in capital letters.

- If you don't understand something, leave space and place a question mark in the margin. Then, take advantage of your resources—ask the instructor to explain it after class, discuss it with a classmate, or consult your textbook—and fill in the blank when the idea is clear.

- Take notes until the instructor stops speaking. If you stop writing a few minutes before the class is over, you might miss critical information.

- Make your notes as legible and organized as possible—you can't learn from notes that you can't read or understand. But don't be too fussy; you can always rewrite and improve your notes.

- Consider that your notes are part, but not all, of what you need to learn. Using your text to add to your notes after class makes a superior, "deeper and wider" set of information to study.

Reviewing and Revising Your Notes

Even the most comprehensive notes in the world won't do you any good unless you review them. The crucial act of reviewing helps you solidify the information in your memory so that you can recall it and use it. It also helps you link new information to information you already know, which is a key step in building new ideas. The review and revision stage of note taking should include time for planning, critical thinking, adding information from other sources, summarizing, and working with a study group.

Plan a Review Schedule

When you review your notes affects how much you are likely to remember. Reviewing right after the lecture but not again until the test, reviewing here and there without a plan, or cramming it all into one crazy night does not allow you to make the most of your abilities. Do yourself a favor by planning your time strategically.

Review within a day of the lecture. Reviewing while the material is still fresh in your mind helps you to remember it. You don't have to sit down for two hours and focus on every word. Just set some time aside to reread your notes, if you can, and perhaps write questions and comments on them. If you know you have an hour between classes, for example, that is an ideal time to work in a quick review.

Review regularly. Try to schedule times during the week for reviewing notes from that week's class meetings. For example, if you know you always have from 2 P.M. to 5 P.M. free every Tuesday and Thursday afternoon, you can plan to review notes from two courses on Tuesday and from two others on Thursday. Having a routine helps ensure that you look at material regularly.

Review with an eye toward tests. When you have a test coming up, step up your efforts. Schedule longer review sessions, call a study group meeting, and review more frequently. Shorter sessions of intense review work interspersed with breaks may be more effective than long hours of continuous studying. Some students find that recopying their notes before an exam or at an earlier stage helps cement key concepts in memory.

Read and Rework Using Critical Thinking

The critical-thinking mind actions help you make the most of your notes.

- *Recall.* Read your notes to learn information, clarify points, write out abbreviations, and fill in missing details.

- *Similarity.* Consider what similar facts or ideas the information brings to mind. Write them in the margins or white space on the page if they are helpful to you.

- *Difference.* Consider how the information differs from what you already know. Is there a discrepancy you should examine? If something seems way off base, could you have written it down inaccurately?

- *Cause and effect.* Look at how ideas, facts, and statements relate to one another. See if any of them have cause-and-effect relationships. You might even want to use another color pen to draw a line linking related ideas or facts on the page.

- *Example to idea.* Think about what new ideas you can form from the information in your notes. If any come to mind, write them in your notes or on a separate page. If particular information seems to fit together more specifically than your notes initially indicate, you may want to add headings and subheadings, and insert clarifying phrases or sentences.

- *Idea to example.* Think carefully about the ideas in your notes. What do they mean? Do examples in your notes support or negate them? If you have no examples in your notes as written, add them as you review.

- *Evaluation.* Use evaluation skills to select and underline or highlight the most important ideas and information. Think about why they are important and work to understand them as completely as possible.

Revise Using Other Sources

Revising and adding to your notes using material from your texts, other required course readings, and the Internet is one of the best ways to build your understanding and link new information to information you already know. Try using the following critical-thinking actions when you add to your notes:

- Brainstorm and write down examples from other sources that illustrate central ideas in your notes.

- Pay attention to similarities between your text materials and class notes (ideas that appear in both are probably important to remember).

- Think of facts or ideas from the reading that can support and clarify ideas from your notes.

- Consider what in your class notes differs from your reading, and why.

- Write down any new ideas that come up when reviewing your notes.

- Look at cause-and-effect relationships between material from your notes and reading material. Note how ideas, facts, and examples relate to one another.

Summarize

Writing a summary of your notes is another important review technique. Summarizing involves critically evaluating which ideas and examples are most important and then rewriting the material in a shortened form, focusing on those important ideas and examples.

You may prefer to summarize as you review, with the notes in front of you. If you are using the Cornell system (see page 178), you summarize in the space saved at the bottom of the page. Other ideas include summarizing on a separate page that you insert in your loose-leaf binder or summarizing on the back of the previous page (this is possible if you only take notes on one side of the paper).

Another helpful review technique is to summarize your notes from memory after you review them. This gives you an idea of how well you have retained the information. You may even want to summarize as you read, then summarize from memory, and compare the two summaries.

Work with Study Groups

When you work with a study group, you have the opportunity to review both your personal notes and those of other members of the class. This can be an enormous help if, for example, you lost concentration during part of a lecture and your notes don't make much sense. You and another student may even have notes that contradict each other or have radically different information. When this happens, try to reconstruct what the instructor said and, if necessary, bring in a third group member to clear up the confusion. See Chapter 5 for more on effective studying in groups.

You can take notes in many ways. Different note-taking systems suit different people and situations. Explore each system and choose what works for you.

Which *note-taking system* should you use?

There is more than one way to take good notes. You benefit most from the system that feels most comfortable to you and makes the most sense for the course content. For example, you might take notes in a different style for a history class than for a foreign language class. The most common note-taking systems include outlines, the Cornell system, and think links.

As you consider each system, remember your learning styles from Chapter 2. In each class, choose a system that takes both your learning styles and the class material into account. For example, a visual learner may take notes in think link style most of the time, but may find that only the Cornell style works well for a particular chemistry course. Experiment to discover what works best in any situation.

Taking Notes in Outline Form

When a reading assignment or lecture seems well organized, you may choose to take notes in outline form. When you use an outline, you construct a line-by-line representation, with certain phrases set off by varying indentations, showing how ideas relate to one another and are supported by facts and examples.

Formal outlines indicate ideas and examples using Roman numerals, capital and lowercase letters, and numbers. When you are pressed for time, such as during class, you can use an informal system of consistent indenting and dashes instead. Formal outlines also require at least two headings on the same level—that is, if you have a IIA you must also have a IIB. Figure 6.3 shows an outline on civil rights legislation.

Guided Notes

From time to time, an instructor may give you a guide, usually in the form of an outline, to help you take notes in the class. This outline may be on a page that you receive at the beginning of the class, on the board, on an overhead projector, or even posted on-line prior to the class.

Although guided notes help you follow the lecture and organize your thoughts, they do not replace your own notes. Because they are more of a basic outline of topics than a comprehensive coverage of information, they require that you fill in what they do not cover in detail. If your mind wanders because you think that the guided notes are all you need, you may miss important information.

When you receive guided notes on paper, write directly on the paper if there is room. If not, use a separate sheet and copy the outline categories that the guided notes suggest. If the guided notes are on the board or overhead, copy them, leaving plenty of space in between for your own notes.

Figure 6.3   **Sample formal outline.**

CIVIL RIGHTS LEGISLATION: 1860–1968

I. Post–Civil War Era
   A. Fourteenth Amendment, 1868: equal protection of
       the law for all citizens
   B. Fifteenth Amendment, 1870: constitutional
       rights of citizens regardless of race, color, or
       previous servitude
II. Civil Rights Movement of the 1960s
   A. National Association for the Advancement of
       Colored People (NAACP)
       1. Established in 1910 by W.E.B. DuBois and
           others
       2. Legal Defense and Education fund fought
           school segregation
   B. Martin Luther King Jr., champion of nonviolent
       civil rights action
       1. Led bus boycott: 1955–1956
       2. Marched on Washington, D.C.: 1963
       3. Awarded NOBEL PEACE PRIZE: 1964
       4. Led voter registration drive in Selma,
           Alabama: 1965
   C. Civil Rights Act of 1964: prohibited discrimination
       in voting, education, employment, and public
       facilities
   D. Voting Rights Act of 1965: gave the government
       power to enforce desegregation
   E. Civil Rights Act of 1968: prohibited discrimination
       in the sale or rental of housing

Using the Cornell Note-Taking System

The Cornell note-taking system, also known as the T-note system, was developed more than 45 years ago by Walter Pauk at Cornell University.[3] The system is successful because it is simple—and because it works. It consists of three sections on ordinary notepaper:

- Section 1, the largest section, is on the right. Record your notes here in informal outline form.

- Section 2, to the left of your notes, is the *cue column*. Leave it blank while you read or listen; then fill it in later as you review. You might fill it with comments that highlight main ideas, clarify meaning, suggest examples, or link ideas and examples. You can even draw diagrams.

- Section 3, at the bottom of the page, is the *summary area*. Here you use a sentence or two to summarize the notes on the page. When you review, use this section to reinforce concepts and provide an overview.

When you use the Cornell system, create the note-taking structure before class begins. Picture an upside-down letter T and use Figure 6.4 as your guide.

- Start with a sheet of standard loose-leaf paper. Label it with the date and title of the lecture.

- To create the cue column, draw a vertical line about 2.5 inches from the left side of the paper. End the line about 2 inches from the bottom of the sheet.

- To create the summary area, start at the point where the vertical line ends (about 2 inches from the bottom of the page) and draw a horizontal line that spans the entire paper.

Figure 6.4 shows how a student used the Cornell system to take notes in an introductory business course.

Creating a Think Link

A *think link,* also known as a mind map, is a visual form of note taking. When you draw a think link, you diagram ideas by using shapes and lines that link ideas and supporting details and examples. The visual design makes the connections easy to see, and the use of shapes and pictures extends the material beyond just words. Many learners respond well to the power of visualization. You can use think links to brainstorm ideas for paper topics as well.

VISUALIZATION
The interpretation of verbal ideas through the use of mental visual images.

One way to create a think link is to start by writing your topic in the middle of a sheet of paper and putting a circle around it. Next, draw a line from the circled topic and write the name of one major idea at the end of the line. Circle that idea also. Then, jot down specific facts related to the idea, linking them to the idea with lines. Continue the process, connecting thoughts to one another by using circles, lines, and words. Figure 6.5 shows a think link on a sociology concept called social stratification.

Figure 6.4 Sample Cornell system notes.

October 3, 200X, p. 1

UNDERSTANDING EMPLOYEE MOTIVATION

Why do some workers have a better attitude toward their work than others?	Purpose of motivational theories
	  — To explain role of human relations in motivating employee performance
	  — Theories translate into how managers actually treat workers

Some managers view workers as lazy; others view them as motivated and productive.	2 specific theories
	  — Human resources model, developed by Douglas McGregor, shows that managers have radically different beliefs about motivation.
	    — Theory X holds that people are naturally irresponsible and uncooperative
	    — Theory Y holds that people are naturally responsible and self-motivated

Maslow's Hierarchy
 	
self-actualization needs (challenging job)
esteem needs (job title)
social needs (friends at work)
security needs (health plan)
physiological needs (pay)
	— Maslow's Hierarchy of Needs says that people have needs in 5 different areas, which they attempt to satisfy in their work.
	    — Physiological need: need for survival, including food and shelter
	    — Security need: need for stability and protection
	    — Social need: need for friendship and companionship
	    — Esteem need: need for status and recognition
	    — Self-actualization need: need for self-fulfillment
	Needs at lower levels must be met before a person tries to satisfy needs at higher levels.
	—Developed by psychologist Abraham Maslow

Two motivational theories try to explain worker motivation. The human resources model includes Theory X and Theory Y. Maslow's Hierarchy of Needs suggests that people have needs in 5 different areas: physiological, security, social, esteem, and self-actualization.

Figure 6.5 Sample think link.

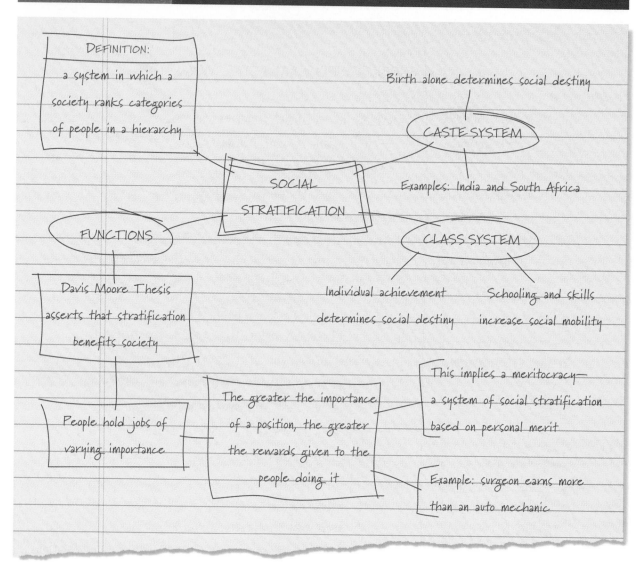

This is only one of many think link styles; other examples include stair steps (showing connecting ideas that build to a conclusion) and a tree shape (roots as causes and branches as effects). Look back to Figure 5.4 on page 141 for a type of think link sometimes referred to as a "jellyfish." You can design any think link that makes sense to you.

A think link may be tough to construct in class, especially if your instructor talks quickly. In this case, use another note-taking system during class. Then, make a think link as you review your notes.

Using Other Visual Note-Taking Strategies

Several other note-taking strategies help you organize your information and are especially useful to visual learners. These strategies may be too involved to complete quickly during class, so you may want to use them when taking notes on a text chapter or when rewriting your notes for review.

Time lines. A time line can help you organize information—such as dates of French Revolution events or eras of different psychology practices—into chronological order. Draw a vertical or horizontal line on the page and connect each item to the line, in order, noting the dates.

Tables. There are tables throughout this text that show information through vertical or horizontal columns. Use tables to arrange information according to particular categories.

Hierarchy charts. These charts can help you understand information in terms of how each piece fits into the hierarchy. A hierarchy chart could show levels of government, for example, or levels of the scientific classification of animals and plants. One version of a hierarchy is called a *matrix*—a table that has categories listed across the top and left side. Each box inside shows information that relates to the categories above and beside it. Table 4.2 on page 108 is an example of a matrix.

HIERARCHY

A graded or ranked series.

Once you choose a note-taking system, your success depends on how well you use it. Personal shorthand will help you make the most of whatever system you choose.

How can you *write faster* when taking notes?

SHORTHAND

A system of rapid handwriting that employs symbols, abbreviations, and shortened words to represent words, phrases, and letters.

When taking notes, many students feel that they can't keep up with the instructor. Using some personal shorthand (not standard secretarial shorthand) can help you push your pen faster. Shorthand is writing that shortens words or replaces them with symbols. Because you are the only intended reader, you can misspell and abbreviate words in ways that only you understand.

The only danger with shorthand is that you might forget what your writing means. To avoid this problem, review your shorthand notes while your abbreviations and symbols are fresh in your mind. If there is any confusion, spell out words as you review.

Here are some suggestions that will help you master this important skill:

1. Use the following standard abbreviations in place of complete words:

w/	with	cf	compare, in comparison to
w/o	without	ff	following
→	means; resulting in	Q	question
←	as a result of	p.	page
↑	increasing	*	most importantly
↓	decreasing	<	less than

∴	therefore	>	more than
∵ or b/c	because	=	equals
≈	approximately	%	percent
+ or &	and	Δ	change
−	minus; negative	2	to; two; too
NO. or #	number	vs	versus; against
i.e.	that is,	e.g.	for example
etc.	and so forth	c/o	care of
ng	no good	lb	pound

2. Shorten words by removing vowels from the middle of words:

    prps   =   purpose
    Crvtte   =   Corvette (as on a vanity license plate for a car)

3. Substitute word beginnings for entire words:

    assoc   =   associate; association
    info   =   information

4. Form plurals by adding s:

    prblms   =   problems
    prntrs   =   printers

5. Make up your own symbols and use them consistently:

    b/4   =   before
    2thake   =   toothache

6. Use key phrases instead of complete sentences ("German—nouns capped" instead of "In German, all nouns are capitalized.")

Finally, throughout your note taking, remember that the primary goal is for you to generate materials that help you learn and remember information. No matter how sensible any note-taking strategy, abbreviation, or system might be, it won't do you any good if it doesn't help you reach that goal. Keep a close eye on what works for you and stick to it.

If you find that your notes aren't comprehensive, legible, or focused enough, think critically about how you might improve them. Can't read your notes? You might have been too sleepy, or you might have a handwriting issue. Confusing gaps in the information? You might be distracted in class, have an instructor who skips around, or have a lack of understanding of the course material. Put your problem-solving skills to work and brainstorm solutions from the variety of strategies in this chapter. With a little time and effort, your notes will truly become a helpful learning tool in school and beyond.

Once you have figured out how to effectively record what you hear, your next task is to remember it so that you can use it. The following information about memory will help you remember what you learn so that you can put it to use.

How does *memory* work?

Your memory enables you to use the knowledge you take in. Human memory works like a computer. Both have essentially the same purpose: to encode, store, and retrieve information.

- During the *encoding* stage, information is changed into usable form. On a computer, this occurs when keyboard entries are transformed into electronic symbols and stored on a disk. In the brain, sensory information becomes impulses that the central nervous system reads and codes. You are encoding, for example, when you study a list of chemistry formulas.

"The true art of memory is the art of attention."

SAMUEL JOHNSON

- During the *storage* stage, information is held in memory (the mind's version of a computer hard drive) for later use. In this example, after you complete your studying of the formulas, your mind stores them until you need to use them.

- During the *retrieval* stage, memories are recovered from storage by recall, just as a saved computer program is called up by name and used again. In this example, your mind retrieves the chemistry formulas when you have to take a test or solve a problem.

Memories are stored in three different storage banks. The first, called *sensory memory,* is an exact copy of what you see and hear and lasts for a second or less. Certain information is then selected from sensory memory and moves into *short-term memory,* a temporary information storehouse that lasts no more than 10 to 20 seconds. You are consciously aware of material in your short-term memory. Whereas unimportant information is quickly dumped, important information is transferred to *long-term memory*—the mind's more permanent information storehouse.

Having information in long-term memory does not necessarily mean that you will be able to recall it when needed. Particular techniques can help you improve your recall.

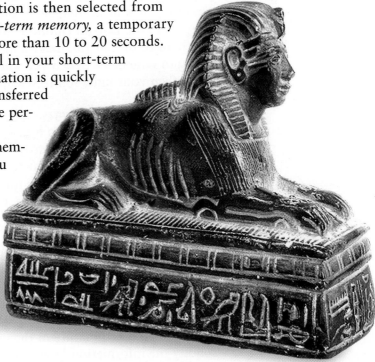

How can you *improve* your memory?

Most forgetting occurs within minutes after memorization. In a classic study conducted in 1885, researcher Herman Ebbinghaus memorized a list of meaningless three-letter words such as CEF and LAZ. Within one hour, he measured that he had forgotten more than 50 percent of what he learned. After two days, he knew less than 30 percent. Although his recall remained fairly stable after that, the experiment showed how fragile memory can be—even when you take the time and energy to memorize information.[4]

People with superior memories may have an inborn talent for remembering. More often, though, they have mastered techniques for improving recall. Remember that techniques aren't a cure-all for memory difficulties. If you have a learning disability, the following strategies may help but may not be enough. Seek specific assistance if you consistently have trouble remembering.

Use Specific Strategies

As a student, your job is to understand, learn, and remember information—everything from general concepts to specific details. The following suggestions will help improve your recall.

Have purpose and intention. Why can you remember the lyrics to dozens of popular songs, but not the functions of the pancreas? Perhaps this is because you want to remember the lyrics, you connect them to a visual image, or you have an emotional tie to them. To achieve the same results at school or on the job, make sure you have a purpose for what you are trying to remember. When you know why it is important, you are able to strengthen your intention to remember it.

Understand what you memorize. Information that has meaning is easier to recall than gibberish. This basic principle applies to everything you study—from biology and astronomy to history and English literature. If something you need to memorize makes no sense, consult textbooks, fellow students, or an instructor for an explanation. Use organizational tools, such as outlines (see page 176) or think links (see page 178), to make logical connections between different pieces of information.

Recite, rehearse, and write. When you *recite* material, you repeat it aloud to remember it. Reciting helps you retrieve information as you learn it and is a crucial step in studying (see Chapter 5). *Rehearsing* is similar to reciting but is done silently. It is the process of repeating, summarizing, and associating information with other information. *Writing* is rehearsing on paper. The physical nature of the acts of speaking and writing help to solidify the information in your memory.

Study during short but frequent sessions. Research shows that you can improve your chances of remembering material if you learn it more than once. Study in short sessions followed by brief rest periods, rather than studying continually with little or no rest. Even though studying for an hour straight may feel productive, you'll probably remember more from three 20-minute sessions. Try studying between classes or during other breaks in your schedule.

Separate material into manageable sections. When material is short and easy to understand, studying it from start to finish may work. With longer material, however, you may benefit from dividing it into logical sections, mastering each section, putting all the sections together, and then testing your memory of all the material.

Use a tape recorder selectively. If permitted in class, you can record lectures. Unless you have a learning disability that makes note taking difficult, take notes just as you would if the tape recorder were not there. Later, you can listen to the tapes to clarify your notes and help you remember important ideas. You can also make your own study tapes: Use your tape recorder to record study questions, leaving 10 to 15 seconds between questions so that you can answer out loud. Record the correct answer after the pause for quick feedback.

Use Visual Aids

Any kind of visual representation of study material can help you remember. Try converting material into a think link or outline. Use any visual that helps you recall it and link it to other information. If you have handouts of visuals that coordinate with class topics, have them ready as you study. Pay close attention to figures and tables in your texts; they help to remind you of important information.

Flash cards (easily made from index cards) are a great visual memory tool. They give you short, repetitive review sessions that provide immediate feedback. Use the front of each card to write a word, idea, or phrase you want to remember. Use the back side for a definition, explanation, and other key facts. Figure 6.6 shows two flash cards for studying psychology.

| Figure 6.6 | Sample flash cards. |

Here are some additional suggestions for making the most of your flash cards:

- Carry the cards with you and review them frequently.
- Shuffle the cards and learn the information in various orders.
- Test yourself in both directions (e.g., first look at the terms and provide the definitions or explanations; then turn the cards over and reverse the process).

Use Critical Thinking

Your knowledge of the critical-thinking mind actions can help you remember information. Many of the mind actions use the principle of *association*—considering new information in relation to information you already know. The more you can associate a piece of new information with your current knowledge, the more likely you are to remember it.

Imagine that you have to remember information about a specific historical event—for example, the signing of the Treaty of Versailles, the agreement that ended World War I. You might put the mind actions to work in the following ways:

 Recall everything that you know about the topic.

 Think about how this event is *similar* to other events in history, either recent events or events from long ago.

 Consider what is *different* and unique about this treaty in comparison to other treaties.

 Explore the *causes* that led up to this event, and look at the event's *effects*.

 From the general *idea* of treaties that ended wars, explore other *examples* of such treaties.

 Think about *examples* of what happened during the treaty signing, and from those examples come up with *ideas* about the tone of the event.

Looking at the facts of the event, *evaluate* how successful you think the treaty was.

PERSONAL TRIUMPH

even the most painful memory can be an inspiration for learning and change. Nathalie Piraino's experience as a refugee from Rwanda has led her to achieve educational goals and to strive to create a lasting memorial for those she left behind.

I grew up in Rwanda with my family. Although we had nothing materially, my papa passed on many important values to me. One of the most enduring is that he believed in higher education. When I was a child, we were forced to leave our home as a result of ethnic strife and were displaced into the south of the country. We lived in a refugee camp for two years with very little to eat.

As poor as we were, my father always made sure we had enough coffee beans or other products to sell in order to have the cash to purchase notebooks. We had to do many chores before and after school, but he always had oil for our lanterns so we could study at night. He would walk many kilometers on mountainous paths to attend school meetings. His participation boosted my self-esteem.

In 1993, I left my country and began taking classes shortly after I arrived in the United States. College was a dream come true for me. But my happiness was short lived.

In 1994, Rwanda erupted into a volcano of violence. When I began receiving the news, I cried a river of tears. My family had been massacred. The men who killed my mother worked on our farm. I remember that she would serve them food before us. She said, "If it weren't for the workers, we wouldn't be able to eat." She respected all people. I dropped classes because I couldn't focus. At night, I couldn't sleep because of recurring nightmares. I frantically called

Nathalie Piraino, English student;
Community College of Baltimore County—Essex Campus

organizations, doing everything I could, to try and save a life in my beloved country. Then, in 1995, my husband and I went to Rwanda. Even though I knew it would be incredibly painful, I also knew I needed closure. I couldn't believe what I saw. I couldn't recognize where my home used to be. I saw skeletons of children, some still with their shoes on. No one can ever describe the horror that went on there.

Last year, I experienced a major episode of depression, and once again, I had to audit my college courses. With the help of medicine and therapy, I'm feeling better now. I don't think you ever completely recover from traumas like these, but there are healthy things you can do to cope.

I have three goals in my life. The first is to adopt my niece, now 16 and living in an orphanage in Rwanda, who survived the massacre by hiding in a swamp for 36 days with her brother and eating leaves. She desperately needs love and therapy. The second is to help raise money to erect a monument for my people. My husband and I visited the Holocaust museum. I want to help erect such a memorial for my people in an effort to honor their lives. My third goal is to complete my degree in writing so that I can write a book about this tragedy. I owe it to myself and to my family to get an education. This is something my father wanted for his children. Faith is a survival tool my father gave me. By faith, I will fulfill his dream and mine.

Take a moment to consider . . .

- How much you value your education, and what sacrifice you may have made for the sake of that education.

- How you feel your being educated will benefit others in your life.

You don't have to use every mind action in every memory situation. Choose the ones that help you most. The more information and ideas you can associate with the new item you're trying to remember, the more successful at remembering it you will be.

Critical thinking also helps you perform the crucial task of separating main points from less important details. When you select and focus on the most important information, you don't waste time memorizing items you don't really need to know. As you read your texts, ask questions about what is most crucial to remember; then highlight only the most important information and write notes in the margins about central ideas. When you review your lecture notes, highlight or rewrite the most important information to remember.

Use Mnemonic Devices

Mnemonic devices (pronounced neh-MAHN-ick) work by connecting information you are trying to learn with simpler information or information that is familiar. Instead of learning new facts by rote (repetitive practice), associations give you a hook on which to hang and retrieve these facts. Mnemonic devices make information familiar and meaningful through unusual, unforgettable mental associations and visual pictures.

Here's an example of the power of mnemonics. Suppose you want to remember the names of the first six presidents of the United States. The first letters of their last names—Washington, Adams, Jefferson, Madison, Monroe, and Adams—together are W A J M M A. To remember them, you might add an E after the J and create a short nonsense word: *wajemma*.

Visual images, idea chains, acronyms, and songs and rhymes are the more widely used kinds of mnemonic devices. Apply them to your own memory challenges.

Create Visual Images and Associations

Visual images are often easier to remember than images that rely on words alone. The best mental images often involve bright colors, three dimensions, action scenes, inanimate objects with human traits, ridiculousness, and humor.

Memory techniques
that involve associ-
ating new information
with information you
already know.

Turning information into mental pictures helps improve memory, especially for visual learners. To remember that the Spanish artist Picasso painted *The Three Women,* you might imagine the women in a circle dancing to a Spanish song with a pig and a donkey (pig-asso). Don't reject outlandish images—as long as they help you.

Use an Idea Chain to Remember Items in a List

An idea chain is a memory strategy that involves forming exaggerated mental images of a large group of items. The first image is connected to the second image, which is connected to the third image, and so on. Imagine, for example, that you want to remember the seven mind actions that appear in the critical-thinking discussion in Chapter 4: *recall, similarity, difference, cause and effect, example to idea, idea to example,* and *evaluation.* You can use the visual icons to form an idea chain that goes like this:

> The letter R (recall) rolls down a hill and bumps into two similar intersecting circles (similarity), which start rolling and bump into two different intersecting circles (difference). Everything rolls past a sign with two circling arrows on it telling them to keep rolling (cause and effect), and then bump into an "EX" at the bottom of the hill, which turns on a light bulb (example to idea). That light bulb shines on another "EX" (idea to example). The two "EX"s are sitting on either side of a set of scales (evaluation).

ACRONYM

A word formed from
the first letters
of a series of
words, created in
order to help you
remember the
series.

Create Acronyms

Another helpful association method involves the use of the acronym. In history, you can remember the "big three" Allies during World War II—Britain, America, and Russia—with the acronym BAR. The word (or words) spelled don't necessarily have to be real words; for example, see Figure 6.7 for a "name" acronym that often helps students remember the colors of the spectrum.

Other acronyms take the form of an entire sentence in which the first letter of each word in each sentence stands for the first letter of the memorized term. This is also called a *list order acronym.* For example, when

Figure 6.7 **Spectrum acronym.**

red

orange

yellow

green

blue

indigo

violet

R O Y G B I V

science students want to remember the list of planets in order of their distance from the sun (Mercury, Venus, Earth, Mars, Jupiter, Saturn, Uranus, Neptune, and Pluto), they may learn the sentence:

<u>M</u>y <u>v</u>ery <u>e</u>legant <u>m</u>other <u>j</u>ust <u>s</u>erved <u>u</u>s <u>n</u>ine <u>p</u>ickles.

Use Songs or Rhymes

Some of the most classic mnemonic devices are rhyming poems that tend to stick in your mind effectively. One you may have heard is the rule about the order of "i" and "e" in spelling:

I before E, except after C, or when sounded like "A" as in "neighbor" and "weigh."

Four exceptions if you please: either, neither, seizure, seize.

"Memory is the stepping-stone to thinking, because without remembering facts, you cannot think, conceptualize, reason, make decisions, create, or contribute."

HARRY LORAYNE

Make up your own poems or songs, linking tunes or rhymes that are familiar to you with information you want to remember. Thinking back to the "wajemma" example, imagine that you want to remember the presidents' first names as well. You might set those first names—George, John, Thomas, James, James, and John—to the tune of "Happy Birthday." Or, to extend the history theme, you might use the first musical phrase of the National Anthem.

Improving your memory requires energy, time, and work. In school, it also helps to master SQ3R, the textbook study technique that was introduced in Chapter 5. By going through the steps in SQ3R and using the specific memory techniques described in this chapter, you will be able to learn more in less time—and remember what you learn long after exams are over.

In Sanskrit, the classical written language of India and other Hindu countries, these characters read as *sem ma yeng chik,* mean "do not be distracted." This advice can refer to the focus of the work you are currently doing, the concentration required to critically think and talk through a problem, or the mental discipline of meditation, among other things.

Think of this concept as you strive to improve your listening, note taking, and memory techniques. Focus on the task, the person, or the idea at hand. Try not to be distracted by other thoughts, other people's notions of what you should be doing, or any negative messages. Be present in the moment to take in and retain what is happening around you. Do not be distracted.

Building Skills

FOR COLLEGE, CAREER, AND LIFE SUCCESS

The Big Picture *Combining Thinking, Strategy, and Teamwork*

Optimum Listening Conditions

Think of a recent situation (this semester or last semester) in which you were able to understand and retain most of what you heard in the classroom.

Describe the environment (course title, classroom setting, instructor's style, etc.):

_____

_____

_____

Describe your attitude toward the course (including how prepared you feel):

_____

_____

_____

Describe any barriers to listening that you had to overcome in this situation:

_____

_____

_____

Now describe a classroom situation you recently experienced where you feel you didn't retain information well.

Describe the environment (course title, classroom setting, instructor's style, etc.):

_____

_____

_____

Describe your attitude toward the course (including how prepared you feel):

_____
_____
_____

Describe any barriers to listening that were present in this situation:

_____
_____
_____

Examine the two situations. Based on your descriptions, name two conditions that seem crucial for you to listen effectively and retain information.

_____
_____

Describe one way in which you could have improved your listening and retention in the more difficult situation.

_____
_____

Now put your listening skills to work as you interact with others in a study group. Choose one particular meeting of this class when people were likely to take notes—or, if students in your class happen to share other classes together, try using a set of notes from another class. Join with two or three other classmates, all of whom were in class that day, and make a temporary study group. Make enough photocopies of your notes to give one copy to each of the other group members.

First, look over the sets of notes on your own. Think about:

- readability of handwriting
- information covered
- note-taking systems used
- clarity of the ideas and examples

Then, gather together and talk through the four topics, one by one. Approach the notes as though you were in a study group session.

- Can you read each other's handwriting? If not, the information won't be of much use to you.
- Did you cover the same information? If someone missed a topic, someone else can help them fill in the blanks.
- Did you use the same or different note-taking systems? You might gather insight from the way someone else structures their notes.
- Could you understand what the notes were saying? If you are confused about something in your own notes, someone else might have a helpful perspective. If you don't understand someone else's notes, together you can figure out which information is confusing or missing.

Finally, write one change you plan to make in your note taking based on your study group session.

Writing *Discovery Through Journaling*

To record your thoughts, use a separate journal or the lined pages at the end of the chapter.

REMEMBERING. Think about your memory. What do you tend to remember, and memorize, well? What just doesn't stick in your head? Write about your toughest memory challenge. Discuss any strategies from this chapter that you think will help you improve, and plan how you will implement them.

Career Portfolio *Charting Your Course*

MATCHING CAREER TO CURRICULUM. Your success in most career areas depends in part on your academic preparation. Some careers, such as medicine, require very specific curriculum choices (e.g., you have to take a number of biology and chemistry courses to be considered for medical school). Some careers require certain courses that teach basic competencies; for example, to be an accountant, you have to take accounting and bookkeeping. Other career areas, such as many business careers, don't have specific requirements, but employers often look for certain curriculum choices that indicate the mastery of particular skills.

Put your listening and note-taking skills to work as you investigate your options. Choose two of the career areas in which you are interested. For each, interview two people to find out about both required curriculum and beneficial, but not required, courses. Choose one person from your academic setting (e.g., an instructor in a related subject area, a student further along that career track, an academic advisor) and one from the working world (e.g., a person working in that career, a career planning and placement office counselor). Interview each in a setting where you can listen well and take effective notes.

When you have completed your interviews, create two lists—one for each career area—of recommended courses. Write each career at the top of its list. To set off the courses that are absolutely required from those that are simply recommended, mark them with a star.

Assess Yourself *Student Success Strategies*

If you have access to the CD-ROM Strategies for Success, *use the following questions to assess your thoughts and enhance your understanding of the chapter. The questions below represent only some of the activities provided on the CD for the chapter topics—try others if you have time.*

Click on the Note Taking bookmark. Use the following activities to enhance your ability to take good notes:

1. Take the pre-assessment to identify your current understanding of how to take notes successfully.

2. Watch the video and consider how specific note-taking actions involving writing can heighten your learning and retention. In the space provided, answer the question regarding active and passive learning.

3. Click on Activity One: The Cornell System of Note Taking. Read the passage; then, in the T-note fields provided, take notes on the passage using the Cornell system.

4. Take the post-assessment to further evaluate your note-taking knowledge.

 uggested Readings

DePorter, Bobbi and Mike Hernacki. *Quantum Notes: Whole-Brain Approaches to Note Taking.* Chicago, IL: Learning Forum, 2000.

Dunkel, Patricia A., Frank Pialorsi, and Joane Kozyrez. *Advanced Listening Comprehension: Developing Aural & Note-Taking Skills.* Boston, MA: Heinle & Heinle, 1996.

Higbee, Kenneth L. *Your Memory: How It Works and How to Improve It.* Marlowe & Co., 2001.

Lebauer, R. Susan. *Learn to Listen, Listen to Learn: Academic Listening and Note Taking.* Upper Saddle River, NJ: Prentice Hall, 2000.

Levin, Leonard. *Easy Script Express: Unique Speed Writing Methods to Take Fast Notes and Dictation.* Chicago, IL: Legend Publishing, 2000.

Lorayne, Harry. *Super Memory—Super Student: How to Raise Your Grades in 30 Days.* Boston, MA: Little, Brown & Company, 1990.

Lorayne, Harry. *The Memory Book: The Classic Guide to Improving Your Memory at Work, at School, and at Play.* New York: Ballantine Books, 1996.

Robbins, Harvey A. *How to Speak and Listen Effectively.* New York: AMACOM, 1992.

Roberts, Billy. *Educate Your Memory: Improvement Techniques for Students of All Ages.* London: Allison & Busby, 2000.

Roberts, Billy. *Working Memory: Improving Your Memory for the Workplace.* London Bridge Trade, 1999.

 nternet Resources

ForgetKnot: A Source for Mnemonic Devices: http://members.tripod.com/~ForgetKnot/

Prentice Hall Student Success Supersite—Study Skills: www.prenhall.com/success/StudySkl/index.html

E ndnotes

1. Ralph G. Nichols, "Do We Know How to Listen? Practical Helps in a Modern Age," *Speech Teacher* (March 1961), pp. 118–124.

2. Ibid.

3. Walter Pauk, *How to Study in College,* 5th ed. Boston, MA: Houghton Mifflin Company, 1993, pp. 110–114.

4. Herman Ebbinghaus, *Memory: A Contribution to Experimental Psychology,* trans. H. A. Ruger and C. E. Bussenius. New York: New York Teacher's College, Columbia University, 1885.

JOURNAL

name   date

visit: www.prenhall.com/carter NY Times link for this chapter

In this chapter you explore answers to the following questions: • How can preparation improve test performance? • How can you work through test anxiety? • What general strategies can help you succeed on tests? • How can you master different types of test questions? • How can you learn from test mistakes?

IN THIS CHAPTER

Test taking

FOR A RUNNER, a race is the equivalent of a test because it measures ability at a given moment. Doing well in a race requires training similar to the studying you do for exams. The best runners—and test takers—understand that they train not just for the race or test, but to achieve a level of competence that will stay with them. Knowing that you will continue to use the skills on which you are being tested gives you the perspective that *owning* these skills is more important than achieving a perfect score.

Tests provoke anxiety for Peter Changsak (see next page) and for many students. To find the positive side of exams, see them as preparation for life. When you get a job or even work on your budget, you'll apply what you know and put your skills into action—exactly what you do when you take a test. As you will see in this chapter, test taking is about preparation, persistence, and strategy. It's also about conquering fears, paying attention to details, and learning from mistakes.

showing what you know

Peter Changsak, Sheldon-Jackson College, Sitka, Alaska

Tim Nordberg, Executive Director, Chicago Youth Project

How can I combat test anxiety?

Study to learn . . . Good test scores reflect your passion to know what you have studied

I am a Yu'pik Eskimo from a village on the Yukon River. Before attending college, I worked for six years as a clerk at the Native Corporation, a gas station and general store. When the manager passed away, the business offered to make me a manager. Even though I knew how to do much of the work, I didn't feel I was ready, so I decided to go to school for more training.

College life is different from what I am accustomed to. The hardest part has been taking tests. I study hard, but then when I get in class and the test begins, my mind goes blank. When I read, I understand what I'm reading, but as soon as I close the book, I can't remember what I just read. My favorite class is biology lab—probably because we can walk around.

I love mechanics and construction. When I worked at the Native Corporation, we built a new building. I felt like I was a success at work, but I don't feel successful as a student. Sometimes I feel like quitting, but I also think it can help me have more choices if I stick with it. I'm learning how to be a serious student, but it isn't easy. Can you give suggestions about how I can get over my test anxiety?

In many ways my experience in college was similar to yours. I was raised in a car industry town and was the first person in my family to go to college. My first year was hard—I discovered that I read at an eighth grade level. I hated studying and taking tests. During the spring, the college began a building project. I wanted to be outside doing manual work, too. I constantly felt a battle going on within me.

Two factors gave me the endurance to go on: One was seeing my old high school buddies, who seemed stuck in the past, and the second factor was my desire to fulfill my goals. I decided that if I fail, it won't be because I haven't given it my best; I'm not going to fail because I refuse to try.

That summer I took a reading class. School was still not easy that fall, but I was not studying as much out of fear or duty; rather, I was studying to do my best. Classes began to take on a different meaning. I was beginning to learn because I enjoyed the challenge. I took tests to see how well I knew the subject. Today, I still love sports and carpentry, but I also love to learn.

Don't fear failure. Just try to do your best. Concentrate on the task at hand. Study to learn, not to take a test. Good test scores reflect your passion to know what you have studied rather than how good you are at test taking. You are being challenged to survive in new ways, and you are not alone. Ask the student services office to help you through this adjustment process. Ask your advisor if there is a class that teaches study and test-taking tips.

Also, try to remember why you came to college in the first place—to better equip yourself. As you prepare for classes and tests, remind yourself what this experience will do for you someday when it is all behind you. Growing in any area of life isn't always fun and may not seem within reach. But if we give up, we may miss out on a part of us that, in time, would have brought greater rewards.

How can preparation *improve* test performance?

like a runner who prepares for a marathon by exercising, eating right, taking practice runs, and getting enough sleep, you can take steps to master your exams. The primary step, occupying much of your preparation time, is to listen when material is presented, read carefully, and study until you know the material that will be on the test (Chapter 5 examines the art of effective studying). In this sense, staying on top of your class meetings, readings, and assignments over the course of the semester is one of the best ways to prepare for tests. Other important steps are the preparation strategies that follow.

Identify Test Type and Material Covered

Before you begin studying, find out as much as you can about the type of test you will be taking and what it will cover. Try to identify:

- *What topics the test will cover* (Will it cover everything since the semester began or will it be limited to a narrow topic?)
- *The type of questions on the test*—objective (multiple choice, true–false, sentence completion), subjective (essay), or a combination.
- *What material you will be tested on* (Will the test cover only what you learned in class and in the text or will it also cover outside readings?)

Your instructors may answer these questions for you. Even though they may not reveal specific test questions, they might let you know the question format or information covered. Some instructors may even drop hints about possible test questions, either directly ("I might ask a question on this subject on your next exam") or more subtly ("One of my favorite theories is . . .").

Here are a few other strategies for predicting what may be on a test.

Use SQ3R to identify what's important. Often, the questions you write and ask yourself when you read assigned materials may be part of the test. Textbook study questions are also good candidates.

Talk to people who already took the course. Try to find out how difficult the instructor's tests are, whether they focus primarily on assigned readings or on class notes, what materials are usually covered, and what types of questions are asked. Also ask about instructors' preferences. If you learn that the instructor pays close attention to specific facts, for example, use flash cards to drill yourself on major and minor details. If he or she emphasizes a global overview, focus on conceptualization and example-to-idea thinking (see discussion in Chapter 4).

Examine old tests, if they are available. You may find them in class, on-line, or on reserve in the library. Old tests help to answer the following questions:

- Does the instructor focus on examples and details, general ideas and themes, or a combination?
- Can you do well through straight memorization or should you take a critical-thinking approach?
- Are the questions straightforward or confusing and sometimes tricky?
- Do the tests require that you integrate facts from different areas in order to draw conclusions?

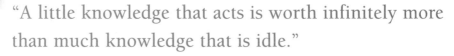

"A little knowledge that acts is worth infinitely more than much knowledge that is idle."

KAHLIL GIBRAN

If you can't get copies of old tests and your instructor doesn't give too many details, use clues from the class to predict test questions. After taking the first exam in the course, you will have more information about what to expect.

Create a Study Plan and Schedule

Once you have identified as much as you can about what will be covered on the test, choose your study materials. Go through your notes, texts, related primary sources, and handouts, and then set aside materials you don't need.

Then, use your time-management skills to prepare a schedule. Consider all of the relevant factors—your study materials, the number of days until the test, and the time you can study each day. If you establish your schedule ahead of time and write it in a date book, you are more likely to follow it.

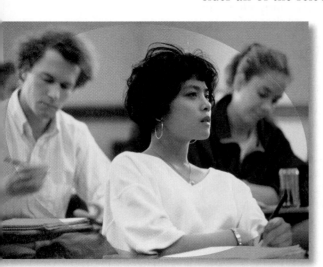

Schedules vary widely according to the situation. For example, if you have three days before the test and no other obligations during that time, you might set two 2-hour study sessions during each day. On the other hand, if you have two weeks before a test, classes during the day, and work three nights a week, you might spread out your study sessions over the nights you have off during those two weeks.

A checklist, like the one in Figure 7.1, helps you get organized and stay on track as you prepare. Use a checklist to assign specific tasks to particular study times and sessions. That way, not only do you know when you have time to study, but you also have defined goals for each study session.

Prepare Through Careful Review

By thoroughly reviewing your materials, you will have the best shot at remembering their contents. Use the following strategies when you study.

Figure 7.1　Pretest checklist.

Course: _____　Instructor: _____

Date, time, and place of test: _____

Type of test *(e.g., is it a midterm or a minor quiz?)*: _____

What the instructor has told you about the test, including the types of test questions, the length of the test, and how much the test counts toward your final grade:

_____

_____

Topics to be covered on the test in order of importance:

1. _____

2. _____

3. _____

4. _____

5. _____

Study schedule, including materials you plan to study *(e.g., texts and class notes)* and dates you plan to complete each:

MATERIAL	DATE OF COMPLETION
1.	
2.	
3.	
4.	
5.	

Materials you are expected to bring to the test *(e.g., your textbook, a sourcebook, a calculator)*:

_____

_____

Special study arrangements *(e.g., plan study group meetings, ask the instructor for special help, get outside tutoring)*:

_____

_____

_____

Life-management issues *(e.g., rearrange work hours)*:

_____

_____

_____

Source: Adapted from Ron Fry, *"Ace" Any Test,* 3rd ed. (Franklin Lakes, NJ: Career Press, 1996), 123–124.

Use SQ3R. The reading method you studied in Chapter 5 provides an excellent structure for reviewing your reading materials.

- *Surveying* gives you an overview of topics.
- *Questioning* helps you focus on important ideas and determine what the material is trying to communicate.
- *Reading* (or, in this case, rereading) reminds you of the ideas and supporting information.
- *Reciting* helps to anchor the concepts in your head.
- *Review* tasks, such as quizzing yourself on the Q-stage questions, summarizing sections you have highlighted, making flash cards for important concepts, and constructing a chapter outline, help you solidify your learning so that you are able to use it at test time and beyond.

Review your notes. Recall the section in Chapter 6 for making your notes a valuable after-class reference. Use the following techniques to effectively review notes:

- *Time your reviews carefully.* Review notes for the first time within a day of the lecture, if you can, and then review again closer to the test day.
- *Mark up your notes.* Reread them, filling in missing information, clarifying points, writing out abbreviations, and highlighting key ideas.
- *Organize your notes.* Consider adding headings and subheadings to your notes to clarify the structure of the information. Rewrite them using a different organizing structure—for example, an outline if you originally used a think link.
- *Summarize your notes.* Evaluate which ideas and examples are most crucial, and then rewrite your notes in shortened form, focusing on those ideas and examples. Summarize your notes in writing or with a summary think link. Try summarizing from memory as a self-test.

Think critically. Using the techniques from Chapter 4, approach test preparation as a critical thinker, working to understand the material rather than just repeat facts. As you study, try to analyze causes and effects, look at issues from different perspectives, and connect concepts that, on the surface, appear unrelated. This work will increase your understanding and probably result in a higher exam grade. Critical thinking is especially important for essay tests that ask you to develop and support a thesis.

Take a Pretest

Use questions from your textbook to create your own pretest. Most textbooks include end-of-chapter questions. If your course doesn't have an assigned text, develop questions from your notes and assigned outside readings. Choose questions that are likely to be covered on the test, then answer them under testlike conditions—in quiet, with no books or notes to help you (unless your exam is open book), and with a clock telling you when to quit.

If the topic or format of a test challenges your stronger or weaker intelligences, these tips will help you make the most of your time and abilities.

INTELLIGENCE	SUGGESTED STRATEGIES	WHAT WORKS FOR YOU? WRITE NEW IDEAS HERE
Verbal–Linguistic	■ Think of and write out questions your instructor may ask on a test. Answer the questions and then try rewriting them in a different format (essay, true–false, and so on). ■ Underline important words in review questions or practice questions.	
Logical–Mathematical	■ Make diagrams of review or practice questions. ■ Outline the key steps involved in topics on which you may be tested.	
Bodily–Kinesthetic	■ Use your voice to review out loud. Recite concepts, terms and definitions, important lists, dates, and so on. ■ Create a sculpture, model, or skit to depict a tough concept that will be on your test.	
Visual–Spatial	■ Create a think link to map out an important topic and its connections to other topics in the material. Study it and redraw it from memory a day before the test. ■ Make drawings related to possible test topics.	
Interpersonal	■ Develop a study group and encourage each other. ■ In your group, come up with as many possible test questions as you can. Ask each other these questions in an oral exam-type format.	
Intrapersonal	■ Brainstorm test questions. Then, come back to them after a break or even a day's time. On your own, take the sample "test" you developed. ■ Make time to review in a solitary setting.	
Musical	■ Play music while you read if it does not distract you. ■ Study concepts by reciting them to rhythms you create or to music.	
Naturalistic	■ Bring your text, lecture notes, and other pertinent information to an outdoor spot that inspires you and helps you to feel confident, and review your material there.	

Prepare Physically

Most tests ask you to work efficiently under time pressure. If your body is tired or under stress, your performance may suffer. If you can, avoid staying up all night. Get some sleep so that you can wake up rested and alert. Remember that adequate sleep can help cement memories by reducing interference from new memories (see Chapter 6).

Eating right is also important. Sugar-laden snacks bring up your energy, only to send you crashing down much too soon. Also, too much caffeine can add to your tension and make it difficult to focus. Eating nothing leaves you drained, but too much food can make you sleepy. The best advice is to eat a light, well-balanced meal before a test. When time is short, grab a quick-energy snack such as a banana, orange juice, or a granola bar.

Make the Most of Last-Minute Studying

Cramming—studying intensively, and often round the clock, right before an exam—often results in information going into your head and popping right back out shortly after the exam is over. Because study conditions aren't always ideal, nearly every student crams during college, especially when a busy schedule leaves only a few hours to prepare. Use these hints to make the most of your study time:

- *Go through your flash cards,* if you have them, one last time.

- *Focus on crucial concepts;* don't worry about the rest. Resist reviewing notes or texts page by page.

- *Create a last-minute study sheet.* On a single sheet of paper, write down key facts, definitions, formulas, and so on. Try to keep the material short and simple. If you prefer visual notes, use think links to map out ideas and supporting examples.

- *Arrive early.* Study the sheet or your flash cards until you are asked to clear your desk.

- *While it is still fresh, record any helpful information on scrap paper.* Do this before looking at the test. Review this information as needed during the test.

After your exam, evaluate the effects cramming had on your learning. Even if you passed, you might remember very little. This low level of retention won't do you much good in the real world where you have to make use of information instead of just recalling it for a test. Think about how you can plan strategically to start earlier and improve the situation next time.

Whether you have to cram or not, you may experience anxiety on test day. Following are some ideas for how to handle test anxiety when it strikes.

How can you work through *test anxiety?*

A certain amount of stress can be a good thing. Your body is alert, and your energy motivates you to do your best (for more on stress and stress management, see Chapter 9). Some students, however, experience incapacitating stress levels before and during exams, especially midterms or finals.

Test anxiety can cause physical symptoms, such as sweating, nausea, dizziness, headaches, and fatigue, as well as psychological symptoms such as the inability to concentrate and feeling overwhelmed. You can minimize your anxiety by working on your preparation and attitude.

TEST ANXIETY

A bad case of nerves that can make it hard to think or to remember.

Preparation

Preparation is the basic defense against anxiety. The more confident you feel about the material, the better you will perform on test day. In this sense, consider all the preparation and study information in this chapter as test anxiety assistance. Also, finding out what to expect on the exam will help you feel more in control. Seek out information about what material will be covered, the question format, the length of the exam, and the points assigned to each question.

Creating a detailed study plan builds knowledge as it combats anxiety. Divide the plan into small tasks. As you finish each, you will increase your sense of accomplishment, confidence, and control. Instead of worrying about the test, take active steps that will help you succeed.

Attitude

Although good preparation is a confidence builder, maintaining a positive *attitude* is equally important. Here are some key ways to maintain an attitude that will help you succeed.

See the test as an opportunity to learn. A test is an opportunity to show what you have learned. All too often, students view tests as contests. If you pass, or "win" a contest, you might feel no need to retain what you've learned. If you fail, or "lose" the contest, you might feel no need to try again. However, if you see the test as a signpost along the way to a greater goal, mastering the material will be more important than "winning."

Understand that tests measure performance, not personal value. Your grade does not reflect your ability to succeed. Whether you get an A or an F, you are still the same person.

Appreciate your instructor's purpose. Instructors don't intend to make you miserable. They test you to give you an opportunity to grow and demonstrate what you have accomplished. They test you so that, in rising to the challenge, you become better prepared for challenges outside of school. Don't hesitate to engage your instructors in your quest to learn and succeed. Visit them during office hours; send them e-mail questions to clarify material and issues before tests.

Seek study partners who challenge you. Your anxiety may get worse if you study with someone who is also anxious. Find someone who can inspire you to do your best. For more on how to study effectively with others in study groups, see Chapter 5.

Set yourself up for success. Expect progress and success—not failure. Take responsibility for creating success through your work and attitude. Know that, ultimately, you are responsible for the outcome.

Practice relaxation. When you feel test anxiety mounting, breathe deeply, close your eyes, and visualize positive mental images such as getting a good grade and finishing with time to spare. Do whatever you have to do to ease muscle tension—stretch your neck, tighten and then release your muscles.

These strategies will help in most test anxiety situations. However, many students have issues surrounding math tests that require special attention.

Coping with Math Anxiety

QUANTITATIVE

Of, relating to, or involving the measurement of amount or number.

Math anxiety is the uncomfortable feeling associated with **quantitative** thinking. Math anxiety is often based on common misconceptions about math, such as the notion that people are born with or without an ability to think quantitatively, or the idea that real quantitative thinkers solve problems in their heads. Some students feel that they can't do math at all, and as a result may give up without asking for help. Use the questionnaire in Figure 7.2 to get an idea of your math anxiety level.

The best way to overcome test-time anxiety is to practice quantitative thinking and thereby increase your confidence. Keeping up with your homework, attending class, preparing well for tests, and doing extra problems will help you feel confident by increasing your familiarity with the material. Figure 7.3 shows additional ways to reduce math anxiety.

Test Anxiety and the Returning Student

If you're returning to school after years away, you may wonder if you can compete with younger students or if your mind is still able to learn. To counteract these feelings of inadequacy, focus on the useful skills you have learned in life. For example, managing work and a family requires strong time-management, planning, and communication skills that can help you plan your study time, juggle school responsibilities, and interact with students and instructors.

In addition, life experiences give you contexts through which you can understand ideas. For example, your relationship experiences may help you understand social psychology concepts and managing your finances may help you understand accounting. If you permit yourself to

Figure 7.2 Explore your math anxiety.

Rate each of the following statements on a scale of 1 (Strongly Disagree) to 5 (Strongly Agree).

① ② ③ ④ ⑤ 1. I don't like math classes and haven't since high school.

① ② ③ ④ ⑤ 2. I do okay at the beginning of a math class, but I always feel it will get to the point where it is impossible to understand.

① ② ③ ④ ⑤ 3. I don't seem to concentrate in math classes. I try, but I get nervous and distracted and think about other things.

① ② ③ ④ ⑤ 4. I don't like asking questions in math class. I'm afraid that the teacher or the other students will think I'm stupid.

① ② ③ ④ ⑤ 5. I stress out when I'm called on in math class. I seem to forget even the easiest answers.

① ② ③ ④ ⑤ 6. Math exams scare me far more than any of my other exams.

① ② ③ ④ ⑤ 7. I can't wait to finish my math requirement so that I'll never have to do any math again.

SCORING KEY: 28–35 You suffer from full-blown math anxiety.

21–27 You are coping, but you're not happy about mathematics.

14–20 You're doing okay.

7–13 So, what's the big deal about math? You have very little problem with anxiety.

Source: Freedman, Ellen (March 1997). *Test Your Math Anxiety* [on-line]. Available at http://fc.whyy.org/CCC/algl/anxtest.htm (March 1998).

Figure 7.3 Ten ways to reduce math anxiety and do well on tests.

1. Overcome your negative self-image about math.

2. Ask questions of your teachers and your friends, and seek outside assistance.

3. Math is a foreign language—practice it often.

4. Don't study mathematics by trying to memorize information and formulas.

5. READ your math textbook.

6. Study math according to your personal learning style.

7. Get help the same day you don't understand something.

8. Be relaxed and comfortable while studying math.

9. "TALK" mathematics. Discuss it with people in your class. Form a study group.

10. Develop a sense of responsibility for your own successes and failures.

Source: Freedman, Ellen (March 1997). *Ten Ways to Reduce Math Anxiety* [on-line]. Available at http://fc.whyy.org/CCC/algl/reduce.htm (March 1998).

feel positive about the knowledge and skills you have acquired, you may improve your ability to achieve your goals.

Parents who have to juggle child care with study time can find the challenge especially difficult before a test. Here are some suggestions that might help:

- *Tell your children why the test is important.* Discuss the situation in concrete terms. For example, doing well in school might mean a high-paying job after graduation, which, in turn, can mean more money for family vacations, summer camps, and less stress over paying bills.
- *Explain the time frame.* Tell them your study schedule and when the test will occur. Plan a reward after your test—going for ice cream, seeing a movie, or having a picnic.
- *Plan activities.* Stock up on games, books, and videos.
- *Find help.* Ask a relative or friend to watch the children during study time, or arrange for your child to visit a friend. Consider trading baby-sitting hours with another parent, hiring a baby-sitter who will come to your home, or enrolling your child in day care.

"Fear is nature's warning sign to get busy."

HENRY C. LINK

When you have prepared by using the strategies that work for you, you are ready to take your exam. Now, you can focus on methods to help you succeed when the test begins.

What general strategies can help you *succeed* on tests?

E ven though every test is different, there are general strategies that will help you handle almost all tests, including short-answer and essay exams.

Write Down Key Facts

Before you even look at the test, write down key information—including formulas, rules, and definitions—that you studied recently. Use the back of the question sheet or a piece of scrap paper for your notes (be sure your instructor knows that this paper didn't come into the test room already filled in). Recording this information at the start makes forgetting less likely.

Begin with an Overview of the Exam

Although exam time is precious, spend a few minutes at the start of the test getting a sense of the kinds of questions you'll be answering, what type of thinking they require, the number of questions in each section, and their point values. Use this information to schedule your time. For example, if a two-hour test is divided into two sections of equal point value—an essay section with 4 questions and a short-answer section with 60 questions—you can spend an hour on the essays (15 minutes per question) and an hour on the short-answer section (1 minute per question). As you calculate, think about the level of difficulty of each section. If you think you can handle the short-answer questions in less than an hour and that you'll need more time for the essays, rebudget your time.

Read Test Directions

Reading test directions carefully can save you trouble. For example, although a history test of 100 true-or-false questions and one essay may look straightforward, the directions may tell you to answer 80 of the 100 questions or that the essay is an optional bonus. If the directions indicate that you are penalized for incorrect answers—meaning that you lose points instead of simply not gaining points—avoid guessing unless you're fairly certain. These questions may do damage, for example, if you earn two points for every correct answer and lose one point for every incorrect answer.

When you read directions, you may learn that some questions or sections are weighted more heavily than others. For example, the short-answer questions may be worth 30 points, whereas the essays are worth 70. In this case, it's smart to spend more time on the essays than on the short answers. To stay aware of the specifics of the directions, circle or underline key words and numbers.

Work from Easy to Hard

Begin with the questions that seem easiest to you. You can answer these questions quickly, leaving more time for questions that require greater effort. If you like to work through questions in order, mark difficult questions as you reach them and return to them after you answer the questions you know. Answering easier questions first also boosts your confidence.

Watch the Clock

Keep track of how much time is left and how you are progressing. You may want to plan your time on a piece of scrap paper, especially if you have one or more essays to write. Wear a watch or bring a small clock with you to the test room. A wall clock may be broken, or there may be no clock at all.

Some students are so concerned about time that they rush through the test and have time left over. Instead of leaving early, spend the remaining time refining and checking your work. You may correct inadvertent errors, change answers, or add more information to an essay.

Master the Art of Intelligent Guessing

When you are unsure of an answer on a short-answer test, you can leave it blank or you can guess. As long as you are not penalized for incorrect answers, guessing helps you. "Intelligent guessing," writes Steven Frank, an authority on student studying and test taking, "means taking advantage of what you do know in order to try to figure out what you don't. If you guess intelligently, you have a decent shot at getting the answer right."[1]

First, eliminate all the answers you know—or believe—are wrong. Try to narrow your choices to two possible answers; then choose the one you think is more likely to be correct. Strategies for guessing the correct answer on a multiple-choice test are discussed later in the chapter.

When you check your work at the end of the test, ask yourself whether you would make the same guesses again. Chances are that you will leave your answers alone, but you may notice something that makes you change your mind—a qualifier that affects meaning, a remembered fact that enables you to answer the question without guessing, or a miscalculation in a math problem.

Follow Directions on Machine-Scored Tests

Machine-scored tests require that you use a special pencil to fill in a small box on a computerized answer sheet. When the computer scans the sheet, it can tell whether you answered the questions correctly.

Taking these tests requires special care. Use the right pencil (usually a number 2) and mark your answer in the correct space, filling the space completely. Periodically, check the answer number against the question number to make sure they match. If you mark the answer to question 4 in the space for question 5, not only do you get question 4 wrong, but your responses for all subsequent questions are off by a line. To avoid this problem, put a small dot next to any number you skip and plan to return to later.

Neatness counts on these tests because the computer can misread stray pencil marks or partially erased answers. If you mark two answers to a question and only partially erase one, the computer will read both responses and charge you with a wrong answer.

Use Critical Thinking to Avoid Errors

Critical thinking can help you work through each question thoroughly and avoid errors. Following are some critical-thinking strategies to use during a test.

Recall facts, procedures, rules, and formulas. Base your answers on the information you recall. Think carefully to make sure your recall is accurate.

Think about similarities. If you don't know how to attack a question or problem, consider similar questions or problems that you have worked on in class or while studying.

Note differences. Especially with objective questions, items that seem different from the material you studied may lead to answers you can eliminate.

Think through causes and effects. For a numerical problem, think about how you plan to solve it and see if the answer—the effect of your plan—makes sense. For an essay question that asks you to analyze a condition or situation, consider both what caused it and what effects it has.

Find the best idea to match the example(s) given. For a numerical problem, decide what formula (idea) best applies to the example or examples (the data of the problem). For an essay question, decide what idea applies to, or links, the examples given.

Support ideas with examples. When you present an idea in an answer to an essay question, be sure to back it up with supporting examples.

Evaluate each test question. In your initial approach to a question, decide what kinds of thinking will best help you solve it. For example, essay questions often require cause-and-effect and idea-to-example thinking, whereas objective questions often benefit from thinking about similarities and differences.

Use Special Techniques for Math Tests

In addition to these general test-taking strategies, here are several techniques that can help you achieve better results on math exams:

- *Read through the exam first.* When you first get an exam, read through every problem quickly. Make notes on how you might attempt to solve the problem if something occurs to you immediately.
- *Analyze problems carefully.* Categorize problems according to type. Take the "givens" into account, and write down any formulas, theorems, or definitions that apply before you begin. Focus on what you want to find or prove, and take the time you need to be precise.
- *Estimate before you begin to come up with a "ballpark" solution.* Work the problem and check the solution against your estimate. The two answers should be close. If they're not, recheck your calculations. You may have made a simple calculation error.
- *Break the calculation into the smallest possible pieces.* Go step-by-step and don't move on to the next step until you are clear about what you've done so far.
- *Recall how you solved similar problems.* Past experience can give you valuable clues to how a particular problem should be handled.
- *Draw a picture to help you see the problem.* This can be a diagram, a chart, a probability tree, a geometric figure, or any other visual image that relates to the problem.
- *Be neat.* When it comes to numbers, mistaken identity can mean the difference between a right and a wrong answer. A 4 that looks like a 9 will be marked wrong.
- *Use the opposite operation to check your work.* Work backward from your answer to see if you are right. Use subtraction to check your addition; use division to check multiplication.
- *Look back at the question to be sure you did everything that was asked.* Did you answer every part of the question? Did you show all required work?

Maintain Academic Integrity

When you take a test honestly, following all the rules of the test, you strengthen the principle of trust between students and instructors, which is at the heart of academic integrity (see Chapter 1). You also receive an accurate reading on your performance, from which you can determine what you know and what you still have to learn. Finally, you reinforce the habit of honesty.

Cheating as a strategy to pass a test or get a better grade robs you of the opportunity to learn the material on which you are being tested, which, ultimately, is your loss. It also makes fair play between students impossible. When one student studies hard for an exam and another cheats and both get the same high grade, the efforts of the hard-working student are diminished. It is important to realize that cheating jeopardizes your future at college if you are caught. You may be seriously reprimanded—or even expelled—if you violate your school's code of academic integrity.

Now that you have explored these general strategies, you can use what you've learned to address specific types of test questions.

How can you *master* different types of *test questions?*

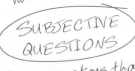

OBJECTIVE QUESTIONS

Short-answer questions that test your ability to recall, compare, and contrast information and to choose the right answer from a limited number of choices.

SUBJECTIVE QUESTIONS

Essay questions that require you to express your answer in terms of your own personal knowledge and perspective.

Every type of test question has a different way of finding out how much you know about a subject. Answering different types of questions is part science and part art. The strategy changes according to whether the question is objective or subjective.

For objective questions, you choose or write a short answer you believe is correct, often making a selection from a limited number of choices. Multiple-choice, fill-in-the-blank, matching, and true-or-false questions fall into this category. Subjective questions demand the same information recall as objective questions, but they also require you to plan, organize, draft, and refine a written response. They may also require more extensive critical thinking and evaluation. All essay questions are subjective. Although some guidelines will help you choose the right answers to both types of questions, part of the skill is learning to "feel" your way to an answer that works.

Multiple-Choice Questions

Multiple-choice questions are the most popular type of question on standardized tests. The following strategies can help you answer them.

Carefully read the directions. Directions can be tricky. For example, whereas most test items ask for a single correct answer, some give you the option of marking several choices that are correct. For some tests, you might be required to answer only a certain number of questions.

Read each question thoroughly. Then, look at the choices and try to answer the question. This strategy reduces the possibility that the choices will confuse you.

Underline key words and phrases. If the question is complicated, try to break it down into small sections that are easy to understand.

Pay attention to words that could throw you off. For example, it is easy to overlook negatives in a question ("Which of the following is not . . .").

If you don't know the answer, eliminate those answers you know or suspect are wrong. Your goal is to leave yourself with two possible answers, which would give you a 50–50 chance of making the right choice. The following questions will help you eliminate choices:

- *Is the choice accurate on its own terms?* If there's an error in the choice—for example, a term that is incorrectly defined—the answer is wrong.

- *Is the choice relevant?* An answer may be accurate, but it may not relate to the essence of the question.

- *Are there any qualifiers?* Absolute qualifiers, like *always, never, all, none,* or *every,* often signal an exception that makes a choice incorrect. For example, the statement "Normal children always begin talking before the age of two" is untrue (most normal children begin talking before age two, but some start later). Analysis has shown that choices containing conservative qualifiers (e.g., *often, most, rarely,* or *may sometimes be*) are often correct.

- *Do the choices give clues?* Does a puzzling word remind you of a word you know? If you don't know a word, does any part of the word—its prefix, suffix, or root—seem familiar? (See Chapter 5 for information on the meanings of common prefixes, suffixes, and roots.)

Make an educated guess by following helpful patterns. The ideal is to know the material so well that you don't have to guess, but that isn't always possible. Test-taking experts have found patterns in multiple-choice questions that may help you. Here is their advice:

- Consider the possibility that a choice that is *more general* than the others is the right answer.

- Consider the possibility that a choice that is *longer* than the others is the right answer.

- Look for a choice that has a middle value in a range (the range can be from small to large or from old to recent). It is likely to be the right answer.

- Look for two choices that have similar meanings. One of these answers is probably correct.

- Look for answers that agree grammatically with the question. For example, a fill-in-the-blank question that has an *a* or *an* before the blank gives you a clue to the correct answer.

Make sure you read every word of every answer. Instructors have been known to include answers that are almost right, except for a single word. Focus especially on qualifying words such as *always, never, tend to, most, often,* and *frequently.*

When questions are keyed to a reading passage, read the questions first. This will help you focus on the information you need to answer the questions.

Here are some examples of the kinds of multiple-choice questions you might encounter in an Introduction to Psychology course[2] (the correct answer follows each question):

1. Arnold is at the company party and has had too much to drink. He releases all of his pent-up aggression by yelling at his boss, who promptly fires him. Arnold normally would not have yelled at his boss, but after drinking heavily he yelled because
   A. parties are places where employees are supposed to be able to "loosen up"
   B. alcohol is a stimulant
   C. alcohol makes people less concerned with the negative consequences of their behavior
   D. alcohol inhibits brain centers that control the perception of loudness

(The correct answer is C)

2. Which of the following has not been shown to be a probable cause of or influence on the development of alcoholism in our society?
   A. intelligence   C. personality
   B. culture   D. genetic vulnerability

(The correct answer is A)

3. Geraldine is a heavy coffee drinker who has become addicted to caffeine. If she completely ceases her intake of caffeine over the next few days, she is likely to experience each of the following EXCEPT
   A. depression   C. insomnia
   B. lethargy   D. headaches

(The correct answer is C)

True-or-False Questions

True-or-false questions test your knowledge of facts and concepts. Read them carefully to evaluate what they truly say. If you're stumped, guess (unless you're penalized for wrong answers).

Look for qualifiers in true-or-false questions—such as *all, only,* and *always* (the absolutes that often make a statement false) and *generally, often, usually,* and *sometimes* (the conservatives that often make a statement true)—that can turn a statement that would otherwise be true into one that is false or vice versa. For example, "The grammar rule 'I before E except after C' is always true" is false, whereas "The grammar rule 'I before E except after C' is usually true" is true. The qualifier makes the difference.

Here are some examples of the kinds of true-or-false questions you might encounter in an Introduction to Psychology course (the correct answer follows each question).

Are the following questions true or false?

1. Alcohol use is clearly related to increases in hostility, aggression, violence, and abusive behavior. (True)

2. Marijuana is harmless. (False)

3. Simply expecting a drug to produce an effect is often enough to produce the effect. (True)

4. Alcohol is a stimulant. (False)

Matching Questions

Matching questions ask you to match the terms in one list with the terms in another list, according to the directions. For example, the directions may tell you to match a communicable disease with the pathogen that usually causes it. The following strategies will help you handle these questions.

Make sure you understand the directions. The directions tell you whether each answer can be used once or more than once.

Work from the column with the longest entries. This saves time because you are looking at each long phrase only once as you scan the column with the shorter phrases for the match.

Start with the matches you know. On your first run-through, mark these matches immediately with a penciled line, waiting to finalize your choices after you've completed all the items. Keep in mind that if you can use an answer only once, you may have to change answers if you reconsider any of your original choices.

Finally, tackle the matches you're not sure of. On your next run-through, focus on the more difficult matches. Look for clues and relationships you might not have thought of at first. Think back to class lectures, notes, and study sessions and try to visualize the correct response.

Consider the possibility that one of your sure-thing answers is wrong. If one or more phrases seem to have no correct answer, look back at your easy matches to be sure that you did not jump too quickly. See if another phrase can be used instead, thus freeing up an answer for use in another match.

Fill-in-the-Blank Questions

Fill-in-the-blank questions, also known as sentence completion questions, ask you to supply one or more words or phrases with missing information that completes the sentence. These strategies will help you make the right choices.

Be logical. Insert your answer; then reread the sentence from beginning to end to be sure it is factually and grammatically correct and makes sense.

Note the length and number of the blanks. Use these as important clues, but not as absolute guideposts. If two blanks appear right after one another, the instructor is probably looking for a two-word answer. If a blank is longer than usual, the correct response may require additional space. However, if you are certain of an answer that doesn't fit the blanks, trust your knowledge and instincts.

Pay attention to how blanks are separated. If there is more than one blank in a sentence and the blanks are widely separated, treat each one separately. Answering each as if it were a separate sentence-completion question increases the likelihood that you will get at least one answer correct. Here is an example:

> When Toni Morrison was awarded the _____ Prize for Literature, she was a professor at _____ University.
>
> (Answer: Morrison received the Nobel Prize and is a professor at Princeton University.)

In this case, and in many other cases, your knowledge of one answer has little impact on your knowledge of the other answer.

Think out of the box. If you can think of more than one correct answer, put them both down. Your instructor may be impressed by your assertiveness and creativity.

Make a guess. If you are uncertain of an answer, make an educated guess. Use qualifiers like *may, sometimes,* and *often* to increase the chance that your answer is at least partially correct. Have faith that after hours of studying, the correct answer is somewhere in your subconscious mind and that your guess is not completely random.

Essay Questions

An essay question allows you to express your knowledge and views more extensively than a short-answer question. With the freedom to express your views, though, comes the chal-

PERSONAL TRIUMPH

everyone has to face tests in life. From the difficulty of those tests can come important lessons and incredible drive. Rusmir Music has come from war-torn Bosnia to a stellar academic performance in his adopted country and an ability to proudly assert his differences.

Talk about square pegs: This year's No. 2 graduate at Holy Cross, a Roman Catholic college in Worcester, Massachusetts, is an openly gay Muslim from Bosnia.

Rusmir Music, 23, is a chemistry major who sings racy Madonna lyrics at every opportunity. He wears T-shirts with slogans rare on this J. Crew campus. He sprinkles glitter on his face, and often spikes his hair (which he used to bleach blond) into horns.

"That's why I think I'm here—I like to shock people, push their limits," Mr. Music said. "I can't say it was easy, but it was worth it. I am who I am today because I had to fight."

Born in Brcko, Bosnia, Mr. Music left home for Croatia in 1992, shortly before the bridge to his village was bombed. He lived with his mother and twin younger siblings in Nasice for four years, the only Muslim refugees in a Catholic town, biking five miles to a job checking coats at a nightclub. English lessons began in fifth grade, but Mr. Music got fluent watching soap operas like "Santa Barbara" and "Beverly Hills, 90210."

At 17, he joined a program that sent Bosnian students to live with American families, arriving in San Francisco on Super Bowl Sunday. He soon won a scholarship to Holy Cross—his host brother's alma mater—and people he met through the private United States high school where he spent three semesters added $30,000 to cover room, board and books.

Helen Whall, a professor of English, met Mr. Music when he signed up for her freshman seminar, "Shakespeare the Loyal Rebel." She

Source: Jodi Wilgoren, "Holy Cross: Fighting for the Right to Live on the Edge," New Yo said that course's title summed up the essence of her best student. His favorite Shakespearean character, she said, is Touchstone, the fool from "As You Like It."

While amassing a grade-point average of 3.93 and getting elected to Phi Beta Kappa in his junior year, Mr. Music served as a resident adviser, worked on plays and helped found Mecca, the Muslim Endeavor to Create Cultural Awareness—as well as the Association of Bisexuals, Gays and Lesbians, known as ABiGaLe.

The buttoned-down community offered few dating opportunities, but plenty of chances to shock his many friends and comfort those on the fringe. "I do talk a lot about sex," he admitted. "I don't necessarily get a lot of sex— I don't get any sex, really—but it's something I think people should be comfortable talking about."

Next year he will pursue a master's degree at New York University, creating an interdisciplinary program focusing on race, gender and sexuality.

Mr. Music's mother canceled plans to attend his graduation Friday, fearful of losing her job in Tusla, so he was on his own, as he has been, really, for years.

"Wherever a voice needed to be heard, where normally you might expect students to be shy and pull back, you could count on Rusmir being there," Professor Whall said. "He's made it O.K. for square pegs to make round holes accommodate them."

Take a moment to consider . . .

- *In what way you feel like you don't quite fit in—like you're a "square peg in a round hole."*
- *How you have handled an event in your life that has tested your ability to adapt.*

Here are examples of fill-in-the-blank questions you might encounter in an Introduction to Astronomy course[3] (correct answers follow questions):

1. A _____ is a collection of hundreds of billions of stars. (galaxy)

2. Rotation is the term used to describe the motion of a body around some _____. (axis)

3. The solar day is measured relative to the sun; the sidereal day is measured relative to the _____. (stars)

4. On December 21, known as the _____ _____, the sun is at its _____ _____. (winter solstice; southernmost point)

lenge to exhibit knowledge and demonstrate your ability to organize and express that knowledge clearly.

Strategies for Answering Essay Questions

The following steps will help improve your responses to essay questions. Many of these guidelines reflect methods for approaching any writing assignment. That is, you undertake an abbreviated version of a basic writing process as you plan, draft, revise, and edit your response. The primary differences here are that you are writing under time pressure and that you are working from memory.

1. *Start by reading the questions.* Decide which to tackle (if there's a choice). Then, focus on what each question is asking and the mind actions you need to use. Read the directions carefully and do everything that you are asked to do. Some essay questions may contain more than one part. Knowing what you have to accomplish, budget your time accordingly. For example, if you have 1 hour to answer 3 questions, you might budget 20 minutes for each question and break that down into stages (3 minutes for planning, 15 minutes for drafting, 2 minutes for revising and editing).

2. *Watch for action verbs.* Certain verbs can help you figure out how to think. Figure 7.4

Figure 7.4   Common action verbs on essay tests.

Analyze—Break into parts and discuss each part separately.	**Explain**—Make the meaning of something clear, often by making analogies or giving examples.
Compare—Explain similarities and differences.	**Illustrate**—Supply examples.
Contrast—Distinguish between items being compared by focusing on differences.	**Interpret**—Explain your personal view of facts and ideas and how they relate to one another.
Criticize—Evaluate the positive and negative effects of what is being discussed.	**Outline**—Organize and present the main examples of an idea or sub-ideas.
Define—State the essential quality or meaning. Give the common idea.	**Prove**—Use evidence and argument to show that something is true, usually by showing cause and effect or giving examples that fit the idea to be proven.
Describe—Visualize and give information that paints a complete picture.	**Review**—Provide an overview of ideas and establish their merits and features.
Discuss—Examine in a complete and detailed way, usually by connecting ideas to examples.	**State**—Explain clearly, simply, and concisely, being sure that each word gives the image you want.
Enumerate/List/Identify—Recall and specify items in the form of a list.	**Summarize**—Give the important ideas in brief.
Evaluate—Give your opinion about the value or worth of something, usually by weighing positive and negative effects, and justify your conclusion.	**Trace**—Present a history of the way something developed, often by showing cause and effect.

explains some words commonly used in essay questions. Underline these words as you read the question, clarify what they mean, and use them to guide your writing.

3. *Plan your essay.* Brainstorm ideas and examples. Create an informal outline or think link to map your ideas and indicate the examples you plan to cite in support.

4. *Draft your essay.* Start with a thesis statement that states clearly what your essay will say. Then, devote one or more paragraphs to the main points in your outline. Back up the general statement that starts each paragraph with evidence in the form of examples, statistics, and so on. Use simple, clear language, and look back at your outline to make sure you cover everything. Wrap it up with a short, pointed conclusion. Because you probably won't have time for further drafts, try to be as complete and organized as possible as you write.

5. *Revise your essay.* Make sure you have answered the question completely and have included all of your points. Look for ideas you left out, ideas you didn't support with examples, paragraphs with faulty structure, and confusing sentences. Make cuts or changes or add sentences in the

margins, indicating with an arrow where they fit. Try to be as neat as possible when making last-minute changes.

6. *Edit your essay.* Check for mistakes in grammar, spelling, punctuation, and usage. No matter your topic, being technically correct in your writing makes your work more impressive.

Neatness is a crucial factor in essay writing. If your instructor can't read your ideas, it doesn't matter how good they are. You might consider printing and skipping every other line if you know your handwriting is a problem. Avoid writing on both sides of the paper if it makes your work hard to read. If your handwriting is dismal, ask if it is possible to take the test on a laptop computer.

Here are some examples of essay questions you might encounter in an Interpersonal Communication course. In each case, notice the action verbs from Figure 7.4.

1. Summarize the role of the self-concept as a key to interpersonal relationships and communication.

2. Explain how internal and external noise affects the ability to listen effectively.

3. Describe three ways that body language affects interpersonal communication.

(Figure 7.5 shows an essay that responds effectively to question 3.)

How can you *learn from* test *mistakes?*

The purpose of a test is to see how much you know, not merely to achieve a grade. Making mistakes, or even failing a test, is human. Rather than ignoring mistakes, examine them and learn from them as you learn from mistakes on the job and in relationships. Working through your mistakes helps you avoid repeating them on another test. The following strategies will help.

Try to identify patterns in your mistakes. Look for the following:

- *Careless errors.* In your rush to complete the exam, did you misread the question or directions, blacken the wrong box on the answer sheet, inadvertently skip a question, write illegibly?

Figure 7.5 Response to an essay question.

QUESTION: Describe three ways that body language affects interpersonal communication.

Body language plays an important role in interpersonal communication and helps shape the impression you make, especially when you meet someone for the first time. Two of the most important functions of body language are to contradict and reinforce verbal statements. When body language contradicts verbal language, the message conveyed by the body is dominant. For example, if a friend tells you that she is feeling "fine," but her posture is slumped, her eye contact minimal, and her facial expression troubled, you have every reason to wonder whether she is telling the truth. If the same friend tells you that she is feeling fine and is smiling, walking with a bounce in her step, and has direct eye contact, her body language is accurately reflecting and reinforcing her words.

The nonverbal cues that make up body language also have the power to add shades of meaning. Consider this statement: "This is the best idea I've heard all day." If you were to say this three different ways—in a loud voice while standing up; quietly while sitting with arms and legs crossed and looking away; and while maintaining eye contact and taking the receiver's hand—you might send three different messages.

Finally, the impact of nonverbal cues can be greatest when you meet someone for the first time. Although first impressions emerge from a combination of nonverbal cues, tone of voice, and choice of words, nonverbal elements (cues and tone) usually come across first and strongest. When you meet someone, you tend to make assumptions based on nonverbal behavior such as posture, eye contact, gestures, and speed and style of movement.

In summary, nonverbal communication plays a crucial role in interpersonal relationships. It has the power to send an accurate message that may belie the speaker's words, offer shades of meaning, and set the tone of a first meeting.

- *Conceptual or factual errors.* Did you misunderstand a concept or never learn it? Did you fail to master certain facts? Did you skip part of the text or miss classes in which ideas were covered?

If you have time, rework the questions you got wrong. Based on instructor feedback, try to rewrite an essay, recalculate a math problem from the original question, or redo questions following a reading selection. If you see patterns of careless errors, promise yourself that you'll be more careful in the future and that you'll save time to double-check your work. If you pick up conceptual and factual errors, rededicate yourself to better preparation.

After reviewing your mistakes, fill in your knowledge gaps. If you made mistakes on questions because you didn't know or understand them, develop a plan to comprehensively learn the material. Solidifying your knowledge can help you on future exams and in life situations that involve the subject you're studying. You might even consider asking to retake the exam. The score might not count, but you may find that focusing on learning, rather than on grades, can improve your knowledge.

"The secret of a leader lies in the tests he has faced over the whole course of his life and the habit of action he develops in meeting those tests."

GAIL SHEEHY

Talk to your instructors. You can learn a lot from consulting an instructor about specific mistakes you made or about subjective essays on which you were marked down. Respectfully ask the instructor for an explanation of grades or comments. In the case of a subjective test where the answers are often not clearly right or wrong, ask for specifics about what you could have done to earn a better grade. Take advantage of this opportunity to find out solid details about how you can do better next time.

If you fail a test, don't throw it away. Keep it as a reminder that many students have been in your shoes and that you have room to improve if you supply the will to succeed.

sine qua non

Although Latin is no longer spoken and is considered a "dead" language, it plays an important role in modern English because many English words and phrases have Latin roots. The Latin phrase *sine qua non* (pronounced sihn-ay kwa nahn) means, literally, "without which not." In other words, a *sine qua non* is "an absolutely indispensable or essential thing."

Think of mastery as the *sine qua non* of test taking. When you have worked hard to learn, review, and retain information, you are well prepared for tests, no matter what form they take. Focus on knowledge to transform test taking from an intimidating challenge into an opportunity to demonstrate your mastery.

Building Skills

FOR COLLEGE, CAREER, AND LIFE SUCCESS

The Big Picture   *Combining Thinking, Strategy, and Teamwork*

Strategic Test Analysis

Take a detailed look at your performance on a particular test, in any course, that you have taken in the last month.

1. Write what you think of your test performance and grade. Were you pleased or disappointed? Briefly explain why.

_____

_____

_____

2. Next, list the test preparation activities that helped you on the exam—strategies that had positive effects.

_____

_____

_____

3. Finally, be strategic about the future. What will you do differently the next time you face a test?

_____

_____

_____

Put your test-taking knowledge to work in a group setting. Form a study group with two or three other students. When your instructor announces the next exam, ask each study group member to record everything he or she does to prepare for the exam, including:

- learning what to expect on the test (topics and material that will be covered, types of questions that will be asked)
- examining old tests
- creating and following a study schedule and checklist
- using SQ3R to review material

- taking a pretest
- getting a good night's sleep before the exam
- doing last-minute cramming
- mastering general test-taking strategies
- mastering test-taking strategies for specific types of test questions (multiple-choice, true/false, matching, fill-in-the-blank, essay)

After the exam, come together to compare preparation regimes. What important differences can you identify in the routines followed by group members? How do you suspect that different routines affected test performance and outcome? On a separate piece of paper, for your own reference, write down what you learned from the test preparation habits of your study mates that may help you as you prepare for upcoming exams.

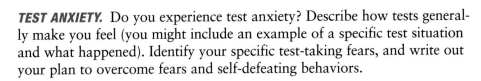

Writing *Discovery Through Journaling*

To record your thoughts, use a separate journal or the lined pages at the end of the chapter.

TEST ANXIETY. Do you experience test anxiety? Describe how tests generally make you feel (you might include an example of a specific test situation and what happened). Identify your specific test-taking fears, and write out your plan to overcome fears and self-defeating behaviors.

Career Portfolio *Charting Your Course*

ON-THE-JOB TESTING. Depending on what careers you are considering, you may encounter one or more tests. Some are for entry into the field (e.g., medical boards); some test your proficiency on particular equipment (e.g., a proficiency test on Microsoft Word); and some move you to the next level of employment (e.g., a technical certification test to become a certified actuary). Choose one career you are thinking about and investigate what tests are involved as you advance through different stages of the field. Be sure to look for tests in any of the areas described above. On a separate piece of paper, write down everything you find out about each test involved. For example:

- what it tests you on
- when, in the course of pursuing this career, you would need to take the test
- what preparation is necessary for the test (including course work)
- whether the test needs to be retaken at any time (e.g., airline pilots usually need to be recertified every few years)

Finally, see if you can review any of the tests you will face if you pursue this career. For example, if your career choice requires proficiency on a specific computer program, your college's career or computer center may have the test available.

If you have access to the CD-ROM Strategies for Success, *use the following questions to assess your thoughts and enhance your understanding of the chapter. The questions below represent only some of the activities provided on the CD for the chapter topics—try others if you have time.*

Click on the Test Taking bookmark. Use the following activities to broaden your knowledge of what it takes to succeed on tests:

1. Take the pre-assessment to clarify your perspective on test taking.

2. Watch the video and think about your own habits. Do you cram? What effects has it had on your learning? In the field provided, write a response to the questions on the video page.

3. Click on Activity Two: Practice Your Test Taking Skills. Print and read the article carefully, using the SQ3R method. Then take the test that follows and submit your results to see how you did.

4. Take the post-assessment to see how these activities have improved your knowledge of test taking.

uggested Readings

Browning, William G., Ph.D. *Cliffs Memory Power for Exams*. Lincoln, NE: Cliffs Notes Inc., 1990.

Frank, Steven. *Test Taking Secrets: Study Better, Test Smarter, and Get Great Grades*. Holbrook, MA: Adams Media Corporation, 1998.

Fry, Ron. *"Ace" Any Test, 3rd ed*. Franklin Lakes, NJ: Career Press, 1996.

Hamilton, Dawn. *Passing Exams: A Guide for Maximum Success and Minimum Stress*. Herndon, VA: Cassell Academic, 1999.

Kesselman, Judy and Franklynn Peterson. *Test Taking Strategies*. New York: NTC/Contemporary Publishing, 1981.

Luckie, William R. and Wood Smethurst. *Study Power: Study Skills to Improve Your Learning and Your Grades*. Cambridge, MA: Brookline Books, 1997.

nternet Resources

Prentice Hall Student Success Supersite (testing tips in study skills section): www.prenhall.com/success

Florida State University (list of sites offering information on test-taking skills): http://osi.fsu.edu/hot/testtaking/skills.htm

NetStudyAids.com—(study aids, skills, guides, and techniques): www.netstudyaids.com/

University of Minnesota Duluth (study strategies home page): www.d.umn.edu/student/loon/acad/strat/

ndnotes

1. Steven Frank, *The Everything Study Book*. Holbrook, MA: Adams Media Corporation, 1996, p. 208.

2. Many of the examples of objective questions used in this chapter are from Gary W. Pigrem, Test Item File for Charles G. Morris, *Understanding Psychology, 3rd ed*. Upper Saddle River, NJ: Prentice Hall, 1996.

3. Questions from Eric Chaisson and Steve McMillan, *Astronomy Today, 2nd ed*. Upper Saddle River, NJ: Prentice Hall, 1996, p. 27.

JOURNAL

name   date

visit: www.prenhall.com/carter NY Times link for this chapter

III

Creating Success

IN THIS CHAPTER

In this chapter you explore answers to the following questions: • Why is it important to embrace diversity? • How can critical thinking help you explore diversity? • How can minority students make the most of college? • How can you communicate effectively? • How do you make the most of personal relationships? • How can you handle conflict?

relating to others

RICHARD PAN'S EXPERIENCES (see next page) reveal a great deal about the tension people feel as they attempt to define their place within the diverse student body that characterizes most colleges. Richard is astute enough to realize that any decision he makes will be met with criticism from students who share his background and from those who are different, and that—in the end—his choices must be his own.

In this chapter, you explore how having a strong network of relationships can help you grow as a person and progress toward your goals. You see how your ability to open your mind can positively affect the way in which you perceive and relate to others. Special attention is paid to the choices minority students, like Richard, face. You also explore communication problems and strategies, techniques for enhancing personal relationships, and methods for handling different forms and levels of conflict.

communicating in a diverse world

Richard Pan, Columbia University, New York, New York

Jo Anne Roe, Spanish Instructor, Oak Park-River Forest High School, Oak Park, Illinois

How can I deal with diversity?

. . . follow the Golden Rule: treat other people the way you want them to treat you.

I was born in Taiwan and came to the United States when I was 12. At my high school in California, everyone mingled well. When I started college, however, I noticed a difference. The Asian kids hung out only with other Asians, and the Caucasians did the same. I'm used to hanging out with all sorts of people, but now I feel this tension, as if Asians are thinking, "Why is he bothering with them?"

During a summer work program, I roomed with a Chinese-American who advised me to avoid being friends with people from different ethnic groups. Although I don't feel comfortable with his advice, I do think you get judged by all sides when you try to be friends with everybody. Sometimes I feel like I'm having an identity crisis. I ask myself, "Which side am I on?" Do you have any ideas about how I could do better managing this problem?

It is wonderful that you have developed the ability to mingle with and enjoy the company of people from diverse backgrounds. This is a skill that many people do not possess; it is a skill that will be immensely valuable for your personal and professional future. Your comfort in a multicultural setting reflects self-assurance, maturity, and a clearly defined sense of identity.

The problem that you face—prejudice—does not originate within you, rather, it is being imposed upon you. To accuse one specific group of having a monopoly on this practice would be a denial of the truth. Misunderstanding of, apprehension toward, and nonacceptance of others who are different are facets of an elemental and, sadly, universal flaw in the human psyche. And because it is so painful, it is natural for people to guard themselves against its damage. I imagine that the other Asian-Americans are advising you out of sincere concern for you not to be hurt by people with whom they have had negative encounters in the past. The bottom line is that you are not at fault!

The best advice that I can offer to you is to follow the "Golden Rule": Treat other people the way you want them to treat you. In following the wisdom of this refrain, you neither compromise your own outlook on life nor give in to the fears and insecurities of other people, and you maintain human dignity in general. Continue as you are and be patient. Eventually, you will begin to see gradual and positive changes in the actions of your friends, directly due to the impact you will have made on them through your positive, accepting attitude.

Why is it important to *embrace diversity?*

W hether you grew up in a small town, a suburb, or a large city, inevitably you will encounter people who are nothing like anyone you've ever met. They may be of a different race or mix of races, have different religious beliefs, or express their sexuality in nontraditional ways. With society becoming more diverse, the likelihood of these encounters is increasing. As Figure 8.1 shows, the population of the United States not only grew by nearly 27.5 million between 1990 and 2000, it also became more of a "gorgeous mosaic"—a metaphor first coined by David Dinkins, New York City's first African-American mayor, to describe the city's diversity.

According to the 2000 census, one in four Americans is a minority group member, compared with one in five in 1980. And, for the first time, with the census allowing people to choose from an array of racial identities—white, black, Asian, American Indian, Alaska native, Pacific Islander and Hawaiian native, or "some other race"—Americans now describe themselves in terms of 63 different racial categories, compared with only five in 1990.[1]

The Diversity Within You

To think about the concept of diversity, look first within yourself. You are a complex jumble of internal and external characteristics that makes you markedly different than everyone else. Just as no two snowflakes are alike, no two people are alike—even identical twins.

> *Your example:* Take a minute to write down the characteristics that best describe you (e.g., Cuban-American, blonde, laid-back, only child, 24 years old, interested in rap music, training to be an exercise physiologist, fraternity member, good sense of humor).

_____

_____

_____

_____

Everything about you—your gender, race, ethnicity, sexual orientation, age, unique personality, talents, and skills—adds up to who you are. Accepting your strengths and weaknesses, your background and group identity is a sign of psychological health. You have every reason to feel proud and to make no

Figure 8.1

Minorities are changing the face of the United States.

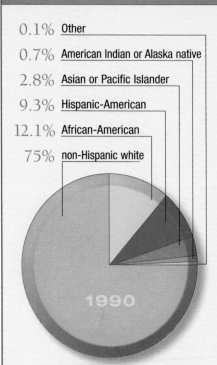

- 0.1% Other
- 0.7% American Indian or Alaska native
- 2.8% Asian or Pacific Islander
- 9.3% Hispanic-American
- 12.1% African-American
- 75% non-Hispanic white

1990

Total population 253,979,140

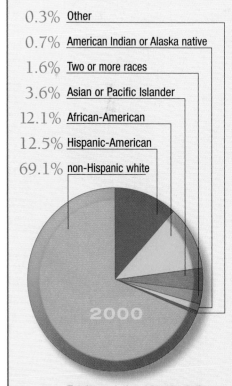

- 0.3% Other
- 0.7% American Indian or Alaska native
- 1.6% Two or more races
- 3.6% Asian or Pacific Islander
- 12.1% African-American
- 12.5% Hispanic-American
- 69.1% non-Hispanic white

2000

Total population 281,421,906

Source: U.S. Census Bureau. Data from 2000 Census of the Population.

Figure 8.2

How the student body is expected to change by 2015.

5% Asian-American

11% Hispanic

13% African-American

71% White

5% Asian-American
11% Hispanic
13% African-American
71% White
1995

8% Asian-American

13% African-American

15% Hispanic

63% White

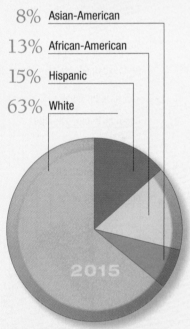

8% Asian-American
13% African-American
15% Hispanic
63% White
2015

(Percentages do not equal 100 because of rounding)

Source: Data from Educational Testing Service. Adapted from Jodi Wilgoren, "Swell of Minority Students Is Predicted at Colleges," *The New York Times*, May 24, 2000, A16.

apologies for your choices, as long as they do not intentionally hurt anyone.

Diversity on Campus

College campuses reflect society, so diversity on campus is on the upswing. Most students will notice different races and ethnicities around them at school, and projections are for greater population shifts to come. As Figure 8.2 shows, while white students made up 71 percent of the student population in 1995, their percentage is expected to drop to 63 percent in 2015. During the same 20-year period, Hispanic-American and Asian-American students will grow more numerous, while African-American enrollment will hold steady at about 13 percent. Some areas show even more dramatic trends. By 2015, whites will be a *minority* on campuses in California, the District of Columbia, Hawaii, and New Mexico.[2]

Minorities are becoming more visible because of their sheer numbers. Enrollment on campuses nationwide is expected to jump from 14.3 million in 1997 to 19 million in 2015, with African American, Hispanic-American, and Asian-American students responsible for 80 percent of the growth.

How will increasing diversity affect your life at school? Almost certainly, you will meet people like the following:

- Classmates and instructors who are bi- or multiracial or come from families with more than one religious tradition.
- Classmates and instructors who speak English as a second language and who may be immigrants.
- Classmates who are older than "traditional" 18- to 22-year-old students.
- Classmates and instructors who are in wheelchairs and those with other disabilities.
- Classmates who adopt different lifestyles—often expressed in the way they dress, their interests, and leisure activities.

In addition, you may see posters on campus for diverse clubs, such as those for African-Americans, Asian-Americans, Hispanic-Americans, gays and lesbians, and religious organizations including those for Christians, Jews, and Muslims. Your school may also have campus-wide ethnic, racial, and gay and lesbian pride celebrations.

Your example: Describe a person you've met recently who is a member of a group or groups with which you have little experience. Did you react to that person primarily as an individual or as a group member?

_____

_____

_____

_____

Every time you meet someone new, you have a *choice* about how to relate—or whether to relate at all. No one can force you to interact or to adopt a particular attitude because it is "right." Considering two important responsibilities may help you analyze your options:

Your responsibility to yourself is to carefully consider your feelings. Observe your reactions to others. Then, use critical thinking to make decisions that are fair to others and right for you.

Your responsibility to others lies in treating people with tolerance and respect. You won't like everyone, but acknowledging that others have a right to their opinions builds understanding. Being open-minded rather than closed-minded about others is necessary for relationships to thrive.

"Minds are like parachutes. They only function when they are open."

SIR JAMES DEWAR

Table 8.1 demonstrates the dramatic difference between an open-minded and a closed-minded approach to diversity.

Accepting others depends on being able to answer the following question with a firm yes: *Do I always give people a chance no matter who they are?* Prejudice, stereotyping, and discrimination often get in the way of fairness to others. Your problem-solving skills will help you overcome these barriers.

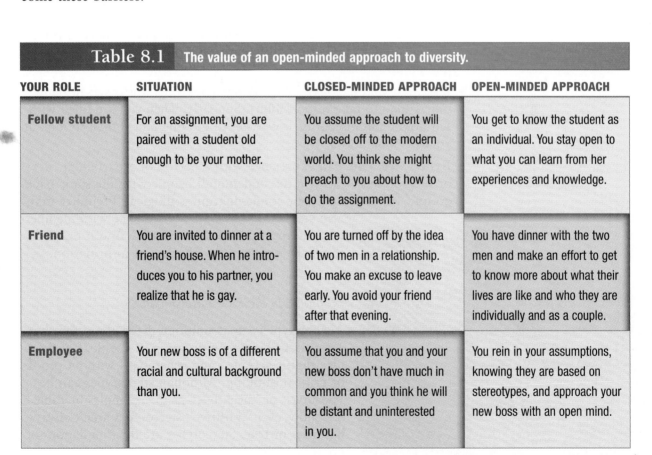

Table 8.1	The value of an open-minded approach to diversity.		
YOUR ROLE	**SITUATION**	**CLOSED-MINDED APPROACH**	**OPEN-MINDED APPROACH**
Fellow student	For an assignment, you are paired with a student old enough to be your mother.	You assume the student will be closed off to the modern world. You think she might preach to you about how to do the assignment.	You get to know the student as an individual. You stay open to what you can learn from her experiences and knowledge.
Friend	You are invited to dinner at a friend's house. When he introduces you to his partner, you realize that he is gay.	You are turned off by the idea of two men in a relationship. You make an excuse to leave early. You avoid your friend after that evening.	You have dinner with the two men and make an effort to get to know more about what their lives are like and who they are individually and as a couple.
Employee	Your new boss is of a different racial and cultural background than you.	You assume that you and your new boss don't have much in common and you think he will be distant and uninterested in you.	You rein in your assumptions, knowing they are based on stereotypes, and approach your new boss with an open mind.

How can critical thinking help you *explore diversity?*

Negative responses to diversity are based on prejudice and stereotypic thinking, which, in turn, can lead to discrimination and hate. As you read, think about what you can do to prevent some of the worst parts of human nature from taking hold within yourself and others.

Understand Prejudice, Discrimination, and Hate

Prejudice occurs when people *prejudge* others, usually on the basis of external characteristics such as gender, race, sexual orientation, and religion. Particular prejudices are so pervasive that they have their own names: *racism* (prejudice based on race), *sexism* (prejudice based on sex), and *ageism* (prejudice based on age) are just a few. Here are some reasons why people judge others before they know anything about them:

- *Family and culture.* Children learn attitudes, including intolerance and hate, from their parents, peers, and community. They may also learn to feel superior to others.

- *Fear of differences.* When people who grew up in the midst of prejudice encounter others from different backgrounds, those differences are too unsettling.

- *Insecurity and jealousy.* When things go wrong, it is easier to blame others than to take responsibility. Similarly, when you are filled with self-doubt and insecurity, it is easier to devalue others than to look at your personal flaws.

- *Experience.* One bad experience with a person of a particular race or religion may lead you to condemn all people with the same background, even though your condemnation is illogical. Prejudice may also stem from having no experience with members of a minority group. Some people find it easy to think the worst in the absence of information.

Prejudice Is Based on Stereotypes

A stereotype is an assumption made about the characteristics of a person or group of people. It is an idea that is accepted and generalized without proof or critical thinking. Although stereotypes can be "positive" or "negative," as the examples in Table 8.2 show, even "positive" stereotypes aren't always harmless or true. Stereotypes are the foundation for prejudiced thinking.

PREJUDICE

A preconceived judgment or opinion, formed without just grounds or sufficient knowledge.

STEREOTYPE

A standardized mental picture that represents an over-simplified opinion or uncritical judgment.

Table 8.2 Positive and negative stereotypes involve generalizations that may not be true.

POSITIVE STEREOTYPE	NEGATIVE STEREOTYPE
All women are nurturing.	Women are too emotional for business.
African-Americans are the best athletes.	African-Americans do poorly in school.
Hispanic-Americans are very family oriented.	Hispanic-Americans have too many kids.
White people are successful in business.	White people are cold and power hungry.
Gay people are artistic.	Gay people sleep around.
Because people with disabilities have been through so much, they are sensitive to the suffering of others.	People with disabilities can't hold jobs.
Older people have wisdom.	Older people can't learn new skills.
Asian-Americans are good in math and science.	Asian-Americans are poor leaders.

What are some reasons for stereotypes?

- *A desire for patterns and logic.* People often try to make sense of the world by using the labels, categories, and generalizations that stereotypes provide.
- *The media.* The more people see stereotypical images—the airhead beautiful blonde, the jolly fat man—the easier it is to believe that stereotypes are universal.
- *Laziness.* Labeling a group according to a characteristic they seem to have in common takes less energy than exploring unique qualities within individual group members.
- *A need to justify your actions.* Labeling people allows you to justify acts of discrimination. If you think women are poor in math, you won't ask any to join your math study group.

Your example: Describe a stereotype that you have witnessed in others or seen in the media that influences the way people treat each other.

_____

_____

_____

Stereotypes communicate the message that you don't respect others enough to discover who they really are. Although stereotyping a stranger is "easy," it comes at a high interpersonal cost. You never experience the personality, character, talents, sense of humor, or intelligence of others if you immediately plug them into stereotypical categories.

Prejudice Causes Discrimination

Prejudice—and the stereotypes it is based on—can lead to discrimination. *Discrimination* is made up of concrete actions that deny people equal employment, educational, and housing opportunities, and treat people as second-class citizens. As Sheryl McCarthy, an African-American columnist for *New York Newsday,* a daily newspaper, explains, "Nothing is quite so basic and clear as having a cab go right past your furiously waving body and pick up the white person next to you."[3]

If you are the victim of discrimination, it is important to know that federal law is on your side: You cannot be denied basic opportunities and rights because of your race, creed, color, age, gender, national or ethnic origin, religion, marital status, potential or actual pregnancy, or potential or actual illness or disability (unless the illness or disability prevents you from performing required tasks and unless accommodations are not possible).

Unfortunately, the law is often broken with the result that many people suffer the impact of discrimination. Some people don't report violations, fearing reprisals. Others aren't aware that discrimination has occurred or that there are laws to protect them from its consequences.

The many faces of prejudice and discrimination are showing up on college campuses. Students may not want to work with students of other races. Members of campus clubs may reject prospective members because of their religion. Outsiders may harass students attending gay and lesbian alliance meetings. Students may find that instructors judge their abilities and attitudes according to their gender, weight, or body piercings. Actions like these block mutual understanding and respect and can derail you from the pursuit of knowledge, which is at the heart of education.

Your example: Have you personally witnessed discriminatory acts at your school or been a victim of discrimination? If so, briefly describe what happened.

_____

_____

_____

Hate Crimes: The Awful Consequences of Prejudice

When prejudice turns violent and ugly, it often manifests itself in hate crimes directed at racial, ethnic, and religious minorities and homosexuals:

> HATE CRIME
>
> A crime motivated by a hatred of a specific characteristic thought to be possessed by the victim.

- In Wyoming in 1998, Matthew Shepard, a gay college student, was kidnapped and tied to a fence where his captors beat and abandoned him. He died of his injuries.

- In 1999, Eric Harris and Dylan Klebold opened fire in Columbine High School in Littleton, Colorado, killing 12 students and one teacher and wounding others. Their writings revealed their desire to harm minorities, athletes, and others different from them.

- In 1999, Buford O. Furrow entered the North Valley Jewish Community Center near Los Angeles, California, and shot three preschool children and two adults because they were Jewish. He then shot and killed a Filipino-American letter carrier.

The increase in hate crimes in recent years—particularly the substantial rise of these crimes on college campuses—is alarming. According to the latest statistics compiled by the U.S. Department of Education, campus hate crimes increased from 1,312 in 1997 to 2,067 in 1999, with more than 90 percent of the offenses involving assaults.[4]

The increase is linked, in part, to the Internet, which has given a "safe haven" to groups that espouse hate. The Internet gives hate-filled individuals a platform to express their racism, anti-Semitism, homophobia (hatred of gays), misogyny (hatred of women), and other prejudices. Some sites even promote prejudices to children through games and other interactive formats.

Your experience: Are you familiar with Internet sites that preach hate? Why do you think people visit these sites?

_____

_____

_____

Be Part of the Solution

As you know from Chapter 4, the best and most lasting solutions come when you address the causes rather than the effects of behavior. Therefore, the best way to fight discrimination and hate crimes is to work to eliminate prejudice.

Start with Yourself

If you can gradually broaden your horizons, you will benefit immensely—and so will the world. *Think critically about any prejudices you have.* Ask yourself: Am I prejudiced against any group or groups? How did I develop this prejudice? How does it affect me and others? How can I change the way I think?

Dr. Martin Luther King, Jr. believed in the power of critical thinking to change ingrained attitudes. He said:

> The tough-minded person always examines the facts before he reaches conclusions: in short, he postjudges. The tender-minded person reaches conclusions before he has examined the first fact; in short, he prejudges and is prejudiced. . . . There is little hope for us until we become tough minded enough to break loose from the shackles of prejudice, half-truths, and down-right ignorance.[5]

As you think critically, realize that the opinions of family, friends, and the media may sometimes lead you to adopt attitudes that you haven't thought through. Think about the attitudes you *want* to hold and make choices that are right for you and fair to others.

Try to avoid judgments based on external characteristics. If you meet a woman in a wheelchair, try not to define her only in terms of her disability. Rather, make the effort to learn who she really is. She may be an accounting major, a daughter, and a mother. She may love baseball, politics, and science fiction novels. These characteristics—not her wheelchair—describe who she is.

Cultivate relationships with people of different cultures, races, perspectives, and ages. Through personal experience and reading, find out how other people live and think, and see what you can learn from them. Then, take concrete actions: Choose a study partner from a different ethnic or racial background. Go to synagogue with a Jewish friend; go to a mosque with a Muslim friend. If you are uncomfortable doing this, start by respecting people who are different from you and allowing them to live peacefully and privately.

Explore who you are. Learn about your personal ethnic and cultural heritage by talking with family and reading. Then, share your knowledge with others.

Learn from history. Read about the atrocities of slavery, the Holocaust, and the "ethnic cleansing" in Kosovo. Cherish your freedom and seek continual improvement at home and in the world.

Be sensitive to the needs of others. Ask yourself what you would feel and do if you were in another person's shoes.

Help others in need. Newspaper columnist Sheryl McCarthy wrote about an African-American who, in the midst of the 1992 Los Angeles riots, saw an Asian-American man being beaten and helped him to safety: "When asked why he risked grievous harm to save an Asian man he didn't even know, the African-American man said, 'Because if I'm not there to help someone else, when the mob comes for me, will there be someone there to save me?'"[6] Continue the cycle of kindness.

Take personal responsibility. Avoid blaming problems on people who are different from you.

Recognize that people everywhere have the same basic needs. Everyone loves, thinks, hurts, hopes, fears, and plans. Strive to find out what is special about others instead of how they fit your preconceived idea of who they are. People are united through their essential humanity.

Encountering Others Who Are Prejudiced

What should you do when someone you know makes prejudiced remarks or takes actions that discriminate against you or others? It can be hard to stand up to someone and risk a confrontation, even though right—and the law—are on your side. You may choose to say nothing, make a small comment, or get help. If you approach an authority, start with the person who can most directly affect the situation—an instructor or supervisor. At each decision stage, weigh all of the positive and negative effects that are possible as a result of your action and evaluate whether the action is wise for you and others.

It is everyone's responsibility to sound the alarm on hate crimes. Let the authorities know if you suspect that a crime is about to occur. Join campus protests. Express your opinion by writing letters to the editor of your school newspaper and attend lectures sponsored by the Anti-Defamation League and other organizations that encourage acceptance and tolerance.

How can minority students
make the most of college?

W ho fits into the category of "minority student" at your school? The term *minority* includes students of color; students who are not part of the majority Christian religions; and gay, lesbian, and bisexual students. However, even for members of these groups, there is no universal "minority" experience. Each person's experiences are filtered through the lens of his or her background.

Most colleges have special organizations and support services that center on minority groups. Among these are specialized student associations, cultural centers, arts groups with a minority focus, residence halls for minority students, minority fraternities and sororities, and political-action groups. Your level of involvement with these groups depends on whether you are comfortable within a community of students who share your background or whether you want to extend your social connections.

Define Your Experience

When you start school and know no one, it's natural to gravitate to people with whom you share common ground. You may choose to live with a roommate from the same background, sit next to other minority students in class, and attend minority-related social events and parties. However, if you define your *entire* college experience by these ties, you may be making a choice that limits your understanding of others, thereby limiting your opportunities for growth.

Many minority students adopt a balanced approach, involving themselves in activities with members of their group, as well as with the college mainstream. For example, a student may be a member of the African-American Students Association and also join clubs for all students such as the campus newspaper or an athletic team. Such students believe that both worlds have much to offer.

To make choices as a minority student on campus, ask yourself these questions:

- Do I want to limit, as much as possible, my social interactions to people who share my background? How much time do I want to spend pursuing minority-related activities? Do I want to focus my studies on a minority-related field, such as African-American studies?

- Do I want to minimize my ties with my minority group and be "just another student"? Will I care if other minority students criticize my choices?

- Do I want to achieve a balance in which I spend part of my time among people who share my background and part with students from other groups?

You may feel pressured to make certain choices based on what your peers do—but if these decisions go against your gut feelings, they are almost always a mistake. Your choice should be right for you, especially because it will determine your college experiences. Plus, the attitudes and habits you develop now may have implications for the rest of your life—in your choice of friends, where you decide to live, your work, and even your family. Think long and hard about the path you take, and always follow your head and heart.

Understand Stereotype Vulnerability

Some minority students deal with the adjustment to college by distancing themselves from the qualities they think others associate with their group. In this phenomenon, called *stereotype vulnerability,* students avoid facing a problem because they think that admitting it perpetuates a group stereotype.[7] For example, an immigrant to the United States may resist tutoring in English for fear of seeming like just another foreigner. Such avoidance cuts people off from assistance and communication that could connect them with others and improve their lives.

In another side of stereotype vulnerability, people refuse help because they believe that these offerings are motivated by pity: "She considers me disadvantaged because I'm from Taiwan"; "He feels sorry for me because of my learning disability." These defensive responses are based on assumptions about what the other person is thinking. Frequently, the person who offers help has the honest desire to aid another human being.

If you see stereotype vulnerability in yourself, you may be trying to deny who you are in an attempt to fit into the larger culture. This inevitably brings trouble because the task you have set out to accomplish is impossible. Instead, if you need help, approach someone who can give it and allow that person to get to know you. The helper will see you not as a representative of a group but as an individual.

"I have a dream that one day on the red hills of Georgia the sons of former slaves and the sons of former slave owners will be able to sit down together at the table of brotherhood."

MARTIN LUTHER KING, JR.

The concept of diversity examined so far in this chapter has focused on the need to accept and embrace the multiculturalism that defines the United States and students' experiences in college. However, some forms of diversity are more subtle, including differences in the way people communicate. While one person may be direct and disorganized, another may be analytic and organized, and a third may hardly say a word. Just as there is diversity in skin color and ethnicity, there is also diversity in the way people communicate.

Accepting diversity includes accepting differences in communication style and working to understand them. This is especially important because successful relationships depend on effective communication. If you strive to express yourself clearly and interpret what others say in the way they intend, you can connect with people in all aspects of your life.

How can you *communicate* effectively?

C lear spoken communication promotes success at school, at work, and in your personal relationships. Clarity comes from understanding communication styles, learning to give and receive criticism, becoming knowledgeable about body language, and developing techniques to solve specific communication problems.

Adjusting to Communication Styles

When you speak, your goal is for listeners to receive the message as you intended. Problems arise when one person has trouble "translating" a message that comes from someone with a different style of communication.

Your knowledge of the Personality Spectrum (see Chapter 2) will help you understand different styles of communication. Particular communication styles tend to accompany dominance in particular dimensions. Recognizing specific styles in yourself and others will help you communicate more effectively.

Identifying Your Styles

Following are some communication styles that tend to be associated with the four dimensions in the Personality Spectrum. No one style is better than another. Successful communication depends on understanding your personal style and becoming attuned to the styles of others.

Thinker-dominant communicators focus on facts and logic. As speakers, they tend to rely on logic to communicate ideas and prefer quantitative concepts to those that are conceptual or emotional. As listeners, they often do best with logical messages. They may also need time to process what they have heard before responding. Written messages—on paper or via e-mail—are often useful because writing can allow for time to put ideas together logically.

Organizer-dominant communicators focus on structure and completeness. As speakers, they tend to deliver well-thought-out, structured messages that fit into an organized plan. As listeners, they often appreciate a well-organized message that has tasks defined in clear, concrete terms. As with Thinkers, a written format is often an effective form of communication to or from an Organizer.

Giver-dominant communicators focus on concern for others. As speakers, they tend to cultivate harmony and work toward closeness in their relationships. As listeners, they often appreciate messages that emphasize personal connection and address the emotional side of the issue. Whether speaking or listening, they often favor direct, in-person interaction over written messages.

Adventurer-dominant communicators focus on the present. As speakers, they tend to convey a message as soon as the idea arises and then move on to the next activity. As listeners, they appreciate up-front, short, direct messages that don't get sidetracked. Like Givers, they tend to communicate and listen more effectively in person.

Use this information not as a label but as a jumping-off point for your self-exploration. Just as people tend to demonstrate characteristics from more than one Personality Spectrum dimension, communicators may demonstrate different styles. Think about the communication styles associated with your dominant Personality Spectrum dimensions. Consider, too, how you tend to communicate and how others generally respond to you. Are you convinced only in the face of logical arguments? Are you attuned most to feelings? Use what you discover to get a better idea of what works best for you.

Speakers Adjust to Listeners

Listeners may interpret messages in ways you never intended. Think about how you can address this problem as you read the following example involving a Giver-dominant instructor and a Thinker-dominant student (the listener):

> Instructor: "Your essay didn't communicate any sense of your personal voice."
>
> Student: "What do you mean? I spent hours writing it. I thought it was on the mark."

- *Without adjustment:* The instructor ignores the student's need for detail and continues to generalize. Comments like, "You need to elaborate. Try writing from the heart. You're not considering your audience," will probably confuse and discourage the student.

- *With adjustment:* Greater logic and detail will help. For example, the instructor might say: "You've supported your central idea clearly, but you didn't move beyond the facts into your interpretation of what they mean. Your essay reads like a research paper. The language doesn't sound like it is coming directly from you."

Listeners Adjust to Speakers

As a listener, you can improve understanding by being aware of stylistic differences and translating the message into one that makes sense to you. The following example of an Adventurer-dominant employee speaking to an Organizer-dominant supervisor shows how adjusting can pay off.

> Employee: "I'm upset about the e-mail you sent me. You never talked to me and just let the problem build into a crisis. I don't feel I've had a chance to defend myself."

- *Without adjustment:* If the supervisor is annoyed by the employee's insistence on direct personal contact, he or she may become defensive: "I told you clearly what needs to be done, and my language wasn't a problem. I don't know what else there is to discuss."

- *With adjustment:* In an effort to improve communication, the supervisor responds by encouraging the in-person, real-time exchange that is best for the employee. "Let's meet after lunch so you can explain to me how we can improve the situation."

Using techniques corresponding to your stronger intelligences boosts your communication skills both as a speaker and as a listener.

INTELLIGENCE	SUGGESTED STRATEGIES	WHAT WORKS FOR YOU? WRITE NEW IDEAS HERE
Verbal–Linguistic	■ Find opportunities to express your thoughts and feelings to others—either in writing or in person. ■ Remind yourself that you have two ears and only one mouth. Listening is more important than talking.	
Logical–Mathematical	■ Allow yourself time to think through solutions before discussing them—try writing out a logical argument on paper and then rehearsing it orally. ■ Accept the fact that others may have communication styles that vary from yours and that may not seem logical.	
Bodily–Kinesthetic	■ Have an important talk while walking or performing a task that does not involve concentration. ■ Work out physically to burn off excess energy before having an important discussion.	
Visual–Spatial	■ Make a drawing or diagram of points you want to communicate during an important discussion. ■ If your communication is in a formal classroom or work setting, use visual aids to explain your main points.	
Interpersonal	■ Observe how you communicate with friends. If you tend to dominate the conversation, brainstorm ideas about how to communicate more effectively. ■ Remember to balance speaking with listening.	
Intrapersonal	■ When you have a difficult encounter, take time alone to evaluate what happened and to decide how you can communicate more effectively next time. ■ Remember that, in order for others to understand clearly, you may need to communicate more than you expect to.	
Musical	■ Play soft music during an important discussion if it helps you, making sure it isn't distracting to the others involved.	
Naturalistic	■ Communicate outdoors if that is agreeable to all parties. ■ If you have a difficult exchange, imagine how you might have responded differently had it taken place outdoors.	

Although adjusting to communication styles helps you speak and listen more effectively, you also need to understand the nature of criticism and learn to handle criticism as a speaker and listener.

Constructive and Nonconstructive Criticism

CONSTRUCTIVE

Promoting improvement or development.

Criticism can be either constructive or nonconstructive. *Constructive criticism* involves goodwill suggestions for improvement, promoting the hope that things will be better. In contrast, *nonconstructive criticism* focuses on what went wrong, doesn't offer alternatives or help, and is often delivered negatively, creating bad feelings and defensiveness.

Consider a case in which someone has continually been late to study group sessions. The group leader can comment in either of these ways:

- *Constructive.* The group leader talks privately with the student: "I've noticed that you've been late a lot. Because our success depends on what each of us contributes, we are all depending on your contribution. Is there a problem that is keeping you from being on time? Can we help?"

- *Nonconstructive.* The leader watches the student arrive late and says, in front of everyone, "Nice to see you could make it. If you can't start getting here on time, we might look for someone else who can."

Which comment would encourage you to change your behavior? When offered constructively and carefully, criticism can help bring about important changes.

While at school, your instructors will constructively criticize your class work, papers, and exams. On the job, constructive criticism comes primarily from supervisors and coworkers. No matter the source, positive comments can help you grow as a person. Be open to what you hear, and always remember that most people want to help you succeed.

Offering Constructive Criticism

When offering constructive criticism, use the following strategies to be effective:

- *Criticize the behavior rather than the person.* Avoid personal attacks—they inevitably result in defensive behavior. In addition, make sure that a behavior is within a person's power to change. Chronic lateness can be changed if the person has poor time-management skills; it can't be changed if a physical disability slows the person down.

- *Define specifically the behavior that bothers you.* Focus on the facts. Substantiate with specific examples and avoid emotions. Avoid dragging in other complaints. People can hear criticisms better if they are discussed one at a time.

- *Suggest new approaches.* Talk about different ways of handling the situation. Help the person see options he or she may have never considered.

- *Use a positive approach and hopeful language.* Express the conviction that changes will occur and that the person can turn the situation around.

- *Stay calm and be brief.* Avoid threats, ultimatums, or accusations. Use "I" messages that help the person see how his or her actions are affecting you.
- *Offer help in changing the behavior.* Do what you can to make the person feel supported.

Receiving Criticism

When you find yourself on criticism's receiving end, use the following techniques:

- *Use critical thinking to analyze the comments.* Listen carefully, and then carefully evaluate what you heard. Does it come from a desire to help or from jealousy or frustration? Try to let nonconstructive comments go without responding.
- *If the feedback is constructive, ask for suggestions on how to change your behavior.* Ask, "How would you like me to handle this in the future?"
- *Summarize the criticism and your response to it.* Make sure everyone understands the situation in the same way.
- *Plan a specific strategy.* Decide how to change and take concrete steps to make it happen.

Criticism, as well as other thoughts and feelings, may be communicated through nonverbal communication. You will become a more effective communicator if you understand what body language may be saying.

The Role of Body Language

Considered by many to be the most "honest" form of communication because of its capacity to express people's real feelings, body language often reveals a great deal though gestures, eye movements, facial expressions, body positioning and posture, touching behaviors, vocal tone, and use of personal space. Although reading body language is far from an exact science, understanding its basics will help you use it to your advantage as you speak and listen.

Figure 8.3 shows examples of body language that are associated with specific meanings in our culture. Keep in mind that culture influences how body language is interpreted. For example, in the United States, looking away from someone may be a sign of anger or distress; in Japan, the same behavior is usually a sign of respect.

How Body Language Works

Here are some important principles of body language.

Nonverbal communication strongly influences first impressions. First impressions emerge from a combination of verbal and nonverbal cues. Nonverbal elements, including tone of voice, posture, eye contact, and speed and style of movement, usually come across first and strongest.

Figure 8.3 | Body language provides possible communication clues.

Firm handshake:
capability, friendliness

Body turned away:
lack of interest

Hands on hips:
readiness, toughness

Open sitting posture:
interest or agreement

Body language can reinforce or contradict verbal statements. When you greet a friend with a smile and a strong handshake, your body language reinforces your words of welcome. When, on the other hand, your body language contradicts your words, your body generally tells the real story. For example, if right before finals a friend asks how you feel, a response of "fine" is confusing if your arms are folded tightly across your chest and your eyes are averted. These cues communicate tension, not well-being.

Nonverbal cues shade meaning. The statement, *"This is the best idea I've heard all day,"* can mean different things depending on vocal tone. Said sarcastically, the words may mean that the speaker considers the idea a joke. In contrast, the same words said while sitting with your arms and legs crossed and looking away may communicate that you dislike the idea, but are unwilling to say so. Finally, if you maintain eye contact and take the receiver's hand while speaking, you may be communicating that the idea is close to your heart.

Nonverbal cues may reveal a lie. Signs that a lie is being told include behaviors that end as soon as the lie ends (the speaker stops fidgeting, averting her glance, or licking her lips), unusual vocal qualities (changes in vocal tone and sentence structure), and jabbering (an unconscious attempt to hide a lie in a load of information).

Using Body Language to Your Advantage

The following strategies will help you maximize your awareness of body language so that you can use it—as a speaker and a listener—to your advantage.

Become aware. Pay attention to what other people are really saying through their nonverbal cues and to what you communicate through your own cues.

Match your words with your body language. Try to monitor your personal body language when you deliver important messages. For example, if you really want to communicate satisfaction to an instructor, look the instructor in the eye and speak enthusiastically.

Note cultural differences. Cultural factors influence how nonverbal cues are interpreted. For example, in Arab cultures, causal acquaintances stand close together when speaking, while in the United States, the same distance is reserved for intimate conversation. Similarly, in the United States, people get right down to business in meetings, while in Asian cultures, business is preceded by personal conversation that builds trust and relationships.[8] With any cross-cultural conversation, you can discover what seems appropriate by paying attention to what the other person does on a consistent basis.

No matter how much you know about verbal and nonverbal communication, you will still encounter communication problems. Here are strategies for solving some common ones.

Solving Communication Problems

Although every communication situation is different, many communication problems have common threads that are easy to identify. As you study the problems described next, think about whether you are "guilty" of any of them. If you are, try applying these strategic fixes.

Problem: Being too passive or aggressive in the way you communicate.
Solution: Take the middle ground. Be assertive.

No matter what your dominant learning styles, you tend to express yourself in one of three ways—through *aggressive, passive,* and *assertive communication.* The assertive style will help you communicate in the clearest, most productive way. Assertive communicators are likely to get their message across without attacking others or sacrificing their own needs, while still giving listeners the opportunity to speak.

By contrast, aggressive communicators focus primarily on their own needs. They can become angry and impatient when those needs are not immediately satisfied. Passive communicators deny themselves power by focusing almost exclusively on the needs of others, often experiencing unexpressed frustration and tension in the process.

Table 8.3 compares the characteristics of these communicators. Assertive behavior strikes a balance between aggression and passivity.

To become more assertive, aggressive communicators should take time before speaking, use "I" statements that accept personal responsibility, listen to others, and avoid giving orders. Similarly, passive

ASSERTIVE

Able to declare and affirm one's own opinions while respecting the rights of others to do the same.

Table 8.3　Assertiveness fosters clear communication.

AGGRESSIVE	PASSIVE	ASSERTIVE
Loud, heated arguing	Concealing one's own feelings	Expressing feelings without being nasty or overbearing
Physically violent encounters	Denying one's own anger	Acknowledging emotions but staying open to discussion
Blaming, name-calling, and verbal insults	Feeling that one has no right to express anger	Expressing oneself and giving others the chance to express themselves equally
Walking out of arguments before they are resolved	Avoiding arguments	Using "I" statements to defuse arguments
Being demanding: "Do this"	Being noncommittal: "You don't have to do this unless you really want to . . ."	Asking and giving reasons: "I would appreciate it if you would do this, and here's why . . ."

communicators who want to become more assertive might try to acknowledge anger or hurt, express opinions, exercise their right to make requests, and know that their ideas and feelings are important.

Problem: Attacking the receiver.
Solution: Send "I" messages.

When a conflict arises, often the first instinct is to pinpoint what someone else did wrong. Unfortunately, accusations put others on the defensive as they shut down communication.

"I" messages help you communicate your needs rather than attacking someone else. Creating these messages involves nothing more than some simple rephrasing: "You didn't lock the door!" becomes "I felt uneasy when I came to work and the door was unlocked." Similarly, "You never called last night" becomes "I was worried about you when I didn't hear from you last night."

"Do not use a hatchet to remove a fly from your friend's forehead."

CHINESE PROVERB

"I" statements soften the conflict by highlighting the effects that the other person's actions have on you, rather than focusing on the person or the actions themselves. When you focus on your own responses and needs, your receiver may feel freer to respond, perhaps offering help and even acknowledging mistakes.

Problem: Choosing bad times to communicate.
Solution: Be sensitive to the cues in your environment.

When you have something to say, choose a time when you can express yourself clearly. Spoken too soon, ideas can come out sounding nothing like you intended. Left simmering too long, your feelings can spill over into other issues. Rehearsing mentally or talking your thoughts through with a friend can help you choose the most effective strategy, words, and tone.

Good timing also requires sensitivity to your listener. Even a perfectly worded message won't get through to someone who isn't ready to receive it. If you try to talk to your instructor when she is rushing out the door, she won't pay attention to what you are saying. If a classmate calls to discuss a project while you are cramming for an exam, his point will be lost. Pay attention to mood as well. If a friend had an exhausting week, it's smart to wait before asking a favor.

The way you communicate has a major impact on your relationships with friends and family. Successful relationships are built on self-knowledge, good communication, and hard work.

How do you make the most of *personal* relationships?

Personal relationships with friends, classmates, spouses and partners, and parents can be sources of great satisfaction and inner peace. Relationships have the power to motivate you to do your best in school, on the job, and in life.

When things go wrong with relationships, however, nothing in your world may seem right. You may be unable to eat, sleep, or concentrate. Because of this, relationship strategies can be viewed as all-around survival strategies that add to your mental health. Sigmund Freud, the father of modern psychiatry, defined mental health as the ability to love and to work.

Use Positive Relationship Strategies

Here are some strategies for improving your personal relationships.

Make personal relationships a high priority. Life is meant to be shared. In some marriage ceremonies, the bride and groom share a cup of wine, symbolizing that the sweetness of life is doubled by tasting it together and the bitterness is cut in half when shared by two.

Invest time. You devote time to education, work, and sports. Relationships benefit from the same investment. In addition, spending time with people you like can relieve stress.

Spend time with people you respect and admire. Life is too short to hang out with people who bring you down or encourage you to do things that go against your values. Develop relationships with people whose choices you admire and who inspire you to fulfill your potential.

If you want a friend, be a friend. If you treat others with the kind of loyalty and support that you appreciate yourself, you are likely to receive the same in return.

Work through tensions. Negative feelings can fester when left unspoken. Instead of facing a problem, you may become angry about something else or irritable in general. Get to the root of a problem by discussing it, compromising, forgiving, and moving on.

Take risks. It can be frightening to reveal your deepest dreams and frustrations, to devote yourself to a friend, or to fall in love. However, if you open yourself up, you stand to gain the incredible benefits of companionship, which for most people outweigh the risks.

Don't force yourself into a pattern that doesn't suit you. Some students date exclusively and commit early. Some students prefer to socialize in groups. Some students date casually. Be honest with yourself—and others—about what you want in a relationship, and don't let peer pressure change your mind.

Keep personal problems in their place. Try to separate your problems from your schoolwork. Mixing the two may hurt your performance, while doing nothing to solve your problem.

If a relationship fails, find ways to cope. When an important relationship becomes strained or breaks up, use coping strategies to help you move on. Some people need time alone; others need to be with friends and family. Some seek counseling. Some throw their energy into school or exercise. Some cry. Whatever you do, believe that in time you will emerge from the experience stronger.

PERSONAL TRIUMPH

making a connection with others can be difficult, especially if you start out feeling exceptionally different. Gustavo Minaya spoke no English when he came to a completely unfamiliar United States as a child. Through learning and getting involved in activities, he has found his niche.

I am native of Peru. When I was six years old, my mother told me that we were going to America for a better life. My father was already living in the United States, so my mother went to the embassy to apply for a visa, but our visa was denied. In desperation, she decided to hire "coyotes." These are people who know secret routes to the United States. Their job was to help us cross the border.

Our journey began at night with cold train rides. At different points, we stopped to eat or to get on a different train. Along the way, other families joined us. At the Mexico–Texas border, the "coyotes" instructed us to walk under a highway. Once we were out again in the open, everyone began running for the U.S. border. Helicopters were circling overhead with their search lights on, and people were shouting. It was pandemonium.

Exhausted, we made it across the border and onto a van, where people were stacked on top of each other. At another border check, my mother and I were arrested and taken into custody by immigration officers who took our fingerprints. They arranged to have us transported to an emergency shelter run by the American Red Cross. Meanwhile, my Dad completed the paperwork for legal immigration, and we joined him a few months later.

Of course, I didn't know English. When I started school in the second grade, I looked different than the other kids, and I sounded different because of my accent. Some of the kids picked on me. I cried a lot back then. The next year, I took English as a Second Language (ESL) classes. Gradually, I learned English and began to feel like I fit in.

Gustavo Minaya, Freshman, Business Administration; Community College of Baltimore County—Essex Campus

When I look back over my experiences, I believe the one thing that has helped me adjust to the changes is friendliness. I like to make people laugh, and I go into things with a positive attitude. Being friendly with other students, and people in general, has helped me gain a sense of belonging.

My main advice to international students who want to make the most of their education is to participate in campus activities. You can join a club or work on campus, maybe at the school store or library. This way you meet new people, and you'll learn English faster. You can't fit in if you isolate yourself.

Participation is also important for developing leadership skills. I look at clubs and other campus activities as opportunities to enhance my education. For example, I joined the International Student Association (ISA) and am now the president. During the meetings, I give my ideas and show my support by volunteering for projects. I've discovered that one of my strengths is bringing people together for a good cause.

I'm very proud of my parents for how hard they worked to make a better life for me and my brothers and sisters. In my native country of Peru, you can work as hard as you want, but it gets you nowhere. Some of the smartest people there are taxicab drivers because they can't find jobs doing anything else. Here, if you are willing to work, you can have a profession and achieve what you want. I plan to achieve as much as I can.

Take a moment to consider . . .

- *What important opportunity you feel that living in this country offers you, whether you are an immigrant or native-born.*

- *How you plan to "gain a sense of belonging" at your school.*

Choose Communities That Enhance Your Life

Personal relationships often take place in the context of communities, or groups, that include people who share your interests—for example, martial arts groups, bridge clubs, sororities, fraternities, athletic teams, and political groups. It is common to have ties to several communities, often with one holding your greatest interest.

Try to affiliate with communities that are involved in life-affirming activities. You will surround yourself with people who are responsible and character-rich and who may be your friends and professional colleagues for the rest of your life. You may find among them your future husband, wife, or partner; best friend; the person who helps you land your first job; your doctor, accountant, real estate agent, and so on. So much of what you accomplish in life is linked to your network of personal contacts, so start now to make positive connections.

If you find yourself drawn toward communities that are negative and even harmful, such as groups that haze pledges or gangs, stop and think before you get in too deep. Be aware of cliques that bring out negative qualities including aggression, hate, and superiority. Use critical thinking to analyze why you are drawn to these groups. In many people, fears and insecurities spur these relationships. Look into yourself to understand the attraction and to resist the temptation to join. If you are already involved and want out, believe in yourself and be determined. Never consider yourself a "victim."

The biggest threat to personal relationships is conflict, which can result in anger and even violence. With effort, you can manage conflict successfully—and stay away from those who cannot.

How can you handle *conflict?*

onflicts, both large and small, arise when there is a clash of ideas or interests. You may have small conflicts with a housemate over a door left unlocked or a sink filled with dirty dishes. You may have major conflicts with your partner about finances or with an instructor about a failing grade. Conflict, as unpleasant as it can be, is a natural element in the dynamic of getting along with others. No relationship is conflict free.

Conflict Resolution Strategies

When handled poorly, conflicts create anger and frustration. All too often, people deal with these negative feelings through avoidance (a passive tactic that shuts down communication) or escalation (an aggressive tactic that often leads to fighting). Avoidance doesn't make the problem go away—in fact, it often makes things worse—and a shouting match destroys the opportunity to problem solve.

Conflict resolution strategies use calm communication and critical thinking to avoid extreme reactions. Think through the conflicts in your relationships by using what you know about problem solving (see Chapter 4):

1. *Identify and analyze the problem.* Determine the severity of the problem by looking at its effects on everyone involved. Then, find and analyze its causes.

2. *Brainstorm possible solutions.* Consider as many angles as you can, without judgment. Try to apply what you did in similar situations.

3. *Explore each solution.* Evaluate each solution, including its possible benefits and risks. Look at options from the perspective of others as you try to determine which would cause the least stress. Make sure everyone has a chance to express an opinion.

4. *Choose, carry out, and evaluate the solution you decide is best.* Translate the solution into actions, and then evaluate what happens. Decide whether you made the best choice, and make mid-course corrections, if necessary.

Your efforts to resolve conflict will work only if you begin with good will and motivation. Also needed is a determination to focus on the problem rather than on placing blame. All people get angry at times—at people, events, and themselves. However, excessive anger—out-of-control, loud, irrational, and sometimes physical—has the power to contaminate relationships, stifle communication, and turn friends and family away.

Managing Anger

People who continually respond to disappointments and frustrations by shouting, cursing, or even physically lashing out find that emotions get in the way of personal happiness and school success. It is hard to concentrate on American history when you are raging over being cut off in traffic. It is hard to focus during a study group if you can't let go of your anger with a group member who forgot a book.

For years, psychologists believed that venting your anger—letting it all hang out—would help you deal with your feelings even if you hurt others in the process. They now realize that instead of helping, bouts of uncontrolled rage intensify your aggression as you increasingly lose control. Angry outbursts do nothing to resolve problems and may actually make things worse.

What can you do when you feel yourself losing control or when anger turns into rage that you just can't drop? First, remember that it doesn't help to explode. Then, try one of these anger-management techniques until you calm down.

Relax. Calm down by breathing deeply while slowly repeating a calming word or phrase, such as "Take it easy" or "It's just not worth it" or "Relax."

Try to change the way you process what is happening. Instead of reacting to the frustration of being closed out of a course by cursing and yelling, change the way you think. Say to yourself, "I'm frustrated and upset, but it's not the end of the world. I'll talk to my advisor about taking the course next semester. And besides, getting angry is not going to get me a seat in the class."

Change your environment. Take a walk, go to the gym, see a movie. Take a break from what's upsetting you. Try to build break time into your daily schedule. You'll decompress from the pressures of school and be better able to handle problems without blowing up.

Change your language. Language can inflame anger, so turn your language down a notch. Instead of barking orders to your lab partner, such as "Hand me the flask right now or my experiment will be ruined," calmly say, "My experiment is at a crucial point. Thanks for handing me the flask as soon as you can." The person to whom you are talking is more likely to do what you ask if you stay in control.

Think before you speak. When angry, most people tend to say the first thing that comes to mind, even if it's mean. Inevitably, this escalates the hard feelings and the intensity of the argument. Instead, count to 10—slowly—if necessary, until you are in control.

Try not to be defensive. No one likes to be criticized, and it's natural to respond by fighting back. It's also self-defeating. Instead, try to hear the message that's behind the criticism. Ask questions to make sure you understand the other person's point. If you focus on the problem—and if the other person works with you—anger will take a back seat.

Do your best to solve a problem, but remember that not all problems can be solved. Analyze a challenging situation, make a plan, resolve to do your best, and begin. If you fall short, you will know you did all you could and be less likely to turn your frustration into anger.

Get help if you can't keep your anger in check. If you try these techniques and still find yourself lashing out, you may need the help of a counselor. Many schools have licensed mental health professionals available to students, but it's up to you to set up an appointment.

Anger directed primarily at women sometimes takes the form of sexual harassment. When this anger turns violent, it involves partners in destructive relationships. Anger also fuels rape, including date rape.

Sexual Harassment

The facts. Sexual harassment covers a wide range of behavior, divided into the following types:

- *Quid pro quo harassment* refers to a request for some kind of sexual favor or activity in exchange for something else. It is a kind of bribe or threat. ("If you don't do X for me, I will fail you/fire you/make your life miserable.")

- *Hostile environment harassment* indicates any situation where sexually charged remarks, behavior, or displayed items cause discomfort. Harassment of this type ranges from lewd conversation or jokes to the display of pornography.

Both men and women can be victims of sexual harassment, although the most common targets are women. Sexist attitudes can create an environment in which men feel they have the right to make statements that degrade women. Even though physical violence is not involved, the fear and mental trauma associated with harassment are harmful.

How to cope. If you feel degraded by anything that goes on at school or work, address the person who you believe is harassing you. If you are uncomfortable doing that, speak to an authority. Try to avoid assumptions—perhaps the person is unaware that the behavior is offensive. On the other hand, the person may know exactly what is going on and even enjoy your discomfort. Either way, you are entitled to ask the person to stop.

Violence in Relationships

The facts. Violent relationships among students are increasing. Here are some chilling statistics from the Corporate Alliance to End Partner Violence, a Bloomington, Illinois–based advocacy group.[9]

- One in five college students has experienced and reported at least one violent incident while dating, from being slapped to more serious violence.

- In three out of four violent relationships, problems surface after the couple has dated for a while.

- In six out of ten cases, drinking and drugs are associated with the violence.

Women in their teens and twenties, who make up the majority of women in college, are more likely to be victims of domestic violence than older women. There are a number of reasons for this, says law professor and domestic violence expert Sally Goldfarb. First, many college students accept traditional sex roles that place the woman in a subservient position. Second, when trouble occurs, students are likely to turn to friends, rather than professional counselors or the law. Third, peer pressure makes them uneasy about leaving the relationship; they would rather be abused than alone. And finally, because of their inexperience in dating, they may believe that violent relationships are "normal."[10]

How to cope. Start by recognizing the warning signs of impending violence including possessive, jealous, and controlling behavior; unpredictable mood swings; personality changes associated with alcohol and drugs; and outbursts of anger. If you see a sign, think about ending the relationship.

If you are being abused, your safety and sanity depend on seeking help. Call a shelter or abuse hotline and talk to someone who understands. Seek counseling at your school or at a community center. If you need medical attention, go to a clinic or hospital emergency room. If you believe that your life is in danger, get out. Then, get a restraining order that requires your abuser to stay away from you.

Rape and Date Rape

The facts. Any intercourse or anal or oral penetration by a person against another person's will is defined as rape. Rape is primarily a controlling, violent act of rage, not a sexual act.

Rape, especially acquaintance rape or date rape, is a problem on many campuses. Any sexual activity during a date that is against one partner's will constitutes date rape, including situations where one partner is too drunk or drugged to give consent. Currently appearing on campuses is a drug called Rohypnol, known as Roofies, that is sometimes used by date rapists to sedate their victims and is difficult to detect in a drink.

Campus Advocates for Rape Education (C.A.R.E.), an organization at Wheaton College, describes the collateral damage caused by date rape. "One's trust in a friend, date, or acquaintance is violated. As a result, a victim's fear, self-blame, guilt, and shame are magnified because the assailant is known."[11]

How to cope. Beware of questionable situations or drinks when on a date with someone you don't know well or who you suspect is unstable or angry. If you are raped, get medical attention immediately. Don't shower or change clothes; doing so destroys evidence. Next, talk to a close friend or counselor. Consider reporting the incident to the police or to campus officials, if it occurred on campus. Finally, consider pressing charges, especially if you can identify your assailant. Whether or not you take legal action, continue to get help through counseling, a rape survivor group, or a hot line.

DATE RAPE

Sexual assault perpetrated by the victim's escort during an arranged social encounter.

kente

The African word *kente* means "that which will not tear under any condition." *Kente* cloth is worn by men and women in African countries such as Ghana, Ivory Coast, and Togo. There are many brightly colored patterns of *kente,* each beautiful, unique, and special.

Think of how this concept applies to people. Like the cloth, all people are unique, with brilliant and subdued aspects. Despite mistreatment or misunderstanding by others, you need to remain strong so that you don't tear, allowing the weaker fibers of your character to show through. The *kente* of your character can help you endure, stand up against injustice, and fight peacefully, but relentlessly, for the rights of all people.

Building Skills
FOR COLLEGE, CAREER, AND LIFE SUCCESS

The Big Picture   *Combining Thinking, Strategy, and Teamwork*

Diversity Discovery

Express your own personal diversity. Describe yourself in response to the
following questions:

How would you identify yourself? Write words or short phrases that
describe you.

_____

_____

_____

Name one or more facts about yourself that would not be obvious to
someone who just met you.

_____

_____

_____

Name two values or beliefs that govern how you live, what you pursue,
or with whom you associate.

_____

_____

_____

Describe a particular choice you have made that tells something about
who you are.

_____

_____

_____

Now, join with a partner in your class. Choose someone you don't know well. Your goal is to communicate what you have written to your partner and for your partner to communicate to you in the same way. Talk to each other for 10 minutes, and take notes on what the other person says. At the end of that period, join together as a class. Each person will describe his or her partner to the class.

Name something you learned about your partner that intrigued and even surprised you.

_____

_____

_____

What did you learn that went against any assumptions you may have made about that person?

_____

_____

_____

Working on your own, look back at the communication styles on pages 241–242. Write the two styles that fit you best.

1. _____

2. _____

Of these two styles, which one has more positive effects on your ability to communicate? What are those effects?

_____

_____

_____

Which style has more negative effects?

_____

_____

_____

Think through, and briefly describe, a strategy that will help you improve your communication skills by minimizing those negative effects.

_____

_____

_____

Writing *Discovery Through Journaling*

To record your thoughts, use a separate journal or the lined page at the end of the chapter.

NEW PERSPECTIVE.[12] Imagine that you must change either your gender or your racial/ethnic group. Which would you change and why? What do you anticipate would be the positive and negative effects of the change—in your social life, in your family life, on the job, and at school?

Career Portfolio *Charting Your Course*

COMPILING A RÉSUMÉ. What you have accomplished in various work and school situations will be important for you to emphasize as you strive to land a job that is right for you. Whether on the job, in school, in the community, or at home, your roles help you gain knowledge and experience.

Use two pieces of paper. On one, list your education and skills information. On the other, list job experience. For each job, record job title, the dates of employment, and the tasks that this job entailed (if the job had no particular title, come up with one yourself). Be as detailed as possible—it's best to write down everything you remember. When you compile your résumé, you can make this material more concise. Keep this list current by adding experiences and accomplishments as you go along.

Using the information you have gathered and Figure 8.4 as your guide, draft a résumé for yourself. Remember that there are many ways to construct a résumé; consult other resources, such as those listed in the bibliography, for different styles. You may want to reformat your résumé according to a style that your career counselor or instructor recommends, that best suits the career area you plan to enter, or that you like best.

Keep your résumé draft on hand—and on a computer disk. When you need to submit a résumé with a job application, update the draft and print it out on high-quality paper.

Here are some general tips for writing a résumé:

- Always put your name and contact information at the top. Make it stand out.

- State an objective if it is appropriate—if your focus is specific or you are designing this résumé for a particular interview or career area.

- List your post-secondary education, starting from the latest and working backward. This may include summer school, night school, seminars, and accreditations.

- List jobs in reverse chronological order (most recent job first). Include all types of work experience (full-time, part-time, volunteer, internship, and so on).

Figure 8.4   Sample résumé.

Désirée Williams

237 Custer Street, San Francisco, CA 92017 • 650/555-5252 (w) or 415/555-7865 (h) • fax: 707/555-2735 • e-mail: desiree@zzz.com

EDUCATION

2000 to present   San Francisco State University, San Francisco, CA

Pursuing a B.A. in the Spanish BCLAD (Bilingual, Cross-Cultural Language Acquisition Development) Education and Multiple Subject Credential Program. Expected graduation: June, 2004

PROFESSIONAL EMPLOYMENT

10/01 to present   **Research Assistant, Knowledge Media Lab**

Developing ways for teachers to exhibit their inquiry into their practice of teaching in an online, collaborative, multimedia environment.

5/00 to present   **Webmaster/Web Designer**

Worked in various capacities at QuakeNet, an Internet Service Provider and Web Commerce Specialist in San Mateo, CA. Designed several sites for the University of California, Berkeley, Graduate School of Education, as well as private clients such as A Body of Work and Yoga Forever.

9/00 to 6/01   **Literacy Coordinator**

Coordinated, advised, and created literacy curriculum for an America Reads literacy project at Prescott School in West Oakland. Worked with non-reader 4th graders on writing and publishing, incorporating digital photography, Internet resources, and graphic design.

8/00   **Bilingual Educational Consultant**

Consulted for Children's Television Workshop, field-testing bilingual materials. With a research team, designed bilingual educational materials for an ecotourism project run by an indigenous rain forest community in Ecuador.

10/99 to 6/00   **Technology Consultant**

Worked with 24 Hours in Cyberspace, an on-line worldwide photojournalism event. Coordinated participation of schools, translated documents, and facilitated public relations.

SKILLS

Languages: Fluent in Spanish.

Proficient in Italian and Shona (majority language of Zimbabwe).

Computer: Programming ability in HTML, Javascript, Pascal, and Lisp. Multimedia design expertise in Adobe Photoshop, Netobjects Fusion, Adobe Premiere, Macromedia Flash, and many other visual design programs.

Personal: Perform professionally in Mary Schmary, a women's a cappella quartet. Have climbed Mt. Kilimanjaro.

- When you describe your work experience, use action verbs and focus on what you have accomplished, rather than on the description of assigned tasks.

- Have references listed on a separate sheet. You may want to put "References upon request" at the bottom of your résumé.

- Use formatting (larger font sizes, different fonts, italics, bolding, and so on) and indents selectively to help the important information stand out.

- Get several people to look at your résumé before you send it out. Other readers will have ideas that you haven't thought of and may pick up errors that you have missed.

Assess Yourself *Student Success Strategies*

If you have access to the CD-ROM Strategies for Success, *use the following questions to assess your thoughts and enhance your understanding of the chapter. The questions below represent only some of the activities provided on the CD for the chapter topics—try others if you have time.*

Click on the **Relating to Others** bookmark. Use the following activities to further develop your perspective on the people with whom you interact from day to day:

1. Take the pre-assessment to get an idea of your perspective on friendships and relationships.

2. Watch the video and consider the importance of self-knowledge and openness to your relationships. In the field provided, reflect on your perception of yourself since you made the transition to college.

3. Click on **Activity One: Explore Your Cultural Background.** Answer the questions in the activity to learn more about how your culture may influence how you communicate with others.

4. Take the post-assessment to reinforce what you have learned about relating to others.

uggested Readings

Bertholf, Stephen D. *What Every College Age Woman Should Know About Relationships.* Wichita, KS: Abbey House Books, 1999.

Blank, Rennee and Sandra Slipp. *Voices of Diversity: Real People Talk About Problems and Solutions in a Workplace Where Everyone Is Not Alike.* New York: American Management Association, 1994.

Dublin, Thomas, ed. *Becoming American, Becoming Ethnic: College Students Explore Their Roots.* Philadelphia, PA: Temple University Press, 1996.

Feagin, Joe R., Hernan Vera, and Nikitah O. Imani. *The Agony of Education: Black Students at White Colleges and Universities.* New York: Routledge, 1996.

Gonzales, Juan L., Jr. *The Lives of Ethnic Americans, 2nd ed.* Dubuque, IA: Kendall/Hunt, 1994.

Hockenberry, John. *Moving Violations.* New York: Hyperion, 1996.

Levey, Marc, Michael Blanco, and W. Terrell Jones. *How to Succeed on a Majority Campus: A Guide for Minority Students.* Belmont, CA: Wadsworth Publishing Co., 1997.

Qubein, Nido R. *How to Be a Great Communicator: In Person, on Paper, and at the Podium.* New York: John Wiley, 1996.

Schuman, David and Dick W. Olufs. *Diversity on Campus.* Boston, MA: Allyn & Bacon, 1994.

Suskind, Ron. *A Hope in the Unseen: An American Odyssey from the Inner City to the Ivy League.* New York: Broadway Books, 1998.

Takaki, Ronald. *A Different Mirror: A History of Multicultural America.* Boston, MA: Little, Brown, and Company, 1994.

Tannen, Deborah. *You Just Don't Understand: Women and Men in Conversation.* New York: Ballantine Books, 1991.

Terkel, Studs. *Race: How Blacks and Whites Think and Feel About the American Obsession.* New York: Free Press, 1995.

Trotter, Tamera and Joycelyn Allen. *Talking Justice: 602 Ways to Build and Promote Racial Harmony.* Saratoga, FL: R & E Publishers, 1993.

Internet Resources

Prentice Hall Student Success Supersite (see success stories from students from a diversity of backgrounds): www.prenhall.com/success

Asian-American Resources: www.ai.mit.edu/people/irie/aar/

Britannica Guide to Black History: http://blackhistory.eb.com

Latino USA: www.latinousa.org

Latino Website Pathfinder: www.sscnet.ucla.edu.csrc/

The Sociology of Race and Ethnicity: www.trinity.edu/~mkearl/race.html

Endnotes

1. "For 7 Million, One Census Race Category Wasn't Enough," *The New York Times,* March 13, 2001, pp. A1 and A14.

2. Jodi Wilgoren, "Swell of Minority Students Is Predicted at Colleges," *The New York Times,* May 24, 2000, p. A16.

3. Sheryl McCarthy, *Why Are the Heroes Always White?* Kansas City, MO: Andrews and McMeel, 1995, p. 188.

4. "Campus Killings Fall, but Some Crimes Rise," *The New York Times,* January 21, 2001, p. A25.

5. Martin Luther King, Jr., from his sermon "A Tough Mind and a Tender Heart," *Strength in Love.* Philadelphia: Fortress Press, 1986, p. 14.

6. Sheryl McCarthy, *Why Are the Heroes Always White?*, p. 137.

7. Claude Steele, Ph.D., Professor of Psychology, Stanford University.

8. Louis E. Boone, David L. Kurtz, and Judy R. Block, *Contemporary Business Communication.* Englewood Cliffs, NJ: Prentice Hall, 1994, pp. 49–54.

9. Much of the information in this section is from Tina Kelley, "On Campuses, Warnings About Violence in Relationships," *The New York Times,* February 13, 2000, p. 40.

10. Ibid.

11. U.S. Department of Justice, Bureau of Justice Statistics, "Sex Offenses and Offenders," 1997, and "Criminal Victimization," 1994.

12. Adapted by Richard Bucher, Professor of Sociology, Baltimore City Community College, from Paula Rothenberg, William Paterson College of New Jersey.

JOURNAL

name   date

visit: www.prenhall.com/carter NY Times link for this chapter

GROW

9

Wellness, career, and money

In this chapter you explore answers to the following questions:
- **How do you manage stress?**
- **How can you make smart decisions about substances and sex?**
- **How can you prepare for a successful career?**
- **How can you create a budget that works?**
- **How can you live your mission?**

AS YOU COME TO THE END of your work in this course, you have built up a wealth of knowledge. Like Morgan Packard (see next page), you are facing important decisions about what direction you want your life to take and how you can find a place in the working world. This chapter will help you build life skills that can fuel your success—managing stress, maintaining wellness, preparing for a career, and budgeting your money, including information on financial aid and credit cards. Finally, you revisit your personal mission, exploring how to keep it in sync with life's changes.

building skills for life success

Morgan Packard, Tulane University, New Orleans, Louisiana

Ramona Z. Locke, Vice President, Senior Financial Consultant, Merrill Lynch Private Client Group, Dallas, Texas

How can I find a career I will enjoy?

Use college to discover what you do well; then . . . find the job you are most suited for

I have always had varied interests. Through high school, my extracurricular activities ranged from piano and voice lessons to spending my summers acting in a Renaissance Fair and everything in between. I was also continually motivated to keep a high grade point average; though I love my activities, school is my top priority. So, when it came time to choose a college, I looked for one whose reputation in academics, particularly the English department, was balanced by opportunities to participate in the arts.

Now attending college and majoring in English, I am faced with a problem. Since I was little, one of my favorite escapes has been reading. When I chose my major, I did so based on a subject that interested me and that would prepare me to participate in a profession that I would like to turn into my career, editing and publishing. I'm wondering how I can apply my major along with my interests to allow me to stay flexible in my studies, and how I can use those tools to find and maintain a career I will enjoy.

I think that some of your biggest strengths when you graduate and look for a job will be not only your school affiliation and grades, but those other activities and strengths you acquired along the way. People who strictly adhere to the academic route don't necessarily acquire the skills associated with those activities; they may not have worked in a team environment, which is important in the job market. What is important to businesses today is not your grade point average or your major, but what skills you bring to the table, how flexible you can be to mold and grow into the position for which that company is looking.

I think one of the greatest attributes a person can acquire is to be able to get up in front of a crowd. I've been in the business world long enough to know that you do not have to be brilliant to be a success; however, if you can communicate your ideas, you *will* be successful. I think that your other activities, such as acting, singing, and dancing, will be important and helpful to you down the road. There are so many nontraditional career paths open today. You need to stay flexible and active so that you can be available when the right choice comes along.

Life doesn't work within the bounds of a rigid focus. To be successful and happy, you must learn to take life's curve balls. You must assimilate all of those situations that come your way and find the benefit in them. My analytical background and nature have helped me the most in my current career; I have a bachelor's degree in science and a master's in biochemistry and biophysics. I love what I do now, but that doesn't mean that I couldn't do seven other careers and be happy in them too. Try to come to grips with what you do best and do that because if you are good at it you will enjoy it. Use college to discover what you do well; then, when it comes time to leave, you can find the job you are most suited for and be happy in it, staying flexible and always open to the next opportunity that comes your way.

How do you *manage stress?*

I f you are feeling more stress in your everyday life as a student, you are not alone.[1] Stress levels among college students have increased dramatically, according to an annual survey conducted at the University of California at Los Angeles. More than 30 percent of the freshmen polled at 683 two- and four-year colleges and universities nationwide reported that they frequently felt overwhelmed, almost double the rate in 1985. Stress factors for college students include being in a new environment, facing increased work and difficult decisions, and juggling school, work, and personal responsibilities.

Stress refers to the way in which your mind and body react to pressure—that is, increased workloads (a week of final exams), excitement (being a finalist for the lead in a play), change (new school, new courses), time pressure (spending 20 hours a week working and finding the time to study), illness (having a head cold that wipes you out for a week), or happiness (getting an A in a course when you expected a C). Even positive changes can create some level of stress.

At their worst, stress reactions can make you physically ill. But stress can also supply the heightened readiness you need to do well on tests, finish assignments on time, prepare for a class presentation, or meet new people. Your goal is to find a balance so that you can manage it. Figure 9.1, based on research conducted by Drs. Robert M. Yerkes and John E. Dodson, shows that stress can be helpful or harmful, depending on how much you experience.

| Figure 9.1 | Yerkes–Dodson law: Stress levels affect performance. |

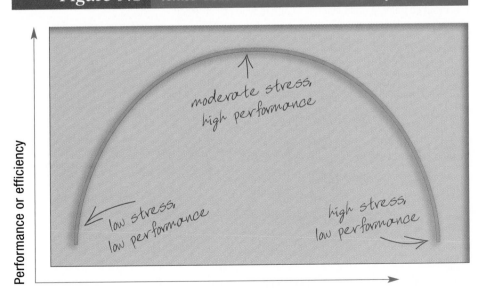

moderate stress, high performance

low stress, low performance

high stress, low performance

Performance or efficiency

Stress or anxiety

Source: From *Your Maximum Mind* by Herbert Benson, M. D., Copyright © 1987 by Random House, Inc. Used by permission of Time Books, a division of Random House, Inc.

Everyone handles stress differently—the strategies linked to your stronger intelligences help you improve your coping skills.

INTELLIGENCE	SUGGESTED STRATEGIES	WHAT WORKS FOR YOU? WRITE NEW IDEAS HERE
Verbal–Linguistic	■ Keep a journal of what makes you stressed. ■ Make time to write letters or e-mail friends or talk with them.	
Logical–Mathematical	■ Think through problems critically using a problem-solving process and devise a plan. ■ Analyze possible positive effects that may result from the stress.	
Bodily–Kinesthetic	■ Choose a physical activity that helps you release tension—running, yoga, team sports—and do it regularly. ■ Plan fun physical activities for your free time—go for a hike, take a bike ride, go dancing with friends.	
Visual–Spatial	■ Take as much time as you can to enjoy beautiful things—art, nature, etc. Visit an exhibit, see an art film, shoot a roll of film with your camera. ■ Use a visual organizer to plan out a solution to a stressful problem.	
Interpersonal	■ Spend time with people who care about you and are very supportive. ■ Practice being a good listener to others who are stressed.	
Intrapersonal	■ Schedule down time when you can think through what is stressing you. ■ Allow yourself five minutes a day for visualizing a positive way in which you want a stressful situation to evolve.	
Musical	■ Play music that "feeds your soul." ■ Write a song about what stresses you out—or about anything that transports your mind.	
Naturalistic	■ Spend as much time as possible in your most soothing places in nature. ■ Listen to tapes of outdoor sounds to help you relax.	

Stress Management Strategies

Stress is a normal part of life. The following strategies will help you avoid overload.

- *Eat right.* A healthy body will help you deal with stress. Eat a balanced, low-fat diet and try to avoid overloading on junk food. Maintain a reasonable weight.

- *Exercise.* Any kind of workout will help you blow off steam. Find a type of exercise you like and make it a regular part of your life.

- *Get sleep.* Avoid the system-wide dysfunction that sleep deprivation can create. Figure out how much sleep you need and do your best to get it.

- *Learn the power of positive thinking.* Think of all you have to do as challenges, not problems.

- *Seek balance.* A balanced life includes time by yourself—for your thoughts, hopes, and plans—and time for relaxation, in whatever form you choose.

- *Address issues specifically.* Think through stressful situations and use problem-solving strategies to decide on a specific plan of action.

- *Develop a schedule, and then stick to it.* Use the techniques you learned in Chapter 3 to schedule time for all the things you have to accomplish and to avoid procrastination.

- *Set reasonable goals.* Goals seem more manageable when approached as a series of small steps.

- *Set boundaries and learn to say "no."* Don't take responsibility for everyone and everything; learn to delegate. Review obligations regularly and let go of activities that have become burdens.

- *Surround yourself with people who are good for you.* Choose friends who are good listeners and who will support you when things get rough.

Feeling overwhelmed by stress is sometimes related to mental health problems such as depression and eating disorders. It is important to recognize these problems and get help if you need it.

Beyond Stress: Recognizing Mental Health Problems

Emotional disorders limit your ability to enjoy life and to cope with its ups and downs. They affect people in all walks of life.

Depression. A depressive disorder is an illness that requires a medical evaluation and is treatable. Symptoms include constant sadness or anxiety, loss of interest in activities that you normally like, eating too much or too little, and low self-esteem. Depression can have a genetic, psychological, physiological, or environmental cause, or a combination of causes.

Anorexia nervosa. This condition, occurring mainly in young women, creates an intense desire to be thin. People with anorexia become dangerously thin through restricting food intake, constant exercise, and use of laxatives, all the time believing they are overweight. An estimated 5 to 7 percent of college undergraduates in the United States suffer from anorexia.[2] Effects of anorexia-induced starvation include loss of menstrual periods in women, impotence in men, organ damage, heart failure, and death.

Bulimia. People who binge on excessive amounts of food, usually sweets and fattening foods, and then purge through self-induced vomiting have bulimia. They may also use laxatives or exercise obsessively. Effects of bulimia include damage to the digestive tract and even heart failure due to the loss of important minerals.

"To keep the body in good health is a duty . . . Otherwise we shall not be able to keep our mind strong and clear."

BUDDHA

Binge eating. Like bulimics, people with binge eating disorder eat large amounts of food and have a hard time stopping. However, they do not purge afterwards. Binge eaters are often overweight and feel unable to control their eating. Binge eaters may suffer from health problems associated with obesity.

Most student health centers and campus counseling centers can provide both medical and psychological help for students with depression or eating disorders. Treatment may involve psychotherapy, drug therapy, and even hospitalization or residence in a treatment center.

Situations involving substances or sex are sources of stress for many college students. The following will help you make decisions that are right for you.

BINGE DRINKING

Having five or more drinks at one sitting.

How can you make *smart decisions* about substances and sex?

You are responsible for the choices you make regarding alcohol, tobacco, drugs, and sexual practices. Think critically, carefully considering the potential positive and negative effects of your actions.

Alcohol

Alcohol is a drug as much as it is a beverage. Of all alcohol consumption, binge drinking is associated with the greatest problems. Here are statistics from a recent survey of college students:[3]

- Forty-three percent of the students surveyed said they are binge drinkers, and 21 percent said that they binge drink frequently.
- Of students who do not binge drink, 80 percent surveyed reported experiencing one or more secondhand effects of binge drinking

(e.g., vandalism, sexual assault or unwanted sexual advances, interrupted sleep or study).[4]

- Students who binge drink are more likely to miss classes, be less able to work, have hangovers, become depressed, engage in unplanned sexual activity, and ignore safe sex practices.[5]

The bottom line is that heavy drinking causes severe problems. The NIAAA estimates that alcohol contributes to the deaths of 100,000 people every year through both alcohol-related illnesses and accidents involving drunk drivers.[6] Heavy drinking can damage the liver, the digestive system, and brain and nervous system. Prolonged use also leads to addiction, making it seem impossible to quit.

Tobacco

College students do their share of smoking. The National Institute on Drug Abuse (NIDA) found that 38.8 percent of college students reported smoking at least once in the year before they were surveyed, and 24.5 percent had smoked once within the month before.[7]

When people smoke they inhale nicotine, a highly addictive drug found in all tobacco products. Nicotine's immediate effects may include an increase in blood pressure and heart rate, sweating, and throat irritation. Long-term effects may include high blood pressure, bronchitis, emphysema, stomach ulcers, and heart conditions. Pregnant women who smoke increase their risk of having infants with low birth weight, premature births, or stillbirths.

Quitting smoking is difficult and should be attempted gradually and, if possible, with the support of friends and family. However, the positive effects of quitting—increased life expectancy, greater lung capacity, and more energy—may inspire any smoker to consider making a lifestyle change. Weigh your options and make a responsible choice.

ADDICTION

Compulsive physiological need for a habit forming substance.

Drugs

The NIDA reports that 31.4 percent of college students have used illicit drugs at least once in the year before being surveyed, and 16 percent in the month before.[8] Drug use can have numerous negative effects, including damage to body and mind, people who accept you for your drug use and not for who you are, and problems and responsibilities that multiply when you emerge from a high. Furthermore, drug use violates the law; you can jeopardize your reputation, your student status, and your employment possibilities if you are caught using drugs or if drug use impairs your school performance. Table 9.1 shows commonly used drugs and their potential effects.

One drug that doesn't fit cleanly into a particular category is MDMA, better known as Ecstasy. The use of this drug, a combination stimulant and hallucinogenic, is on the rise at college parties, raves, and concerts. Its immediate effects include diminished anxiety and relaxation.

Table 9.1 How drugs affect you.

DRUG CATEGORY	DRUG TYPES	HOW THEY MAKE YOU FEEL	PHYSICAL EFFECTS	DANGER OF PHYSICAL DEPENDENCE	DANGER OF PSYCHOLOGICAL DEPENDENCE
Stimulants	Cocaine, amphetamines	Alert, stimulated, excited	Nervousness, mood swings, stroke or convulsions, psychoses, paranoia, coma at large doses	Relatively strong	Strong
Depressants	Alcohol, Valium-type drugs	Sedated, tired, high	Cirrhosis; impaired blood production; greater risk of cancer, heart attack, and stroke; impaired brain function	Strong	Strong
Opiates	Heroin, codeine, other pain pills	Drowsy, floating, without pain	Infection of organs, inflammation of the heart, hepatitis	Yes, with high dosage	Yes, with high dosage
Cannabinols	Marijuana, hashish	Euphoria, mellowness, little sensation of time	Impairment of judgment and coordination, bronchitis and asthma, lung and throat cancers, anxiety, lack of energy and motivation, reduced ability to produce hormones	Moderate	Relatively strong
Hallucinogens	LSD, mushrooms	Heightened sensual perception, hallucinations, confusion	Impairment of brain function, circulatory problems, agitation and confusion, flashbacks	Insubstantial	Insubstantial
Inhalants	Glue, aerosols	Giddiness, lightheadedness	Damage to brain, heart, liver, and kidneys	Insubstantial	Insubstantial

Source: Compiled and adapted from *Educating Yourself about Alcohol and Drugs: A People's Primer* by Marc Alan Schuckit, M.D., Plenum Press, 1995.

When the drug wears off, nausea, hallucinations, shaking, vision problems, anxiety, and depression replace these highs. Long-term users risk permanent brain damage in the form of memory loss, chronic depression, and other disorders.[9]

You are responsible for what you introduce into your body. Read about individual drugs and their effects. Ask yourself: Why do I want to do this? What positive and negative effects might it have? Why do others want me to take drugs? How would drug use affect the people in my life? The more critical analysis you do, the more likely you will make choices that are in your own best interest.

Facing Addiction

If you think you may be addicted to alcohol or drugs, realize that you are the only one who can take the initiative to change. Because substances often cause physical and chemical changes, quitting may involve guiding your body through a painful withdrawal. Many resources can help along the way.

Counseling and medical care. You can find help from school-based, private, government-sponsored, or workplace-sponsored resources. Ask your school's counseling or health center, your personal physician, or a local hospital for a referral.

Detoxification ("detox") centers. If you have a severe addiction, you may need a controlled environment in which to separate yourself completely from drugs or alcohol.

Support groups. You can derive help and comfort from sharing your experiences with others. Alcoholics Anonymous (AA) is the premier support group for alcoholics.

Sex and Critical Thinking

What sexuality means to you and the role it plays in your life are your own business. However, individual sexual conduct can have consequences such as unexpected pregnancy and the transmission of sexually transmitted diseases (STDs). These consequences affect everyone involved in the sexual act and, often, their families. Think critically about sexual issues, and make choices that maintain your health and safety as well as that of others involved.

Birth Control

Using birth control is a choice, and it is not for everyone. If you do choose to use it, evaluate cost, ease of use, reliability, comfort, and protection against STDs, and with your partner make a choice that is comfortable for both of you. For more information, check your library or the Internet, talk to your doctor, or ask a counselor.

Table 9.2 describes some of the most established methods, with effectiveness percentages and STD prevention based on proper and regular use.

Sexually Transmitted Diseases

Sexually transmitted diseases spread through sexual contact (intercourse or other sexual activity that involves contact with the genitals). All are highly contagious. The only birth control methods that offer protection are the male and female condoms (latex or polyurethane only), which prevent skin-to-skin contact. Most STDs can also spread to infants of infected mothers during birth. Have a doctor examine any irregularity or discomfort as soon as you detect it. Table 9.3 describes common STDs.

Table 9.2 Methods of birth control.

METHOD	APPROXIMATE EFFECTIVENESS	PREVENTS STDS?	DESCRIPTION
Abstinence	100%	Only if no sexual activity occurs	Just saying no. No intercourse means no risk of pregnancy. However, alternative modes of sexual activity can still spread STDs.
Condom (male)	94%	Yes, if made of latex	A sheath that fits over the penis and prevents sperm from entering the vagina.
Diaphragm or cervical cap	85%	No	A bendable rubber cap that fits over the cervix and pelvic bone inside the vagina (the cervical cap is smaller and fits over the cervix only). Both must be fitted initially by a gynecologist and used with a spermicide.
Oral contraceptives (the pill)	97%	No	A dosage of hormones taken daily by a woman, preventing the ovaries from releasing eggs. Side effects can include headaches, weight gain, and increased chances of blood clotting. Various brands and dosages; must be prescribed by a gynecologist.
Spermicidal foams, jellies, inserts	84% if used alone	No	Usually used with diaphragms or condoms to enhance effectiveness, they have an ingredient that kills sperm cells (but not STDs). They stay effective for a limited period of time after insertion.
Intrauterine device (IUD)	94%	No	A small coil of wire inserted into the uterus by a gynecologist (who must also remove it). Prevents fertilized eggs from implanting in the uterine wall. Possible side effects include bleeding.
Rhythm method	Variable	No	Abstaining from intercourse during the ovulation segment of the woman's menstrual cycle. Can be difficult to time and may not account for cycle irregularities.
Withdrawal	Variable	No	Pulling the penis out of the vagina before ejaculation. Unreliable, because some sperm can escape in the fluid released prior to ejaculation. Dependent on a controlled partner.

The most serious of the STDs is AIDS (acquired immune deficiency syndrome), which is caused by the human immunodeficiency virus (HIV). Not everyone who tests positive for HIV will develop AIDS, but AIDS has no cure and results in eventual death. Medical science continues to develop drugs to combat AIDS and its related illnesses. However, the drugs can cause severe side effects, many have not been thoroughly tested, and none are cures.

HIV is transmitted through two types of bodily fluids: fluids associated with sex (semen and vaginal fluids) and blood. People have acquired HIV through sexual relations, by sharing hypodermic needles for drug use, and by receiving infected blood transfusions. You cannot become infected unless one of those fluids is involved. Therefore, it is unlikely you can contract HIV from toilet seats, hugging, kissing, or sharing a glass. Other than not having sex at all, a latex condom is the best defense against AIDS. Although some people dislike using condoms, it's a small price for preserving your life.

Table 9.3 Sexually transmitted diseases.

DISEASE	SYMPTOMS	HEALTH PROBLEMS IF UNTREATED	TREATMENTS
Chlamydia	Discharge, painful urination, swollen or painful joints, change in menstrual periods for women	Can cause pelvic inflammatory disease (PID) in women, which can lead to sterility or ectopic pregnancies; infection; miscarriage or premature birth.	Curable with full course of antibiotics; avoid sex until treatment is complete.
Gonorrhea	Discharge, burning while urinating	Can cause PID, swelling of testicles and penis, arthritis, skin problems, infections.	Usually curable with antibiotics; however, certain strains are becoming resistant to medication.
Genital herpes	Blisterlike itchy sores in the genital area, headache, fever, chills	Symptoms may subside and then reoccur, often in response to high stress levels; carriers can transmit the virus even when it is dormant.	No cure; some medications, such as Acyclovir, reduce and help heal the sores and may shorten recurring outbreaks.
Syphilis	A genital sore lasting one to five weeks, followed by a rash, fatigue, fever, sore throat, headaches, swollen glands	If it lasts over four years, it can cause blindness, destruction of bone, insanity, or heart failure; can cause death or deformity of a child born to an infected woman.	Curable with full course of antibiotics.
Human Papilloma Virus (HPV, or genital warts)	Genital itching and irritation, small clusters of warts	Can increase risk of cervical cancer in women; virus may remain in body even when warts are removed and cause recurrences.	Treatable with drugs applied to warts or various kinds of wart removal surgery.
Hepatitis B	Fatigue, poor appetite, vomiting, jaundice, hives	Some carriers will have few symptoms; others may develop chronic liver disease that may lead to other diseases of the liver.	No cure; some will recover, some will not. Bed rest may help ease symptoms. Vaccine is available.

To be safe, have an HIV test done at your doctor's office or at a government-sponsored clinic. Your school's health department may also administer HIV tests, and home HIV tests are available over the counter. If you are infected, first inform all sexual partners and seek medical assistance. Then, contact support organizations in your area or call the National AIDS Hotline at 1-800-342-AIDS.

Health, both mental and physical, is one asset that will serve you well as you move along the path toward success in the workplace. The education you are receiving right now is another. Following are more ideas about preparing for career success.

How can you prepare for a *successful* career?

Everything in this book is geared toward workplace success. Critical thinking, teamwork, writing skills, and long-term planning all prepare you to thrive in any career. Use the following strategies to start getting more specific in your preparation for career success.

Investigate Career Paths

The working world changes all the time. You can get a good idea of what's out there—and what you think of it all—by exploring potential careers and building knowledge and experience.

Explore potential careers. Career possibilities extend far beyond what you can imagine. Brainstorm about career areas. Check your library for books on careers or biographies of people who worked in fields that interest you. Ask instructors, relatives, mentors, and fellow students about careers they are familiar with. Look at Table 9.4 for some of the kinds of questions you might ask as you talk to people or investigate materials. You may discover that a wide array of job possibilities exists for most career fields, and within each job there is a variety of tasks and skills.

Build knowledge and experience. Having specific knowledge and experience is valuable on the job hunt. Courses, internships, jobs, and volunteering are four great ways to build both.

Table 9.4	Critical-thinking questions for career exploration.
What can I do in this area that I like and do well?	Do I respect the company or the industry? The product or service?
What are the educational requirements (certificates or degrees, courses)?	Does this company or industry accommodate special needs (child care, sick days, flex time)?
What skills are necessary?	Do I have to belong to a union?
What wage or salary and benefits can I expect?	Are there opportunities near where I live (or want to live)?
What kinds of personalities are best suited to this kind of work?	What other expectations exist (travel, overtime, etc.)?
What are the prospects for moving up to higher-level positions?	Do I prefer the service or production end of this industry?

- *Courses.* Take a course or two in your areas of interest to see how you react to them. Find out what courses you have to take to major in the field.
- *Internships.* An (internship) is a great way to gain real-world experience you can't get in the classroom. Your career center may be able to help you explore internship opportunities.
- *Jobs.* No matter what you do to earn money while in college, you may discover career opportunities. Someone who answers phones for a newspaper, for example, might be drawn into journalism.
- *Volunteering.* Offering your services to others in need can introduce you to careers and increase your experience. Many employers look favorably on volunteering.

INTERNSHIP

A temporary work program in which a student can gain supervised practical experience in a particular professional field.

Know What Employers Want

When you look for a job in a particular career area, your technical skills, work experience, and academic credentials that apply to that career are important. Beyond those basics, though, other skills and qualities make you an excellent job candidate in any career. Table 9.5 describes these skills.

Stay Current

The working world is always in flux. Stay on top of two issues: growing and declining career areas and workplace trends.

Growing and declining career areas. Rapid workplace change means that a growth area today may be declining tomorrow—witness the sudden drop in Internet company jobs and fortunes in 2001. The U. S. Bureau of Labor projects that the five fastest growing occupations from 1998–2008 will be computer engineer, computer support specialist, systems analyst, database administrator, and desktop publishing specialist—all computer-related occupations.[10] You can keep tabs on these statistics by checking the *Occupational Outlook Handbook,* published by the Bureau of Labor every two years. Find it in your library or look up highlights on the Internet at http://stats.bls.gov/ocohome.htm.

"Whatever you think you can do or believe you can do, begin it. Action has magic, grace, and power in it."

JOHANN WOLFGANG VON GOETHE

Workplace trends. Here are two ways in which companies are responding to workplace change and economic stress:

- *More temporary employment.* The number of temps increased from 800,000 in 1986 to more than 2.5 million in 1997.[11] Temporary jobs offer flexibility and few obligations, but have limited benefits.

Table 9.5 Skills employers seek.

SKILLS	WHY?
Communication	Both good listening and effective communicating are keys to workplace success, as is being able to adjust to different communication styles.
Critical thinking	An employee who can assess workplace choices and challenges critically and recommend appropriate actions stands out.
Teamwork	All workers interact with others on the job. Working well with others is essential for achieving work goals.
Goal setting	Teams fail if goals are unclear or unreasonable. Benefit is gained from setting realistic, specific goals and achieving them reliably.
Acceptance	The workplace is becoming increasingly diverse. A valuable employee is able to work with, and respect all kinds of people.
Leadership	The ability to influence others in a positive way earns you respect and helps advance your career.
Creativity	The ability to come up with new concepts, plans, and products is valuable in the workplace.
Positive attitude	If you show that you have a high level of commitment to all tasks, you may earn the right to tackle more challenging projects.
Integrity	Acting with integrity at work—communicating promptly, being truthful and honest, following rules, giving proper notice, respecting others—enhances your value.
Flexibility	The most valuable employees understand the constancy of change and have developed the skills to adapt to its challenge.
Continual learning	The most valuable employees stay current on changes and trends by reading up-to-the-minute media and taking workshops and seminars.
Emotional intelligence	This includes *personal competence* (self-knowledge, motivation, the ability to control impulses) and *social competence* (social skills plus awareness of the feelings, needs, and concerns of others).[12]

- *New variety in benefits.* Companies are offering benefits such as telecommuting (working from home), job sharing (two employees sharing the duties of one full-time job), and on-site child care.

Staying informed about workplace developments will help you handle job change when it happens. If you think creatively about your marketable skills and job possibilities, you will be able to find new ways to achieve when one job or career does not work out.

Consider Your Learning Style

Your Personality Spectrum assessment results from Chapter 2 are significant to career planning because they provide insight on how you work best with others. Succeeding in your search and in your chosen job depends, in large part, on your ability to communicate and function in a team.

Table 9.6 focuses the four dimensions of the Personality Spectrum on career ideas and strategies. Remember to use this information as a guide, not a label. Take these ideas about your strengths and challenges as a starting point as you consider potential careers.

Now that you've done your homework, it's time to get to the search. What you know, along with the strategies that follow, will help you along the path to a career that works for you.

Searching for a Job—and a Career

Maximize your opportunities by using the resources available to you and being strategic about the process. The information in this section will help you right away if you are one of the many who want or need to work while in school. In the school year 1995–96, 79 percent of undergraduates—four out of five—reported working while in school.[13] Figure 9.2 shows statistics related to working for both community college and four-year college students.

Use Available Resources

The following resources can help you explore possibilities both for jobs you need right away and for postgraduation career opportunities.

Your school's career planning and placement office. Generally, the career planning and placement office deals with postgraduation job placements, whereas the student employment office, along with the financial aid office, has more information about working while in school. At either location you might find job listings, occupation lists, assessments of skills and personality types, sign-up sheets for interviews, and contact information for companies. The career office may hold frequent informational sessions on different topics. Your school may also sponsor job or career fairs that give you a chance to explore job opportunities. Visit the center early in your college career and work with a counselor there to develop a solid career game plan.

Networking. Networking is one of the most important job-hunting strategies. With each person you get to know, you build your

(handwritten annotation:)
NETWORKING
The exchange of information or services among individuals, groups, or institutions.

Figure 9.2

Working students.

Community college students

49.3%
16.7   17.1
10.2 6.7

■ Not employed

■ Worked 1–15 hours

■ Worked 16–20 hours

□ Worked 21–34 hours

□ Worked 35 hours or more

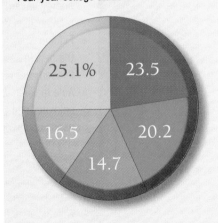

Four-year college students

25.1%   23.5
16.5   20.2
14.7

Source: U.S. Department of Education, National Center for Educational Statistics, *Profile of Undergraduates in U.S. Postsecondary Education Institutions: 1995–1996* (NCES 98-084), May 1998.

Table 9.6 **Personality Spectrum in the working world.**

DIMENSION	STRENGTHS ON THE JOB	CHALLENGES ON THE JOB	LOOK FOR JOBS/CAREERS THAT FEATURE . . .
Thinker	• Problem solving • Development of ideas • Keen analysis of situations • Fairness to others • Efficiency in working through tasks • Innovation of plans and systems • Ability to look strategically at the future	• A need for private time to think and work • A need, at times, to move away from established rules • A dislike of sameness—systems that don't change, repetitive tasks • Not always open to expressing thoughts and feelings to others	• Some level of solo work/think time • Problem solving • Opportunity for innovation • Freedom to think creatively and to bend the rules • Technical work • Big-picture strategic planning
Organizer	• High level of responsibility • Enthusiastic support of social structures • Order and reliability • Loyal • Able to follow through on tasks according to requirements • Detailed planning skills with competent follow-through • Neatness and efficiency	• A need for tasks to be clearly, concretely defined • A need for structure and stability • A preference for less rapid change • A need for frequent feedback • A need for tangible appreciation • Low tolerance for people who don't conform to rules and regulations	• Clear, well-laid-out tasks and plans • Stable environment with consistent, repeated tasks • Organized supervisors • Clear structure of how employees interact and report to one another • Value of, and reward for, loyalty
Giver	• Honesty and integrity • Commitment to putting energy toward close relationships with others • Finding ways to bring out the best in self and others • Peacemaker and mediator • Able to listen well, respect opinions, and prioritize the needs of coworkers	• Difficulty in handling conflict, either personal or between others in the work environment • Strong need for appreciation and praise • Low tolerance for perceived dishonesty or deception • Avoidance of people perceived as hostile, cold, or indifferent	• Emphasis on teamwork and relationship building • Indications of strong and open lines of communication among workers • Encouragement of personal expression in the workplace (arrangement of personal space, tolerance of personal celebrations, and so on)
Adventurer	• Skillfulness in many different areas • Willingness to try new things • Ability to take action • Hands-on problem-solving skills • Initiative and energy • Ability to negotiate • Spontaneity and creativity	• Intolerance of being kept waiting • Lack of detail focus • Impulsiveness • Dislike of sameness and authority • Need for freedom, constant change, and constant action • Tendency not to consider consequences of actions	• A spontaneous atmosphere • Less structure, more freedom • Adventuresome tasks • Situations involving change • Encouragement of hands-on problem solving • Travel and physical activity • Support of creative ideas and endeavors

network and tap into someone else's. Networking contacts—including friends, instructors, coworkers, employers, alumni, and more—may be willing to answer your questions regarding job hunting, challenges and tasks of their jobs, and salary expectations.

Classified ads. Some of the best job listings are in newspapers. Individual ads describe the kind of position available and give a telephone number or post office box for you to contact. Some ads include additional information such as job requirements, a contact person, and the salary or wages offered.

On-line services. The Internet has exploded into one of the most fruitful sources of job listings. There are many different ways to hunt for a job on the Web:

- Look up career-focused and job listing Web sites such as CareerBuilder.com, CareerMosaic, Monster.com, hotjobs.com, JobsOnline, or futurestep.com.
- Access job search databases such as the Career Placement Registry and U. S. Employment Opportunities.
- Check the Web pages of individual associations and companies, which may post job listings.

Employment agencies. Employment agencies are organizations that help people find full-time, part-time, or temporary work. Most employment agencies put you through a screening process. If you pass the tests and interview well, the agency tries to place you in a job. Most employment agencies specialize in particular careers or skills such as computer operation, child care, or food services.

Be Strategic

After you've gathered enough information to narrow your career goals, plan out how to achieve them.

See the big picture. Make a career time line that illustrates the steps toward your goal, as shown in Figure 9.3. Mark years and half-year points (and months for the first year), and write in the steps when you think they should happen. Using what you know about strategic planning, fill in the details about what you will do throughout your plan. Set goals that establish who you will talk to, what courses you will take, what skills you will work on, and what jobs or internships you will investigate. Your path may change, of course; use your time line as a guide rather than as an inflexible plan.

Keep track of details. After you establish your time frame, make a plan for pursuing particular jobs or careers, organizing your approach according to what you need to do and how much time you have. Do you plan to make three phone calls per day? Will you fill out three job applications a week for a month? Keep a record—on 3 × 5 cards, in a computer file, or in a notebook—of people you contact, companies to which you apply,

CONTACT

A person who serves as a carrier or source of information.

Figure 9.3 Career time line.

1 month	Enter community college on a part-time schedule
6 months	Meet with advisor to discuss desired major and required courses
1 year	
	Declare major in secondary education
2 years	Switch to full-time class schedule
3 years	Graduate with associate's degree
	Transfer to 4-year college
4 years	Work part-time as a classroom aide
5 years	Student teaching
	Graduate with bachelor's degree and teaching certificate
6 years	Have a job teaching high school

jobs you rule out, and any response to your communications. Figure 9.4 illustrates a sample file card.

Compile an effective résumé. Your résumé should always be typed or printed on a computer. Design your résumé neatly, using an acceptable format (books or your career office can show you some standard formats—see p. 260 for a sample). Proofread it for errors and have someone else proofread it as well. Type or print it on a heavier bond paper than is used for ordinary copies. Use white or off-white paper and black ink.

Interview well. Be clean, neat, and appropriately dressed. Choose a nice pair of shoes—people notice. Bring an extra copy of your résumé and any other materials that you want to show the interviewer. Avoid chewing gum or smoking. Offer a confident handshake. Make eye contact. Show your integrity by speaking honestly about yourself. After the interview is over, no matter what the outcome, send a formal but pleasant thank-you note right away as a follow-up.

Figure 9.4   Sample file card.

Job/company:	Child-care worker at Morningside Day Care
Contact:	Sally Wheeler, Morningside Day Care,
	17 Parkside Rd, Silver Spring, MD 20910
Phone/fax/e-mail:	(301) 555-3353 phone, (301) 555-3354 fax,
	no e-mail
Communication:	Saw ad in paper, sent résumé & cover letter on Oct. 7
Response:	Call from Sally to set up interview
	—Interview on Oct. 15 at 2 p.m., seemed to get a positive
	response, said she would contact me again by end of the week
Follow-up:	Sent thank-you note on Oct. 16

No matter where your money comes from—financial aid or paychecks from one or more jobs—budgeting skills and strategic planning will help you stretch it as far as it can go.

How can you create a *budget* that *works?*

Budgeting your money is a process that considers your resources (money flowing in) and expenditures (money flowing out) and adjusts the flow so that you come out even or perhaps even ahead. Being able to budget effectively relieves money-related stress and helps you feel more in control. Your biggest expense right now is probably the cost of your education. However, that expense may not hit you fully until after you graduate and begin to pay back your student loans. For now, include in your budget only the part of the cost of your education you are paying while you are in school.

BUDGETING

Making a plan for the coordination of resources and expenditures; setting goals regarding money.

The Art of Budgeting

Budgeting involves a few basic steps: Determining spendable income (how much money you have after taxes), determining how much money you spend, subtracting what you spend from your after-tax income, evaluating the result, and deciding how to adjust your spending or earning based on that result. Budgeting regularly is easiest—most people budget on a month-by-month basis.

Determine Your Spendable Income

Add up all of the money you receive during the year—the actual after-tax money you have to pay your bills. You may earn some of this money every month—from a part-time or full-time job—while other income may come from summer and holiday employment. You may also receive income from gifts, scholarships, or grants. Divide the total by 12 so that you have an idea of your approximate monthly income.

Figure Out How Much You Spend

Examine your basic spending patterns for a month by recording checks you write for fixed expenses like rent and telephone and noting personal expenditures in a small notebook. Indicate any expenditure over five dollars, making sure to count smaller expenditures if frequent (e.g., a thirty-day bus pass). Some expenses, like insurance, are billed only a few times a year. In these cases, convert the expense to monthly by dividing the yearly cost by 12. Here is a list of expenses to consider:

- rent or mortgage
- tuition (after financial aid is taken into account)
- books, lab fees, and other educational expenses
- regular bills (electric, gas, oil, phone, water)
- food, clothing, toiletries, and household supplies
- child care
- transportation and auto expenses (gas, maintenance)
- credit cards and other payments on credit (car payments)
- insurance (health, auto, homeowner's or renter's, life)
- entertainment and related items (cable television, movies, restaurants, books and magazines)
- computer-related expenses, including the cost of your on-line service
- miscellaneous unplanned expenses

PERSONAL TRIUMPH

*W*hat seems at first like a minor well-ness issue can gradually turn into a major problem that makes everything seem hopeless. However, Chip Case found that getting help and looking outside himself to help others can turn a life around and grant newfound perspective.

On the day that I found out I had been awarded the prestigious James R. Gilliam Scholarship from my college, Piedmont Virginia Community College, everything seemed alive. From where I stood in the campus garden, I could see the sun on the bald top of Brown's Mountain above Monticello. Ever since I was a boy, I had dreamed of going to the University of Virginia. I've come a long way to be this close to that dream.

As a child, I was an enthusiastic student, but by the time I was a junior in high school, I became a classic underachiever, smoking pot and going to parties instead of studying. I was arrested for possession of marijuana when I was 17 and for being drunk in public when I was 18, and I failed out of Radford University a year later. At 19, I got my first DUI. During the years following, I worked a series of jobs while continuing to drink. In 1994, I came home from a weekend away to find the apartment I shared with my girlfriend empty and abandoned. Deciding it was time to rededicate myself to the dream of attending UVA, I moved to Charlottesville and enrolled at PVCC. However, after two months, I withdrew from all my classes. I was drinking and depressed. I got my second DUI in 1997.

Two years later, after a second girlfriend broke up with me, I started taking Valium and really drinking. I got a medical leave of absence from work and had a nervous breakdown. The night I went to find her, I got my third DUI and ended up in jail. However, something changed in the subsequent two-and-a-half months I spent locked up. As I watched other inmates

Chip Case, student at Piedmont Virginia
Community College, Charlottesville, Virginia

leaving, I saw that they had nothing and I had the world. I realized I had taken for granted things like a hug from my Mom, a phone call, toothpaste.

I started a 12-step program. I decided to admit not only that I was an alcoholic, but that my whole life was out of control. Quitting drinking was easy. It was dealing with the problems inside that was the challenge.

I still visit that empty place within me. When things get rough, I sometimes want to get drunk to escape. I continue reworking the 12 steps; right now I'm on step number 2. I know I am always one day away from being where I was. I'm really focusing on not worrying, knowing it's going to be OK. I reenrolled at PVCC in August 2000, and celebrated my second year of sobriety in February 2001. Currently I am president of PVCC's Phi Theta Kappa chapter and active in community service.

Becoming happy again and finally being able to help myself has made me want to help others. Alcoholism is a selfish disease. Trying to help makes me forget about myself. When I share my experiences, it in turn helps me. It's a circle.

I'm definitely interested in teaching as a career, also in some sort of service. I'm not sure what route I will take. I do plan, however, to major in government and religious studies when I transfer to a four-year college. Recently I applied to UVA. Even if it doesn't go well, faith, family, and friends are the three most important things in my life. All else is a byproduct of these.

Take a moment to consider . . .

- *What your most difficult personal wellness issue is, and what you plan to do to overcome it.*
- *What you would say are your "three most important things" in life.*

Use the total of all your monthly expenses as a baseline for other months, realizing that your expenditures will vary depending on what is happening in your life.

Determine and Evaluate the Result

Subtract your monthly expenses from your monthly income. Ideally, you have money left over—to save or to spend. If you have a deficit, however, analyze the problem by looking at your budget, spending patterns, and priorities. Use your critical-thinking skills to ask some focused questions.

Question your budget. Did you forget to budget for recurring expenses, or was your budget derailed by an emergency expense that you did not foresee? Is your income sufficient for your needs?

Question your spending patterns and priorities. Did you spend money wisely or did you overspend on luxuries? Are you being hit by high interest payments on your credit card balance?

When you are spending more than you are taking in during a "typical month," you may need to adjust your budget over the long term.

Make Decisions About How to Adjust Spending or Earning

Look carefully at what may cause you to overspend and brainstorm possible solutions that address those causes. Solutions can involve either increasing resources or decreasing spending. To deal with spending, prioritize your expenditures and trim the ones you really don't need to make.

As for resources, investigate ways to take in more money, such as taking a part-time job or hunting down scholarships.

Think critically, too, about the big picture of where your money goes. How does your philosophy about money help or hurt your finances? How can you save now for important purchases you want to make later? Some level of financial sacrifice in the present might be necessary to get you where you want to go in the future. Do whatever you can to "pay yourself" every month—set aside some amount of money in a strategic way to provide for your future needs.

Financial Aid

The cost of education continues to rise; as a result, nearly half of all students receive some kind of aid.[14] Because most sources of financial aid don't seek out recipients, it is up to you to learn how you can finance your education. Visit your school's financial aid office, research what's available, weigh the pros and cons of each option, decide what works best, then apply early. Above all, think critically. Never assume that you are *not* eligible for aid. The types of aid available are loans, grants, and scholarships.

Loans. As the recipient of a student loan, you are responsible for paying back the amount you borrow, plus interest, according to a payment schedule that may stretch over a number of years. The federal government administers or oversees most student loans. To receive aid from any federal program, you must be a citizen or eligible non-citizen and be enrolled in a program that meets government requirements. Federal loan programs include Perkins (for those with exceptional financial need), Stafford (available to students enrolled at least half-time, exceptional need not required), and PLUS (available to students enrolled at least half-time and who are claimed as dependents by their parents).

Grants. Unlike student loans, grants do not require repayment. Grants, funded by federal, state, or local governments as well as private organizations, are awarded to students who show financial need. Federal grant programs include Pell (need-based, available to undergraduates), FSEOG (need-based, administered by individual schools), and work-study (need-based; encourages community service work or work related to your course of study).

Scholarships. Scholarships are awarded to students who show talent or ability in specified areas (academics, sports, the arts, citizenship, or leadership). They may be financed by government or private organizations, schools, or individuals. A relatively new federal program, known as the HOPE Scholarship, gives eligible students a tax credit worth up to $1,500, which reduces the amount of taxes owed on a dollar-for-dollar basis.

It can take work to locate financial aid opportunities because many aren't widely advertised. Start digging at your financial aid office and visit your library, bookstore, and the Internet. The Student Guide to Financial Aid contains everything you need to know about federal grants and loans. You can find it at your school's financial aid office, request it by phone at 1-800-4-FED-AID (1-800-433-3243), or read it on-line (www.ed.gov/prog_info/SFA/StudentGuide/). Guides to funding sources, such as *College Financial Aid for Dummies* by Herm Davis and Joyce Lain Kennedy, catalog thousands of organizations. Check out on-line scholarship search services.

Use common sense when applying for aid. Fill out applications as neatly as possible and submit them on time or early. You can access the Free Application for Federal Student Aid (FAFSA) form at your library, the Federal Student Aid Information Center, through your college financial aid office, or via the U. S. Department of Education's website— http://www.ed.gov/finaid.html.

Managing Credit Cards

College students receive dozens of credit card offers. When used properly, credit cards are a handy alternative to cash. They can provide money for emergencies, a record of purchases, and a strong credit history (if you pay your bills on time) that will help you qualify for loans. However, it takes self-control to avoid overspending, and credit cards can plunge you into debt that can take years to erase.

When you make a purchase on credit, the merchant accepts immediate payment from the credit card issuer and you accept the responsibility to pay the money back. *Every time you charge, you are creating a debt that must be repaid.* The credit card issuer earns money by charging interest on your unpaid balance. To avoid unmanageable debt that can lead to a personal financial crisis, learn as much as you can about credit cards, starting with the important concepts in Table 9.7.

The majority of American citizens have some level of debt, and many people go through periods when they have a hard time keeping up with their bills. Falling behind on payments, however, could result in a poor credit rating that makes it difficult for you to make large purchases or take out loans. Particular resources can help you solve credit problems; two are the National Foundation for Credit Counseling (www.nfcc.org) and Consumer Credit Counseling Service (1-800-338-2227).

The most basic way to stay in control is to pay bills regularly and on time. On credit card bills, pay at least the minimum amount due. If you get into trouble, deal with it in three steps. First, admit that you made a mistake, even though you may be embarrassed. Then, address the problem immediately to minimize damages. Call the creditor and see if you can pay your debt gradually using a payment plan. Finally, examine what got you into trouble and avoid it in the future if you can. Cut up a credit card or two if you have too many. If you clean up your act, your credit history will gradually clean up as well.

CREDITOR

A person or company to whom a debt is owed, usually money.

| Table 9.7 | Learn to be a smart credit consumer. |

WHAT TO KNOW ABOUT . . .	. . . AND HOW TO USE WHAT YOU KNOW
Account balance—a dollar amount that includes any unpaid balance, new purchases and cash advances, finance charges, and fees. Updated monthly on your card statement.	Charge only what you can afford to pay at the end of the month. Keep track of your balance. Hold onto receipts and call customer service if you have questions about recent purchases.
Annual fee—the yearly cost some companies charge for owning a card.	Look for cards without an annual fee or, if you've paid your bills on time, ask your current company to waive the fee.
Annual percentage rate (APR)—the amount of interest charged on your unpaid balance, meaning the cost of credit if you carry a balance in any given month. The higher the APR, the more you pay in finance charges.	Credit card companies compete by charging different APRs, so shop around. Two Web sites with competitive APR information are www.studentcredit.com and www.bankrate.com. Also, watch out for low, but temporary, introductory rates that skyrocket to over 20 percent after a few months. Look for *fixed* rates.
Available credit—the unused portion of your credit line. Determine available credit by deducting your current card balance from your credit limit.	It is important to have credit available for emergencies, so avoid charging to the limit.
Cash advance—an immediate loan, in the form of cash, from the credit card company. You are charged interest immediately and may also pay a separate transaction fee.	Use a cash advance only in emergencies because the finance charges start as soon as you complete the transaction. It is a very expensive way to borrow money.
Credit limit—the debt ceiling the card company places on your account (e.g., $1,500). The total owed, including purchases, cash advances, finance charges, and fees, cannot exceed this limit.	Credit card companies generally set low credit limits for college students. Many students get around this limit by owning more than one card, which increases the credit available but most likely increases problems as well.
Delinquent account—an account that is not paid on time or for which the minimum payment has not been met.	Avoid having a delinquent account at all costs. Not only will you be charged substantial late fees, but you also risk losing your good credit rating, affecting your ability to borrow in the future. Delinquent accounts remain part of your credit record for many years.
Finance charges—the total cost of credit, including interest and service and transaction fees.	Your goal is to incur no finance charges. The only way to do that is to pay your balance in full by the due date on your monthly statement.
Minimum payment—the smallest amount you can pay by the statement due date. The amount is set by the credit card company.	Making only the minimum payment each month can result in disaster if you charge more than you can afford. When you make a purchase, think in terms of total cost, not monthly payments.
Outstanding balance—the total amount you owe on your card.	If you carry a balance over several months, additional purchases are immediately hit with finance charges. Pay cash instead.
Past due—your account is considered "past due" when you fail to mail the minimum required payment on schedule.	Three credit bureaus note past due accounts on your credit history: Experian, Trans Union, and Equifax. You can contact each bureau for a copy of your credit report to make sure there are no errors.

How can you *live your mission?*

Whatever changes occur in your life, continuing to learn will give you a greater sense of security in your choices. Recall your mission statement from Chapter 3. Think about how it may change as you develop. It will continue to reflect your goals, values, and strengths if you work to achieve your personal best.

Your personal best is simply the best that you can do, in any situation. It may not be the best you have ever done. It may include mistakes, for nothing significant is ever accomplished without making mistakes and taking risks. It may shift from situation to situation. Aim to do your best and you will invite growth and success.

In Figure 9.5 you see a blank Wheel of Life. Without looking at your Chapter 1 wheel, evaluate yourself as you are right now, after completing this course: Where would you rank yourself in the eight categories? After you have finished, compare this wheel with your previous wheel. Look at the changes: Where have you grown? How has your self-perception changed? Let what you learn from this new wheel inform you about what you have accomplished and what you plan for the future.

Aim for your personal best in everything you do. As a lifelong learner, you will always have a new direction in which to grow and a new challenge to face. Seek constant improvement in your personal, educational, and professional life, knowing that you are capable of such improvement. Enjoy the richness of life by living each day to the fullest, developing your talents and potential into the achievement of your most valued goals.

"And life is what we make it, always has been, always will be."

GRANDMA MOSES

Figure 9.5 Your new wheel of life.

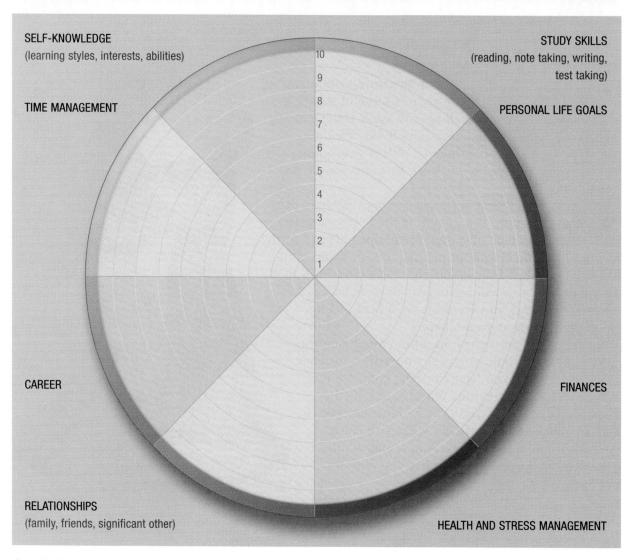

SELF-KNOWLEDGE
(learning styles, interests, abilities)

STUDY SKILLS
(reading, note taking, writing, test taking)

TIME MANAGEMENT

PERSONAL LIFE GOALS

CAREER

FINANCES

RELATIONSHIPS
(family, friends, significant other)

HEALTH AND STRESS MANAGEMENT

Source: Based on "The Wheel of Life" model developed by the Coaches Training Institute, © Co-Active Space 2000.

Kaizen is the Japanese word for "continual improvement." Striving for excellence, finding ways to improve on what already exists, and welcoming change are at the heart of the industrious Japanese spirit. The drive to improve who you are and what you do provides the foundation of a successful future.

Think of this concept as you reflect on yourself, your goals, your lifelong education, your career, and your personal pursuits. Create excellence and quality by continually asking yourself, "How can I improve?" Living by *kaizen* helps you to be a respected friend and family member, a productive and valued employee, and a truly contributing member of society. You can change the world.

Building Skills
FOR COLLEGE, CAREER, AND LIFE SUCCESS

The Big Picture	*Combining Thinking, Strategy, and Teamwork*

Career Possibilities

Choose one of the career areas you have listed as an interest in any other exercise in this book. Follow up on it by using the following leads. List two specific possibilities found using each of the sources below.

Help wanted listings in newspapers, magazines, or Internet databases:

_____

_____

Listings of job opportunities/company contact information at your career center, student employment office, or independent employment agency:

_____

_____

Contacts from friends or family members:

_____

_____

Contacts from instructors, administrators, or counselors:

_____

_____

Current or former employers or coworkers:

_____

_____

Think financial strategy. How might this career area fulfill, or not fulfill, your financial needs? What kind of job or situation in this career area would most likely earn you enough money to live comfortably?

Finally, join with your classmates for a stress brainstorm. Beforehand, by yourself, make a list of stressors—whatever events or factors cause you stress—related to career or finances. As a class, discuss the stressors you have listed. Choose the five most common. Divide into five groups according to who would choose what stressor as his or her most important (redistribute some people if the group sizes are unbalanced). Each group should discuss its assigned stressor, brainstorming solutions and strategies. List your best coping strategies and present them to the class. Groups may want to make extra copies of the lists so that every member of the class has five, one for each stressor.

Writing *Discovery Through Journaling*

To record your thoughts, use a separate journal or the lined pages at the end of the chapter.

CREDIT CARDS. Describe how you use credit cards. What do you buy? How much do you spend? Do you pay in full each month or run a balance? How does using a credit card make you feel? If you would like to change how you use credit, discuss changes you want to make and what effects they might have.

Career Portfolio *Charting Your Course*

PUTTING YOUR WORKING SELF INTO WORDS First, write a job interview letter. To secure a job interview, you may have to write a letter describing your background and explaining your value to the company. To include in your portfolio, write a one-page, three-paragraph cover letter to a prospective employer. (The letter will accompany your résumé.) Be creative—you may use fictitious names, but select a career and industry that interest you. Use the format shown in the sample letter in Figure 9.6.

• *Introductory paragraph:* Start with an attention getter—a statement that convinces the employer to read on. For example, name a person the employer knows who told you to write, or refer to something positive about the company that you read in the paper. Identify the position for which you are applying, and tell the employer that you are interested in working for the company.

- *Middle paragraph:* Sell your value. Try to convince the employer that hiring you will help the company in some way. Center your "sales effort" on your experience in school and the workplace. If possible, tie your qualifications to the needs of the company. Refer indirectly to your enclosed résumé.

- *Final paragraph:* Close with a call to action. Ask the employer to call you, or tell the employer to expect your call to arrange an interview.

Finally, retrieve the mission statement you wrote at the end of Chapter 3. Give yourself a day or so to read it over and think about it. Then, revise it according to the changes that have occurred in you. Add new priorities and goals and delete those that are no longer valid. Continue to update your mission statement so that it reflects your growth and development, helping to guide you through the changes that await you in the future.

Assess Yourself   *Student Success Strategies*

If you have access to the CD-ROM Strategies for Success, use the following questions to assess your thoughts and enhance your understanding of the chapter. The questions below represent only some of the activities provided on the CD for the chapter topics—try others if you have time.

Click on the Managing Your Career bookmark. Use the following activities to clarify your vision of what you want for your future:

1. Take the pre-assessment to explore your views on career planning while in college.
2. Click on Activity One: Investigate Yourself. Making sure your computer is on-line, click on the links provided and take the Emotional Intelligence assessment and the Keirsey Sorter assessment. Then connect your results with potential career plans by answering the rest of the questions in the activity.
3. Click on Activity Three: Journal Reflections. Scroll to the second question, which asks you about what employers value in the people they hire. Type your answer in the field provided.
4. Take the post-assessment to see how ready you are to put your best foot forward in the working world.

Figure 9.6   Sample job interview letter.

First name Last name
1234 Your Street
City, ST 12345

November 1, 2002

Ms. Prospective Employer
Prospective Company
5432 Their Street
City, ST 54321

Dear Ms. Employer:

On the advice of Mr. X, career center advisor at Y College, I am writing to inquire about the position of production assistant at KKKK Radio. I read the description of the job and your company on the career center's employment-opportunity bulletin board, and I would like to apply for the position.

I am a senior at Y College and will graduate this spring with a degree in communications. Since my junior year when I declared my major, I have wanted to pursue a career in radio. For the last year I have worked as a production intern at KCOL Radio, the college's station, and have occasionally filled in as a disc jockey on the evening news show. I enjoy being on the air, but my primary interest is production and programming. My enclosed résumé will tell you more about my background and experience.

I would be pleased to talk with you in person about the position. You can reach me anytime at 555/555-5555 or by e-mail at xxxx@xx.com. Thank you for your consideration, and I look forward to meeting you.

Sincerely,

Sign Your Name Here

First name Last name

Enclosure(s) *(use this notation if you have included a résumé or other item with your letter)*

Suggested Readings

Adams, Robert Lang, et al. *The Complete Résumé and Job Search Book for College Students.* Holbrook, MA: Adams Publishing, 1999.

Bolles, Richard Nelson. *What Color Is Your Parachute? 2001: A Practical Manual for Job Hunters and Career Changers.* Berkeley, CA: Ten Speed Press, 2000.

Detweiler, Gerri. *The Ultimate Credit Handbook.* New York: Plume, 1997.

Goleman, Daniel. *Emotional Intelligence.* New York: Bantam Books, 1997.

Grayson, Paul A., Phil Meilman, and Philip W. Meilman. *Beating the College Blues.* New York: Checkmark Books, 1999.

Johnson, Earvin "Magic." *What You Can Do to Avoid AIDS.* New York: Random House, 1996.

Kennedy, Joyce Lain. *Job Interviews for Dummies.* Foster City, CA: IDG Books Worldwide, Inc., 2000.

Mayo Clinic Family Health Book: The Ultimate Home Medical Reference, 2nd ed. New York: William Morrow, 1996.

McMahon, Susanna. *The Portable Problem Solver: Coping with Life's Stressors.* New York: Dell Publishing, 1996.

The New Wellness Encyclopedia. Edited by the Editors of the University of California at Berkeley Wellness Letter. Boston, MA: Houghton Mifflin, 1995.

Schuckit, Marc Alan. *Educating Yourself about Alcohol and Drugs: A People's Primer.* New York: Plenum Press, 1995.

Selkowitz, Ann. *The College Student's Guide to Eating Well on Campus.* Bethesda, MD: Tulip Hill Press, 2000.

Tyson, Eric. *Personal Finance for Dummies.* Foster City, CA: IDG Books Worldwide, Inc., 2000.

Internet Resources

Prentice Hall Student Success Supersite (fitness and well-being information): www.prenhall.com/success

Columbia University's Health Education Program: www.alice.columbia.edu

It's Your (Sex) Life: www.itsyoursexlife.com/

MayoClinic.com (medical information from this world-renowned medical center): www.mayohealth.org

Monster.com (online job search): www.monster.com

Tripod—Money/Business (financial and career advice, budget counseling): www.tripod.com/money_business/

College Grad Job Hunter (advice on resumes, interviews, and a database of entry-level jobs): www.collegegrad.com

JobWeb (career information site for college students): www.jobweb.org

Prentice Hall Student Success Supersite— Money Matters: www.prenhall.com/success/MoneyMat/index.html

Career Path: www.prenhall.com/success/CareerPath/index.html

Endnotes

1. The following articles were used as sources in this section: Glenn C. Altschuler, "Adapting to College Life in an Era of Heightened Stress," *The New York Times, Education Life,* Section 4A, August 6, 2000, p. 12; Carol Hymowitz and Rachel Emma Silverman, "Can Workplace Stress Get Worse?" *The Wall Street Journal,* January 16, 2001, p. B1; Robert M. Sapolsky, "Best Ways to Reduce Everyday Levels of Stress . . . Bad Ol' Stress," *Bottom Line Personal,* January 15, 2000, p. 13; Kate Slaboch, "Stress and the College Student: A Debate," www.jour. unr.edu/outpost/voices/voi. slaboch.stress.htm, April 4, 2001; University of South Florida, The Counseling Center for Human Development, "Coping with

Stress in College," http://usfweb.usf.edu/counsel/self-hlp/stress.htm, April 4, 2001; Jodi Wilgoren, "Survey Shows High Stress Levels in College Freshmen," *The New York Times,* January 23, 2000, p. NA.

2. Kim Hubbard, Anne-Marie O'Neill, and Christina Cheakalos, "Out of Control," *People,* April 12, 1999, p. 54.

3. H. Wechsler et al., "Changes in Binge Drinking and Related Problems Among American College Students Between 1993 and 1997," *Journal of American College Health,* vol. 47, September 1998, p. 57.

4. Ibid, pp. 63–64.

5. National Institute on Alcohol Abuse and Alcoholism, No. 29 PH 357, July 1995.

6. J. McGinnis and W. Foege, "Actual Causes of Death in the United States," *Journal of the American Medical Association* (JAMA) 270.18, American Medical Association, Nov. 10, 1993, p. 2208.

7. National Institute on Drug Abuse, Capsule Series C-83-08, "Cigarette Smoking," Bethesda, MD: National Institutes of Health, 1994.

8. National Institute on Drug Abuse, "National Survey Results on Drug Abuse from Monitoring the Future Study," Bethesda, MD: National Institutes of Health, 1994.

9. www.usdoj.gov/dea/concern/mdma/mdmaindex.htm; U. S. Department of Justice, Drug Enforcement Administration.

10. U. S. Bureau of Labor. Table 1: Fastest growing occupations covered in the 2000–01 Occupational Outlook Handbook, 1998–2008. Available: http://stats.bls.gov/news.release/ooh.t01.htm. Accessed on-line 6/14/01.

11. Steven Greenhouse, "Equal Work, Less-Equal Perks," *The New York Times,* March 30, 1998, pp. D1, D6.

12. Daniel Goleman, *Working with Emotional Intelligence.* New York: Bantam Books, 1998, pp. 26–27.

13. U. S. Department of Education, National Center for Education Statistics, *Profile of Undergraduates in U. S. Postsecondary Education Institutions: 1995–96,* NCES 98-084, by Laura J. Horn, Jennifer Berktold, Andrew G. Malizio, Project Officer, and MPR Associates, Inc. Washington, DC: U. S. Government Printing Office, 1998, pp. 4, 31.

14. U. S. Department of Education, National Center for Education Statistics, Digest of Educational Statistics 2000. Available: http://nces.ed.gov/pubs2001/digest/ch3.html. Accessed on-line 5/7/01.

JOURNAL

name   date

visit: www.prenhall.com/carter NY Times link for this chapter

Index

Test:
    analysis, 222–223
    anxiety, 198, 205–208, 223
    directions, 209
    performance, 197–224 (*see also*
        Test taking)
    types of, 199–200
Testing, on-the-job, 223
Tests (*see also* Test taking):
    learning from mistakes,
        219–221, 223
    machine-scored, 210
    math, 211
    types of questions, 212–219 (*see
        also* Questions)
Test taking, 197–224
    anxiety, 198, 205–208
    improving performance,
        197–224
    intelligent guessing and, 210
    multiple intelligence and, 203
    physical preparation for, 204
    returning students and, 206, 208
    SQ3R and, 199
    types of questions, 212–219 (*see
        also* Questions)
Thinker, 35, 37, 50, 280
Thinker-dominant communicators,
    241, 242
Think link, 51, 178, 180
Thinking:
    positive, 11–12
    process, 94–99, 116
    quantitative, 206
Time lines, 181
Time:
    assessing how you spend your,
        79–81
    managing, 68–78 (*see also* Time
        management)

taking responsibility for, 73–74
    (*see also* Time management)
    traps, 77–78
Time management, 68–78, 290
    daily and weekly goals and,
        70–71
    flexibility and, 75
    procrastination and, 76–78
    scheduling and, 68–73
    setting priority levels and,
        71–72
Timm, Paul, 61
T-note system, 178, 179
Tobacco, 271
To-do lists, 73
Tolerance, 233
Topic sentence, 143
Transition, 3
Trends, workplace, 277–278
True-false questions, 214–215
Trust, 15
Truth, investigating, 109
Tubal ligation, 274
Type styles, 138

Understanding, seeking, 150

Values, 59–60, 98 (*see also* Evalu-
    ation)
    choice of major and, 44
    choosing and evaluating, 60
    goals and, 66
    sources of, 59–60
Vasectomy, 274
Verbal signposts, 168
Verbal-linguistic intelligence, 31,
    33–34 (*see also* Multiple
    Intelligences)
Verbs, action, 217–218
Violence in relationships, 254–255

Visual:
    aids, 185–186
    associations, 187–188
    focus, 39
Visualization, 180–181
Visual-spatial intelligence, 31,
    33–34 (*see also* Multiple
    Intelligences)
Vocabulary, 127, 158
    expanding your, 134–137
Vocalization, 134
Volunteer work, 277
Vulnerability, stereotype, 240

Wellness:
    mental disorders and, 269
    nutrition and, 269
    sex and, 273–275
    stress management, 267–270
    substance abuse and, 270–273
Wheel of Life, 16, 17, 290
Wheel of thinking, 116
Williams, Jody, 93
Word parts, 134–135
Workload, sharing, 152
Workplace trends, 277–278
World, relating to, 59
Worldview, education and, 6
Writing:
    about your working self,
        292–293
    as memory device, 184
    essay question responses,
        216–220
    journaling, 19, 50, 82, 119,
        157, 192, 223, 259, 292

Yerkes-Dodson law, 267
Yerkes, Robert M., 267
Yuen, Lenora M., 76